Revised 3rd Edition

Elegant Glassware
of the
Depression Era

By Gene Florence

db

COLLECTOR BOOKS

A Division of Schroeder Publishing Co., Inc.

The current values in this book should be used only as a guide. They are not intended to set prices, which vary from one section of the country to another. Auction prices as well as dealer prices vary greatly and are affected by condition as well as demand. Neither the Author nor the Publisher assumes responsibility for any losses that might be incurred as a result of consulting this guide.

Additional copies of this book may be ordered from:

COLLECTOR BOOKS
P.O. Box 3009
Paducah, Kentucky 42001
or
Gene Florence
P.O. Box 22186
Lexington, Kentucky 40522

@$19.95 Add $1.00 for postage and handling.

Copyright: Gene Florence, 1988

This book or any part thereof may not be reproduced without the written consent of the Author and Publisher

DEDICATION

This book is dedicated to my Zenith Z-85 computer which gave up its six year life for this book. In 1981 the first Elegant book was conceived and designed on that computer. There were marvelous, complicated and often frustrating sessions learning to use "Wordstar" to edit and write; there were complicated systems in "Supersort" whereby several hundred listings could be typed and alphabetized after that initial typing. The ability to eliminate duplicate listings (if typed right in the first place) were all marvels of this computer. It didn't matter that measurements had to be converted to decimals to alphabetize, and later be converted back to fractions, or that the computer could not use symbols for inches until after alphabetizing, so those symbols had to be converted twice. All of this was easier than the old "index" card method. Why, I shuddered to remember I had spent 168 hours alphabetizing the Degenhart book by hand! This computer was "the beans"!

After six years of use, "Wordstar" was becoming a friend. Cathy, my wife, originally typed all the books for me; but, after her quilt book, which was also done on the Z-85, she figured it was easier to correct my scribblings from typed computer copy than it was from my so called "handwriting". (I skipped the third grade and missed out on all the practice of script and learned hieroglyphics instead.) It was easier to read my paragraph long, run-on sentences typed than handwritten. It didn't seem to be easier to correct, but easier to read!

In any case, the 8″ double disk drives decided to stop reading the information that was on my disks. All that information stored from the first and second Elegant books was suddenly impossible to access by the computer! Deadline was three weeks away! The disk drives could be shipped to California and I could *possibly* get them back in six or eight weeks. No one uses 8″ drives today and there are no parts available!

My computer repairman suggested using the drives as a boat anchor as a last resort. With no time to spare, my son Chad suggested I use a *good* computer - his XT clone. That meant lessons in a new word processing system called "Leading Edge". It is *easier* to use than "Wordstar"; but after six years, old habits are hard to break. I would push a key meaning to erase a letter and suddenly have 32 repeat letters instead! My son thought it hilarious. My blood pressure elevated.

I contacted Milton Glen in Texas to get a copy of "Wordstar" for his computer, and he sent it by air express so I would get it the next day. Meanwhile, I am plodding away at "Leading Edge". Next day, the package did not arrive and upon tracing it, it was found in Des Moines, Iowa. It seems that Des Moines has zip code 50402 and mine is 40502. A simple mistake changed my method of writing for the whole book!

When the program did finally arrive, my son was away for the weekend. I tried to install it and got some of the most interesting happenings I have ever seen. As I would type, letters would disappear in the line above and suddenly appear in the middle of a blank line. Words would slowly change spellings. "People" would change to "peopla" on my computer screen—without my help! When I printed, the original spelling would show up most of the time, but I couldn't tell what I had written after several lines were typed on the screen itself! It looked like total jibberish!

Being Saturday afternoon, I couldn't get help; so, it was back to "Leading Edge" for the weekend. On Monday, I was able to go to the computer store and get "Wordstar" installed. My son's computer has 640K of memory, but there is a bug in "Wordstar" that tells the computer it doesn't have enough memory to install the program. Sometimes a computer with 256K of memory has to be used to install "Wordstar", and that was my problem. By this time, I had so much information on "Leading Edge" that the computer would not read with "Wordstar"; I had to continue as I was. Computers are fantastic instruments when they work, but they are the most frustrating machines outside a chain saw, I have ever dealt with when they don't! I used to teach data processing back in the days when the IBM 360 was the jewel of the computer world. This little clone will do so much more than that room size antique would do and in shorter time! Believe me, I do speak from some experience.

This book, and the Eighth Depression Glass book (by far the hardest) are finally finished. Now, if I can find a way to transfer all my previous information into a form that can be read by a different computer system, I will be all set for any new frustrations the next time. It's been fun!

3

FOREWORD

"Elegant" glassware, as defined in this book, refers to the handmade and etched glassware that was sold in the department stores and jewelry stores during the Depression era through the 1950's as opposed to the dime store and give-away glass that is known as Depression Glass.

The rapid growth of collecting "Elegant" glassware has been phenomenal and many dealers who wouldn't touch that crystal stuff a few years ago are stocking up on as much "Elegant" as basic Depression Glass.

The success of the first two books has spawned this third book. The term "Elegant" is now standard terminology for glass collectors and dealers.

I hope you enjoy the book; and I hope you will feel the hours of effort taken to give you the best book possible on "Elegant Glassware" were well spent.

PRICING

ALL PRICES IN THIS BOOK ARE RETAIL PRICES FOR MINT CONDITION GLASSWARE. This book is intended to be only A GUIDE TO PRICES. There are regional price differences which cannot be reasonably dealt with herein.

You may expect dealers to pay from thirty to fifty percent less than the prices quoted. My personal knowledge of prices comes from my experience of selling glass in my Grannie Bear Antique Shop in Lexington, from my traveling to and selling at shows in various parts of the United States, and immediately prior to the pricing of this book, from attending the Fostoria, Cambridge and Heisey shows. I readily admit to soliciting price information from persons I know to be expert in these various fields so as to provide you with the latest, most accurate pricing information possible. However, final pricing judgment is mine; so, for any errors (or praises), the buck stops here.

MEASUREMENTS

All measurements are from factory catalog lists. It has been my experience that the actual measurements may vary slightly from those listed, so don't be unduly concerned over slight variations.

ACKNOWLEDGMENTS

There are always numerous people behind the scenes of a book without whose help and encouragement the book would never be done. However, many of the people behind this book have gone above and beyond friendship, or even belief, to see that this work made it to press -- and on time! They have given unstintingly of their time, their glassware, and the knowledge of their special fields of interest. They have helped pack and unpack boxes upon boxes of glass; they have sorted and arranged; they've stayed up nights after grueling show dates to discuss, sort, compile and suggest prices for various items. Much as my ego would like to swell thinking they did all this for me, I have to acknowledge that their driving inspiration was YOU, the public. They each wanted a book of this type available to you, hopefully a good book, filled with information about the better glassware. That's what we all wanted. I hereby acknowledge with much gratitude their efforts in behalf of us all! They include the following beautiful people: Dick and Pat Spencer; Yvonne Spencer Heil; Charles and Cecelia Larson; Earl and Beverly Hines; Bill and Lottie Porter; Gary and Sue Clark; John and Judy Bine; Wayne and Marilyn Ring; Ronnie Marshall; Ralph Leslie; Wanda Farque; and the lady from Pittsburgh who lent the Flanders vase. Her name is locked in computer files that are unreachable now and I apologize to her for omitting her name. Everyone "knows" me, but my memory is failing for names.

The photography "slave" labor (as my wife, not so fondly, calls it) was provided by Dick and Pat Spencer, Beverly Hines, Wanda Farque, Bill and Lottie Porter, Steve Quertermous, Kay Smith, Jane Fryberger and Cathy Florence. I enjoy watching these fine people work! The photography was provided by Tom Clauser and Dana Curtis of Curtis and Mays Studio in Paducah, Kentucky.

Family, especially, need to be acknowledged, particularly my Mom, "Grannie Bear", who spent weeks washing, packing and listing glass for the photography sessions; then there are Charles, Sibyl, Marie, and Chad and Marc who keep home operating and animals alive in our absences and who generally pitch in and do whatever needs doing.

A special thanks to my wife, Cathy, who has tried to make sense out of my writing so you, the reader, may understand what I meant to say in the first place. It has been a long sixteen years of research, travel, packing and unpacking, both the glassware and me. It is hard to remember the years we had together BDG (before Depression Glass); but they have been a fantastic twenty-three years, Cathy.

The editors of COLLECTOR BOOKS, Steve and Jane, as well as the typesetter, Gail Ashburn, need to be commended for their fine work and for the deadline pressures I unwittingly exposed them to with these books. I make them a promise not to do it again this year!

Few people are in a position to really appreciate all the WORK that goes into writing a book; and this one was particularly DIFFICULT because of starting from scratch so to speak.

We are still only denting the surface of ELEGANT glassware; it will take many more years to "mine" it out. Let me know what you find!

INDEX

INDEX BY COMPANY

AMERICAN, Line #2056, Fostoria Glass Company, 1915 - 1986

Colors: crystal; some amber, blue, green, yellow in late 1920's; white, red in 1980's

The closing of Fostoria is finally a fact. Its demise had previously been reported, but that was for the making of the etched, hand made ware and not for the American pattern which was made to the end in 1986. American is still being produced by Lancaster Colony subsidiaries such as Indiana. Not as many pieces are now being made as reported in previous editions; and the quality of the glass is slipping.

Note the picture with the amber cologne. In the foreground are two ice cream saucers of different styles. They are listed in a 1941 catalogue. Behind those is a so called "western style" hat made from the 4" hat. I have one made from a smaller hat also. The size of these hats refers to the height and not the width.

Behind the hat is an item that has been found mostly in England and sent back in containers. The lid has built-in tongs for picking up something from the jar. Speculation is that the "something" was olives or sugar cubes. What makes this so baffling is that one of these bottoms turned up embossed in the base, "Made in England". I did not buy it without the lid, but I did see it. The bottom also comes with a glass lid which is smaller than a coaster. The lids are the hard part to find; completed, these are selling in the $150.00 range.

Prices for the more commonly found pieces of American have slowed somewhat. After all, this pattern was made for seventy years and there was a lot of it made! Many pieces were only made for a few years and those are the pieces most in demand by collectors. Commonly found pieces sell well at mall antiques shows where non-collectors see it and replace pieces that they used to buy from the local department store.

All the items marked with an asterisk below were being sold in some of the outlet stores in April and May of 1987. I visited two stores in Ohio and one in West Virginia for this information.

	Crystal		Crystal
Appetizer, tray, 10½" w/6 inserts	190.00	Bowl, 5½", preserve, 2 hdld., w/cover	50.00
Appetizer, insert, 3¼"	22.50	Bowl, 6", bonbon, 3 ftd.	15.00
Ash tray, 2⅞", sq.	6.00	Bowl, 6", nappy	12.00
Ash tray, 3⅞", oval	9.00	Bowl, 6", olive, oblong	9.00
Ash tray, 5", sq.	25.00	Bowl, 6½", wedding w/cover, sq., ped.	
Ash tray, 5½", oval	12.00	ft., 8" h.	75.00
Basket w/reed handle, 7" x 9"	70.00	Bowl, 6½", wedding, sq., ped. ft., 5¼" h.	35.00
Basket, 10"	25.00*	Bowl, 7", bonbon, 3 ftd.	10.00*
Bell	60.00	Bowl, 7", cupped, 4½" h.	37.50
Bottle, bitters w/tube, 5¾", 4½ oz.	47.50	Bowl, 7", nappy	22.50
Bottle, condiment or catsup w/stopper	80.00	Bowl 8" bonbon, 3 ftd.	17.50
Bottle, cologne w/stopper, 6 oz., 5¾"	50.00	Bowl, 8", deep	42.50
Bottle, cologne w/stopper, 7¼" 8 oz.	52.50	Bowl, 8", ftd.	47.50
Bottle, cordial w/stopper, 7¼", 9 oz.	67.50	Bowl, 8", ftd. 2 hdld. "trophy" cup	70.00
Bottle, water, 44 oz., 9¼"	275.00	Bowl, 8", nappy	12.50*
Bowl, banana split, 9" x 3½"	75.00	Bowl, 8", pickle, oblong	13.00
Bowl, finger, 4½" diam., smooth edge	20.00	Bowl, 8½", 2 hdld.	13.50*
Bowl, 3½", rose	14.00	Bowl, 8½", boat	7.50
Bowl, 3¾", almond, oval	12.50	Bowl, 9", boat, 2 pt.	10.50*
Bowl, 4¼", jelly, 4¼" h.	15.00	Bowl, 9", oval veg.	25.00
Bowl, 4½", 1 hdld.	8.00	Bowl, 9½", centerpiece	27.50
Bowl, 4½", 1 hdld., sq.	8.00	Bowl, 9½", 3 pt., 6" w.	37.50
Bowl, 4½", jelly w/cover, 6¾" h.	18.00	Bowl, 10", celery, oblong	14.00
Bowl, 4½", nappy	10.00	Bowl, 10", deep	16.75
Bowl, 4½", oval	7.00	Bowl, 10", float	35.00
Bowl, 4¾", fruit, flared	15.00	Bowl, 10", oval float	32.50
Bowl, 5", cream soup, 2 hdld.	41.50	Bowl, 10", oval veg., 2 pt.	30.00
Bowl, 5", 1 hdld., tri-corner	11.00	Bowl, 10½", fruit, 3 ftd.	15.00*
Bowl, 5" nappy	7.00*	Bowl, 11", centerpiece	40.00
Bowl, 5" nappy, w/cover	25.00	Bowl, 11", centerpiece, tri-corner	30.00
Bowl, 5", rose	21.00	Bowl, 11", relish/celery, 3 pt.	30.00
Bowl, 5½", lemon w/cover	30.00		

AMERICAN, Line #2056, Fostoria Glass Company, 1915 - 1986 (continued)

	Crystal		Crystal
Bowl, 11½", float	47.50	Creamer, tea, 3 oz., 2⅜" (#2056 ½)	7.50
Bowl, 11½", fruit, rolled edge, 2¾" h. . .	40.00	Creamer, individual, 4¾ oz.	7.50
Bowl, 11½", oval float	45.00	Creamer, 9½ oz.	10.50
Bowl, 11½", rolled edge	37.50	Crushed fruit w/cover & spoon, 10"	325.00
Bowl, 11¾", oval, deep	37.50	Cup, flat	5.00*
Bowl, 12", boat	16.00*	Cup, ftd., 7 oz.	9.00
Bowl, 12", fruit/sm. punch, ped. ft.,		Cup, punch, flared rim	10.00
(Tom & Jerry)	125.00	Cup, punch, straight edge	9.00
Bowl, 12", lily pond	55.00	Decanter w/stopper, 24 oz., 9¼" h.	70.00
Bowl, 12", relish "boat", 2 pt.	19.00	Dresser set: powder boxes w/covers & tray	225.00
Bowl, 13", fruit, shallow	50.00	Flower pot w/perforated cover, 9½" diam.;	
Bowl, 14", punch w/high ft. base (2 gal.)	180.00	5½" h.	350.00
Bowl, 14", punch w/low ft. base	160.00	Goblet, #2056, 2½ oz., wine, hex ft.,	
Bowl, 15", centerpiece, "hat" shape	125.00	4⅜" h.	10.50
Bowl, 16", flat fruit, ped. ft.	105.00	Goblet, #2056, 4½ oz., oyster cocktail,	
Bowl, 18", punch w/low ft. base (3¾ gal.)	235.00	3½" h.	11.00
Box, pomade, 2" square	175.00	Goblet, #2056, 4½ oz., sherbet, flared,	
Box, w/cover, puff, 3⅛" x 2¾"	100.00	4⅜" h.	9.00
Box, w/cover, handkerchief, 5⅝" x 4⅝" .	125.00	Goblet, #2056, 4½ oz., fruit, hex ft.,	
Box, w/cover, hairpin, 3½" x 1¾"	85.00	4¾" h.	9.00
Box, w/cover, jewel, 5¼" x 2¼"	100.00	Goblet, #2056, 5 oz., low ft. sherbet, flared,	
Box, w/cover, jewel, 2 drawer, 4¼" x 3¼"	350.00	3¼" h.	9.00
Box, w/cover, glove, 9½" x 3½"	150.00	Goblet, #2056, 6 oz., low ft. sundae,	
Butter, w/cover, rnd, plate 7¼"	95.00	3⅛" h.	9.00
Butter, w/cover, ¼ lb.	15.00	Goblet, #2056, 7 oz., claret, 4⅞" h.	17.50
Candelabrum, 6½", 2-lite, bell base		Goblet, #2056, 9 oz., low ft., 4⅜" h.	11.00
w/bobeche & prisms	75.00	Goblet, #2056, 10 oz., hex ft. water,	
Candle lamp, 8½", w/chimney, candle		6⅞" h.	12.50
part, 3½"	110.00	Goblet, #2056, 12 oz., low ft. tea,	
Candlestick, twin, 4⅛" h., 8½" spread . .	27.50	5¾" h.	13.00
Candlestick, 2", chamber with fingerhold	20.00	Goblet, #2056½, 4½ oz., sherbet,	
Candlestick, 3", rnd. ft.	13.50	4½" h.	10.00
Candlestick, 4⅜", 2-lite, rnd. ft.	30.00	Goblet, #2056½, 5 oz., low sherbet,	
Candlestick, 6", octagon ft.	20.00	3½" h.	10.00
Candlestick, 6½", 2-lite, bell base	50.00	Goblet, #5056, 1 oz., cordial,	
Candlestick, 6½", round ft.	150.00	3⅛" w/plain bowl	27.50
Candlestick, 7", sq. column	90.00	Goblet, #5056, 3½ oz., claret,	
Candlestick, 7¼", "Eiffel" tower	100.00	4⅝" w/plain bowl	12.00
Candy box w/cover, 3 pt., triangular	60.00	Goblet, #5056, 3½ oz., cocktail,	
Candy w/cover, ped. ft.	15.00*	4" w/plain bowl	12.00
Cheese (5¾" compote) & cracker		Goblet, #5056, 4 oz., oyster cocktail,	
(11½" plate)	45.00	3½" w/plain bowl	10.00
Cigarette box w/cover, 4¾"	30.00	Goblet, #5056, 5½ oz., sherbet,	
Coaster, 3¾"	5.00	4⅛" w/plain bowl	10.00
Comport, 4½" jelly	8.00*	Goblet, #5056, 10 oz., water,	
Comport, 5", jelly, flared	12.00	6⅛" w/plain bowl	12.00
Comport, 6¾", jelly w/cover	30.00	Hair receiver, 3" x 3"	100.00
Comport, 8½", 4" high	35.00	Hat, 2⅛", (sm. ash tray)	11.00
Comport, 9½", 5¼" high	37.50	Hat, 3" tall	22.50
Comport w/cover, 5"	22.50	Hat, 4" tall	35.00
Cookie jar w/cover, 8⅞" h.	250.00	Hurricane lamp, 12" complete	120.00

	Crystal		Crystal
Hurricane lamp base	42.50	Salver, 11″, rnd. ped. ft. (cake stand)	27.50
Ice bucket w/tongs	50.00	Sauce boat & liner	52.50
Ice dish for 4 oz. crab or 5 oz. tomato liner	30.00	Saucer	5.00*
Ice dish insert	5.00	Set: 2 jam pots w/tray	95.00
Ice tub w/liner, 5⅝″	47.50	Set: decanter, 6 - 2 oz. whiskeys on 10½″ tray	185.00
Ice tub w/liner, 6½″	50.00	Set: toddler, w/baby tumbler & bowl	50.00
Jam pot w/cover	40.00	Set: youth, w/bowl, hdld. mug, 6″ plate	65.00
Jar, pickle w/pointed cover, 6″ h.	135.00		
Marmalade w/cover & chrome spoon	35.00	Set, condiment: 2 oils, 2 shakers, mustard w/cover & spoon w/tray	200.00
Mayonnaise, div.	7.50*	Shaker, 3″, ea.	9.50
Mayonnaise w/ladle, ped. ft.	30.00	Shaker, 3½″, ea.	5.50*
Mayonnaise w/liner & ladle	30.00	Shaker, 3¼″, ea.	9.50
Molasses can, 11 oz., 6¾″ h., 1 hdld.	115.00	Shakers w/tray, individual, 2″	15.00
Mug, 5½ oz., "Tom & Jerry", 3¼″ h.	25.00	Sherbet, handled, 3½″ high, 4½ oz.	40.00
Mug, 12 oz., beer, 4½″ h.	32.50	Shrimp bowl, 12¼″	250.00
Mustard w/cover	30.00	Spooner, 3¾″	32.50
Napkin ring	5.00	Strawholder, 10″ w/cover	225.00
Oil, 5 oz.	20.00	Sugar, tea, #2056½, 2¼″	7.50
Oil, 7 oz.	22.00	Sugar, hdld., 3¼″ h.	7.50*
Picture frame	5.50*	Sugar shaker	37.50
Pitcher, ½ gal. w/ice lip, 8¼″, flat bottom	60.00	Sugar, w/o cover	9.00*
Pitcher, ½ gal., 8″, ftd.	50.00	Sugar w/cover, no hand., 6¼″ (cover fits strawholder)	55.00
Pitcher, 1 pt., 5⅜″, flat	22.00	Sugar w/cover, 2 hdld.	17.50
Pitcher, 2 pt., 7¼″, ftd.	50.00	Syrup, 6½ oz., #2056½, Sani-cut server	40.00
Pitcher, 3 pt., 8″, ftd.	47.50	Syrup, 6 oz., non pour screw top, 5¼″ h.	85.00
Pitcher, 3 pt., w/ice lip, 6½″, ftd., "fat"	40.00		
Pitcher, 1 qt., flat	20.00	Syrup, 10 oz., w/glass cover & 6″ liner plate	85.00
Plate, cream soup liner	12.00	Syrup, w/drip proof top	25.00
Plate, 6″, bread & butter	8.00	Toothpick	17.50
Plate, 7″, salad	8.50	Tray, cloverleaf for condiment set	97.50
Plate, 7½″ x 4⅜″ crescent salad	37.50	Tray, tid bit, w/question mark metal hand.	27.50
Plate, 8″, sauce liner, oval	22.50	Tray, 5″ x 2½″, rect.	15.00
Plate, 8½″, salad	8.00	Tray, 6″ oval, hdld.	35.00
Plate, 9″, sandwich (sm. center)	14.00	Tray, pin, oval, 5½″ x 4½″	40.00
Plate, 9½″, dinner	15.00	Tray, 6½″ x 9″ relish, 4 part	35.00
Plate, 10″, cake, 2 hdld.	16.00	Tray, 9½″, service, 2 hdld.	27.50
Plate, 10½″ sandwich (sm. center)	16.00	Tray, 10″, muffin (2 upturned sides)	25.00
Plate, 11½″, sandwich (sm. center)	16.00	Tray, 10″, square, 4 part	75.00
Plate, 12″, cake, 3 ftd.	22.50	Tray, 10″, square	115.00
Plate, 13½″, oval torte	30.00	Tray, 10½″, cake, w/question mark metal hand.	25.00
Plate, 14″, torte	16.75*		
Plate, 18″, torte	75.00	Tray, 10½″ x 7½″, rect.	55.00
Plate, 20″, torte	95.00	Tray, 10½″ x 5″, oval, hdld.	40.00
Platter, 10½″, oval	37.50	Tray, 10¾″, square, 4 part	90.00
Platter, 12″, oval	47.50	Tray, 12″, sand. w/ctr. handle	33.00
Ring holder	100.00	Tray, 12″, round	100.00
Salad set: 10″ bowl, 14″ torte, wood fork & spoon	67.50	Tray, 13½″, oval ice cream	52.50
Salt, individual	5.00	Tray for sugar & creamer, tab. hdld., 6¾″	9.00
Salver, 10″, sq., ped. ft. (cake stand)	60.00		
Salver, 10″, rnd., ped. ft. (cake stand)	50.00		

AMERICAN, Line #2056, Fostoria Glass Company, 1915 - 1986 (continued)

	Crystal		Crystal
Tumbler, hdld. iced tea, 7½"	100.00	Urn, 7½", sq., ped. ft.	30.00
Tumbler, #2056, 2 oz., whiskey, 2½" h. .	11.00	Vase, 4½", sweet pea	75.00
Tumbler, #2056, 3 oz., ftd. cone cocktail		Vase, 6", bud, ftd.	8.00*
2⅞" h.	13.50	Vase, 6", bud, flared	8.00*
Tumbler, #2056, 5 oz., ftd. juice, 4¾" . . .	10.00	Vase, 6", straight side	25.00
Tumbler, #2056, 6 oz., flat old fashioned,		Vase, 6½", flared rim	15.00
3⅜" h.	11.00	Vase, 7", flared	67.50
Tumbler, #2056, 8 oz., flat water, flared,		Vase, 8", straight side	40.00
4⅛" h.	12.00	Vase, 8", flared	77.50
Tumbler, #2056, 9 oz., ftd. water		Vase, 8", porch, 5" diam.	240.00
4⅞" h.	12.00	Vase, 8½", bud, flared	20.00
Tumbler, #2056, 12 oz., flat tea, flared		Vase, 8½", bud, cupped	20.00
5¼" h.	12.00	Vase, 9", w/sq. ped. ft.	37.50
Tumbler, #2056½, 5 oz., straight side		Vase, 9½", flared	85.00
juice	12.00	Vase, 10", cupped in top	150.00
Tumbler, #2056½, 8 oz., straight side		Vase, 10", porch, 8" diam.	150.00
water, 3⅞" h.	12.00	Vase, 10", straight side	90.00
Tumbler, #2056½, 12 oz., straight side		Vase, 10", swung	125.00
tea, 5" h.	12.00	Vase, 10", flared	85.00
Tumbler, #5056, 5 oz., ftd. juice, 4⅛"		Vase, 12", straight side	100.00
w/plain bowl	12.00	Vase, 12", swung	125.00
Tumbler, #5056, 12 oz., ftd. tea, 5½"		Vase, 14", swung	225.00
w/plain bowl	12.00	Vase, 20", swung	275.00
Urn, 6", sq., ped. ft.	25.00		

All items marked with an asterisk were available at outlet stores in April and May 1987 at prices listed.

APPLE-BLOSSOM, Line #3400, Cambridge Glass Company, 1930's

Colors: blue, pink, light and dark green, yellow, crystal, amber

The variety of colors and pieces in Apple-Blossom continues to amaze me. Yellow, which was called "Gold Krystol" by Cambridge, is the most readily found color. I have seen sets that were collected in blue and green, but they were put together with patience and lots of money. I am partial to the blue, but the dark "Emerald Green" often catches my eye. Note the amber stemmed, but yellow-bowled cordial between the amber and yellow pitchers. That was found at the National Cambridge show!

	Crystal	Colors		Crystal	Colors
Bowl, #3025, ftd. finger w/plate	15.00	30.00	Plate, sandwich, 11½", tab hdld.	20.00	33.00
Bowl, #3130, finger w/plate	13.00	25.00	Plate, sandwich, 12½", 2 hdld.	23.00	38.00
Bowl, 5¼", 2 hdld. bonbon	10.00	17.50	Plate, sq. bread/butter	4.00	9.00
Bowl, 5½", 2 hdld. bonbon	10.00	17.50	Plate, sq. dinner	35.00	55.00
Bowl, 5½", fruit "saucer"	8.00	15.00	Plate, sq. salad	9.00	16.00
Bowl, 6", 2 hdld. "basket"			Plate, sq. service	15.00	35.00
(sides up)	12.00	22.00	Platter, 11½"	30.00	50.00
Bowl, 6", cereal	10.00	18.00	Platter, 13½" rect. w/tab handle	35.00	55.00
Bowl, 9", pickle	11.00	20.00	Salt & pepper, pr.	37.50	95.00
Bowl, 10", 2 hdld.	20.00	35.00	Saucer	2.50	5.00
Bowl, 10", baker	20.00	40.00	Stem, #3025, 7 oz., low fancy ft.		
Bowl, 11", fruit, tab hdld.	20.00	40.00	sherbet	11.00	16.00
Bowl, 11", low ftd.	19.00	42.00	Stem, #3025, 7 oz., high sherbet	12.00	18.00
Bowl, 12", relish, 4 pt.	20.00	40.00	Stem, #3025, 10 oz.	17.00	27.00
Bowl, 12", 4 ftd.	25.00	50.00	Stem, #3130, 1 oz., cordial	40.00	65.00
Bowl, 12", flat	28.00	40.00	Stem, #3130, 3 oz., cocktail	15.00	26.00
Bowl, 12", oval, 4 ftd.	25.00	55.00	Stem, #3130, 6 oz., low sherbet	10.00	19.00
Bowl, 12½", console	20.00	40.00	Stem, #3130, 6 oz., tall sherbet	10.00	18.00
Bowl, 13"	20.00	38.00	Stem, #3130, 8 oz., water	14.00	26.00
Bowl, cream soup w/liner plate	13.00	28.00	Stem, #3135, 3 oz., cocktail	13.00	26.00
Butter w/cover, 5½"	100.00	200.00	Stem, #3135, 6 oz., low sherbet	10.00	17.00
Candelabrum, 3-lite, keyhole	17.50	37.50	Stem, #3135, 6 oz., tall sherbet	10.00	19.00
Candlestick, 1-lite, keyhole	12.00	22.00	Stem, #3135, 8 oz., water	14.00	26.00
Candlestick, 2-lite, keyhole	15.00	32.50	Stem, #3400, 6 oz., ftd. sherbet	9.00	18.00
Candy box w/cover, 4 ftd. "bowl"	35.00	100.00	Stem, #3400, 9 oz., water	10.00	26.00
Cheese (compote) & cracker (11½"			Sugar, ftd.	9.00	16.00
plate)	22.00	47.50	Sugar, tall ftd.	9.00	16.00
Comport, 4", fruit cocktail	12.50	20.00	Tray, 11" ctr. hdld. sand.	22.00	37.00
Comport, 7", tall	20.00	42.50	Tumbler, #3025, 4 oz.	12.00	18.00
Creamer, ftd.	11.00	17.50	Tumbler, #3025, 10 oz.	14.00	26.00
Creamer, tall ftd.	11.00	17.50	Tumbler, #3025, 12 oz.	18.00	30.00
Cup	12.00	22.50	Tumbler, #3130, 5 oz., ftd.	11.00	18.00
Fruit/oyster cocktail, #3025, 4½ oz.	11.00	17.50	Tumbler, #3130, 8 oz., ftd.	12.00	20.00
Mayonnaise w/liner & ladle, (4 ftd.			Tumbler, #3130, 10 oz., ftd.	13.00	22.50
bowl)	25.00	55.00	Tumbler, #3130, 12 oz., ftd.	16.00	30.00
Pitcher, 50 oz., ftd., flattened sides	85.00	150.00	Tumbler, #3135, 5 oz., ftd.	10.00	18.00
Pitcher, 64 oz., #3130	100.00	200.00	Tumbler, #3135, 8 oz., ftd.	12.00	22.50
Pitcher, 64 oz., #3025	100.00	200.00	Tumbler, #3135, 10 oz., ftd.	13.00	22.50
Pitcher, 67 oz., squeezed middle,			Tumbler, #3135, 12 oz., ftd.	15.00	30.00
loop hdld.	110.00	250.00	Tumbler, #3400, 2½ oz., ftd.	12.00	25.00
Pitcher, 76 oz.	100.00	225.00	Tumbler, #3400, 9 oz., ftd.	12.00	20.00
Pitcher, 80 oz., ball	110.00	200.00	Tumbler, #3400, 12 oz., ftd.	14.00	25.00
Pitcher w/cover, 76 oz., ftd., #3135	150.00	325.00	Tumbler, 12 oz., flat (2 styles) - 1 mid		
Plate, 6", bread/butter	4.00	9.00	indent to match 67 oz. pitcher	17.00	35.00
Plate, 6", sq., 2 hdld.	7.00	13.00	Tumbler, 6"	15.00	27.50
Plate, 7½", tea	7.00	12.00	Vase, 5"	22.00	35.00
Plate, 8½"	10.00	16.00	Vase, 6", rippled sides	23.00	40.00
Plate, 9½", dinner	35.00	55.00	Vase, 8", 2 styles	30.00	55.00
Plate, 10", grill	18.00	35.00	Vase, 12", keyhole base w/neck indent	35.00	70.00

Note: See Pages 166-167 for stem identification.

BAROQUE, Line #2496, Fostoria Glass Company, 1936 - 1966

Colors: crystal, "Azure" blue, "Topaz" yellow, green

The blue Baroque is harder to find but continues to be more collected than the yellow. Both factors are contributing to price increases. Several blue punch bowls have been discovered in the last two years, but there are no reports of yellow punch bowls to date. Crystal remains the best buy at today's prices, but few collectors are heeding its call.

A couple of green console bowls have been found, but I have not been able to match one with my candlesticks as yet.

Baroque's blanks (#2496) were used on many of Fostoria's etched crystal lines. These can be seen in Chintz and Navarre patterns which are additional Fostoria lines added to this book.

	Crystal	Blue	Yellow
Ash tray	7.50	15.00	13.00
Bowl, cream soup	12.50	-----	-----
Bowl, ftd. punch	250.00	1375.00	-----
Bowl, 3¾", rose	18.00	40.00	35.00
Bowl, 4", hdld. (4 styles)	8.00	16.00	13.50
Bowl, 5", fruit	9.00	16.00	12.50
Bowl, 6", cereal	15.00	27.50	23.50
Bowl, 6", sq.	8.00	15.00	12.00
Bowl, 6½", 2 pt.	9.00	16.00	13.50
Bowl, 7", 3 ftd.	12.50	25.00	20.00
Bowl, 7½", jelly w/cover	25.00	60.00	50.00
Bowl, 8", pickle	8.50	16.50	14.00
Bowl, 8½", hdld.	14.00	26.00	20.00
Bowl, 9½", veg. oval	25.00	45.00	35.00
Bowl, 10", hdld.	15.00	40.00	33.00
Bowl, 10½", hdld., 4 ftd.	17.50	42.00	31.50
Bowl, 10" x 7½"	20.00	-----	-----
Bowl, 10", relish, 3 pt.	17.50	27.50	22.50
Bowl, 11", celery	12.00	22.50	20.00
Bowl, 11", rolled edge	20.00	35.00	30.00
Bowl, 12", flared	21.50	32.50	27.50
Candelabrum, 8¼", 2-lite, 16 lustre	37.50	50.00	40.00
Candelabrum, 9½", 3-lite, 24 lustre	47.50	60.00	45.00
Candle, 7¾", 8 lustre	12.50	25.00	22.50
Candlestick, 4"	8.00	15.00	12.50
Candlestick, 4½", 2-lite	11.00	20.00	17.50
Candlestick, 5½"	9.00	20.00	15.00
Candlestick, 6", 3-lite	15.00	25.00	20.00

	Crystal	Blue	Yellow
Comport, 4¾″	9.00	22.50	16.50
Comport, 6½″	10.00	27.50	19.00
Creamer, 3¼″, indiv.	6.00	11.00	10.00
Creamer, 3¾″, ftd.	7.00	14.00	12.00
Cup	6.50	15.00	11.00
Cup, 6 oz. punch	8.00	17.50	
Ice bucket	27.50	60.00	50.00
Mayonnaise, 5½″, w/liner	15.00	35.00	30.00
Mustard w/cover	22.00	45.00	37.50
Oil w/stopper, 5½″	35.00	325.00	235.00
Pitcher, 6½″	150.00	550.00	425.00
Pitcher, 7″, ice lip	125.00	525.00	375.00
Plate, 6″	3.00	5.00	4.00
Plate, 7″	4.00	9.00	7.00
Plate, 8″	6.00	11.00	9.00
Plate, 9″	15.00	32.00	28.00
Plate, 10″, cake	10.00	21.50	20.00
Plate, 11″, ctr. hdld. sand.	15.00	-----	-----
Plate, 14″, torte	13.00	30.00	25.00
Platter, 12″, oval	22.00	40.00	35.00
Salt & pepper, pr.	30.00	110.00	92.50
Salt & pepper, indiv., pr.	37.50	120.00	85.00
Saucer	2.00	5.00	4.00
Sherbet, 3¾″, 5 oz.	8.00	17.50	15.50
Stem, 6¾″, 9 oz., water	12.50	23.00	18.00
Sugar, 3″, indiv.	5.00	11.00	10.00
Sugar, 3½″, ftd.	6.00	12.00	11.00
Tray, 11″, oval	10.00	21.50	18.00
Tray, 6¼″ for indiv. cream/sugar	6.00	10.00	8.00
Tumbler, 3½″, 6½ oz., old fashioned	15.00	30.00	25.00
Tumbler, 3″, 3½ oz., ftd. cocktail	10.00	20.00	16.00
Tumbler, 3¾″, 5 oz., juice	12.00	30.00	22.00
Tumbler, 4¼″, 9 oz., water	14.00	26.00	21.00
Tumbler, 5¾″, 14 oz., tea	18.00	40.00	30.00
Vase, 6½″	15.00	38.00	32.50
Vase, 7″	15.00	43.00	37.50

BLACK FOREST, Possibly Paden City for Van Deman & Son Late 1920's/Early 1930's

Colors: amber, black, blue, crystal, green, pink, red   See Deerwood for more information.

	Amber	Black	Crystal	Green	Pink	Red
Bowl, 4½", finger				8.00		
Bowl, 11", console	50.00	50.00	35.00	25.00	25.00	
Bowl, 11", fruit	25.00	20.00		20.00	20.00	
Bowl, 13", console		65.00				
Bowl, 3 ftd.			60.00			
Cake plate, 2" pedestal	25.00	25.00		25.00	20.00	
Candlestick, mushroom style	25.00	20.00	15.00	20.00	18.00	
Candlestick double			25.00			
Candy dish w/cover, several styles	75.00	75.00			50.00	
Creamer, 2 styles		25.00	20.00	25.00	25.00	50.00
Comport, 4", low ftd				25.00	25.00	
Comport, 5½", high ftd		30.00		28.00	25.00	
Cup and saucer, 3 styles		65.00			75.00	95.00
Decanter, w/stopper			60.00	75.00	75.00	
Ice Bucket				75.00		
Ice tub, 2 styles	75.00	60.00			50.00	
Mayonnaise, with liner		60.00		50.00	60.00	
Pitcher, 6½", 42 oz.					75.00	
Pitcher, 8", 62 oz.			90.00			
Plate, 6½", bread/butter		22.00		22.00		
Plate, 8", luncheon		20.00			25.00	30.00
Plate, 11", 2 hdld.		30.00		25.00	25.00	
Salt and pepper, pr.			100.00		100.00	
Server, center hdld.	50.00	40.00	35.00	35.00	35.00	
Sherbet or champagne, 4¾"					22.00	
Stem 2 oz., wine, 4¼"			15.00			
Stem 6 oz., champagne, 4¾"			15.00			
Stem, 9 oz., water, 6"			18.00			
Sugar, 2 styles		25.00	20.00	25.00	25.00	50.00
Tumbler, 3 oz., juice, flat or footed, 3½"				25.00	20.00	
Tumbler, 8 oz., old fashioned, 3⅞"					30.00	
Tumbler, 9 oz., ftd., 5½"	20.00					
Tumbler, 12 oz., tea, 5½"				35.00	35.00	
Vase, 6½" (Blue $100.00)		55.00		50.00	50.00	
Vase, 10"		70.00		65.00	65.00	
Whipped cream pail	75.00					

CADENA, Tiffin Glass Company, Early 1930's

Colors: crystal; yellow; some pink

Cadena is a Tiffin pattern that I see only occasionally. I am always looking for cordials and have only been able to find one in crystal. Be sure to keep your eye out for the rarely found cups and saucers in nearly all Tiffin patterns. You will find stemware in all Tiffin lines but the cup and saucer collectors go nuts trying to find these. That means that collectors looking for eight or twelve for their sets are not doing too well!

The pitcher does come with a cover, but it is plain and not etched. That means that many Tiffin pitcher lids are interchangeable. If you can find a non-etched Tiffin pitcher with cover, you can usually buy it very reasonably and use that cover for your etched pitcher.

	Crystal	Yellow
Bowl, cream soup	15.00	22.00
Bowl, finger, ftd.	12.00	17.50
Bowl, grapefruit, ftd.	17.50	32.00
Bowl, 6″, hdld.	10.00	15.00
Bowl, 10″, pickle	12.50	20.00
Bowl, 12″, console	22.50	35.00
Candlestick	13.50	22.00
Creamer	15.00	25.00
Cup	15.00	25.00
Goblet, 4¾″, sherbet	15.00	22.00
Goblet, 5¼″, cocktail	17.50	25.00
Goblet, 5¼″, ¾ oz., cordial	35.00	55.00
Goblet, 6″, wine	22.00	35.00
Goblet, 6½″, champagne	17.00	35.00
Goblet, 7½″, water	20.00	27.50
Mayonnaise, ftd. w/liner	25.00	37.50
Oyster cocktail	15.00	22.00
Pitcher, ftd. w/cover	195.00	285.00
Plate, 6″	5.00	8.00
Plate, 7¾″	7.00	12.00
Plate, 9¼″	30.00	37.50
Saucer	4.00	6.00
Sugar	15.00	23.00
Tumbler, 4¼″, ftd. juice	15.00	25.00
Tumbler, 5¼″, ftd. water	17.00	27.50
Vase, 9″	25.00	45.00

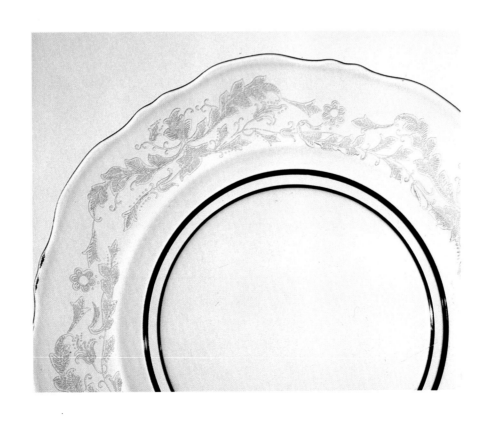

23

CANDLEWICK, Line #400, Imperial Glass Company, 1936 - 1984

Colors: crystal, blue, pink, yellow, black, red, cobalt blue; a few items in color recently

The closing of Imperial was the big news in the last book; but the closing of smaller Viking in 1987 may be fortuitous for Candlewick collectors. Many of the old Candlewick moulds were stored at Viking, having been delivered there from the demise of the Imperial factory. I have not had time to pursue what has happened to these moulds, but you need to be aware of it.

In 1981, I spent six hours at Imperial copying records of mould numbers and information on Candlewick and Cape Cod. I could not use these numbers in my computer because the mould and line numbers messed up the alphabetizing I was doing with all the four hundred pieces I was listing out of catalogues. Since my computer disk drives recently blew up and I had to learn to use my son's computer, I was able to add most of that information into the list this time. Lucille Kennedy and the rest of the staff at the old Imperial factory were always willing to share any Imperial information with you. Imperial had as good a catalogue file on the other glass company competitors as they did of their own glass. That amazed me at first; but in retrospect, it was a good idea to know what the other glass companies were making.

I hope you enjoy seeing all the colored Candlewick this time. There is a strong demand for the red, black, and blue. The two pieces of green were found in Rochester, New York. I have been unable to find out when they were made. There are some very unusual pieces of Candlewick pictured in my book on Rare Depression era glass.

	Crystal		Crystal
Ash tray, eagle, 6½", 1776/1	35.00	Bowl, 5", fruit, 400/1F	9.00
Ash tray, heart, 4½", 400/172	9.00	Bowl, 5", heart w/hand., 400/49H	15.00
Ash tray, heart, 5½", 400/173	13.00	Bowl, 5", square, 400/231	30.00
Ash tray, heart, 6½", 400/174	15.00	Bowl, 5½", heart, 400/53H	12.50
Ash tray, indiv.	5.00	Bowl, 5½", jelly w/cover, 400/59	45.00
Ash tray, oblong, 4½", 400/134/1	6.00	Bowl, 5½", sauce, deep 400/243	25.00
Ash tray, round, 2¾", 400/19	4.50	Bowl, 6", baked apple, rolled edge, 400/53X	15.00
Ash tray, round, 4", 400/33	9.00	Bowl, 6", cottage cheese, 400/85	17.50
Ash tray, 5", round 400/133	8.00	Bowl, 6", fruit, 400/3F	11.00
Ash tray, square, 3¼", 400/651	9.00	Bowl, 6", heart w/hand., 400/51H	17.50
Ash tray, square, 4½", 400/652	12.00	Bowl, 6", mint w/hand., 400/51F	14.00
Ash tray, square, 5¾", 400/653	15.00	Bowl, 6", round, div., 2 hdld, 400/52	20.00
Ash tray, 6", matchbook holder center, 400/60	47.50	Bowl, 6", 2 hdld, 400/52B	10.00
Ash tray set, 3 pc. rnd. nest. (crys. or colors), 400/550	20.00	Bowl, 6", 3 ftd., 400/183	27.50
		Bowl, 6", sq., 400/232	40.00
Ash tray set, 3 pc. sq. nesting, 400/650	36.00	Bowl, 6½", relish, 2 pt., 400/184	18.00
Ash tray set, 4 pc. bridge (cig. hold at side), 400/118	35.00	Bowl, 6½", 2 hdld., 400/181	20.00
		Bowl, 7", round, 400/SF	16.00
Basket, 5", beaded hdld, 400/273	110.00	Bowl, 7", round, 2 hdld., 400/62B	15.00
Basket, 6½", hdld., 400/40/0	27.50	Bowl, 7", relish, sq., div., 400/234	50.00
Basket, 11", hdld., 400/73/0	95.00	Bowl, 7", ivy, high, bead ft., 400/188	70.00
Bell, 4", 400/79	27.50	Bowl, 7", lily, 4 ft., 400/1745	45.00
Bell, 5", 400/108	35.00	Bowl, 7", relish, 400/60	20.00
Bottle, bitters w/tube, 4 oz., 400/117	40.00	Bowl, 7", sq., 400/233	50.00
Bowl, bouillon, 2 hdld., 400/126	17.50	Bowl, 7¼", rose, ftd. w/crimp edge, 400/1326	95.00
Bowl, #3400, finger, ftd	13.50	Bowl, 7½", pickle/celery	15.00
Bowl, #3800, finger	13.50	Bowl, 7½", lily, bead rim, ftd., 400/75N	45.00
Bowl, 4½", nappy, 3 ftd., 400/206	25.00	Bowl, 7½", belled, (console base), 400/127B	37.50
Bowl, 4¾", round, 2 hdld., 400/42B	10.00	Bowl, 7½", pickle/celery, 400/57	15.00
Bowl, 5", cream soup, 400/50	37.50	Bowl, 8", round, 400/7F	22.50

	Crystal
Bowl, 8″, relish, 2 pt., 400/26/1	17.50
Bowl, 8″, cov. veg., 400/65/1	90.00
Bowl, 8½″, rnd., 400/69	27.50
Bowl, 8½″, nappy, 4 ftd., 400/74B	32.50
Bowl, 8½″, 3 ftd., 400/182	55.00
Bowl, 8½″, 2 hdld., 400/72B	20.00
Bowl, 8½″, pickle/celery, 400/58	15.00
Bowl, 8½″, relish, 4 pt., 400/55	18.00
Bowl, 9″, round, 400/10F	30.00
Bowl, 9″, crimp, ftd., 400/67C	42.50
Bowl, 9″, sq., fancy crimp edge, 4 ft., 400/74SC	45.00
Bowl, 9″, heart, 400/49H	85.00
Bowl, 9″, heart w/hand., 400/73H	85.00
Bowl, 10″, 400/13F	32.00
Bowl, 10″, banana, 400/103F	125.00
Bowl, 10″, 3 toed, 400/205	85.00
Bowl, 10″, belled, (punch base), 400/128B . . .	50.00
Bowl, 10″, cupped edge, 400/75F	40.00
Bowl, 10″, deep, 2 hdld., 400/113A	40.00
Bowl, 10″, divided, deep, 2 hdld., 400/114A .	50.00
Bowl, 10″, fruit, bead stem (like compote), 400/103F	70.00
Bowl, 10″, relish, oval, 2h hld, 400/217	22.50
Bowl, 10″, relish, 3 pt., 3 ft., 400/208	57.50
Bowl, 10″ 2 handled, 400/113A	40.00
Bowl, 10½″, belled, 400/63B	60.00
Bowl, 10½″, butter/jam, 3 pt., 400/262	45.00
Bowl, 10½″, salad, 400/75B	35.00
Bowl, 10½″, relish, 3 section, 400/256	22.00
Bowl, 11″, celery boat, oval, 400/46	45.00
Bowl, 11″, centerpiece, flared, 400/13B	35.00
Bowl, 11″, float, inward rim, ftd., 400/75F . .	35.00
Bowl, 11″, oval, 400/124A	30.00
Bowl, 11″, oval w/partition, 400/125A	40.00
Bowl, 12″, round, 400/92B	25.50
Bowl, 12″, belled, 400/106B	75.00
Bowl, 12″, float, 400/92F	37.50
Bowl, 12″, hdld., 400/113B	27.50
Bowl, 12″, shallow, 400/17F	40.00
Bowl, 12″, relish, oblong, 4 sect, 400/215	40.00
Bowl, 13″, centerpiece, mushroom, 400/92F .	47.50
Bowl, 13″, float, 1½″ deep, 400/101	40.00
Bowl, 13½″, relish, 5 pt., 400/209	32.50
Bowl, 14″, belled, 400/104B	85.00
Bowl, 14″, oval, flared, 400/131B	95.00
Butter and jam set, 5 piece, 400/204	130.00
Butter w/cover, rnd, 5½″, 400/144	27.50
Butter w/cover, no beads, California, 400/276	75.00
Butter w/bead top, ¼ lb., 400/161	23.00
Cake stand, 10″, low foot, 400/670	45.00
Cake stand, 11″, high foot, 400/103D	52.50
Calendar, 1947, desk	80.00
Candleholder, 3 way, beaded base, 400/115 . .	65.00
Candleholder, 2-lite, 400/100	16.00
Candleholder, flat, 3½″, 400/280	13.00
Candleholder, 3½″, rolled edge, 400/79R	10.50
Candleholder, 3½″, w/fingerhold, 400/81	25.00
Candleholder, flower, 4″, 2 bead stem, 400/66F	30.00

	Crystal
Candleholder, flower, 4½″, 2 bead stem, 400/66C	25.00
Candleholder 4½″, 3 toed, 400/207	27.50
Candleholder, 3-lite on cir. bead. ctr., 400/147	15.00
Candleholder, 5″, hdld. w/bowled up base, 400/90	35.00
Candleholder, 5″ heart shape, 400/40HC	25.00
Candleholder, 5½″, 3 bead stems, 400/224 . . .	60.00
Candleholder, flower, 5″, (epergne inset), 400/40CV	75.00
Candleholder, 5″, flower, 400/40C	20.00
Candleholder, 6½″, tall, 3 bead stems, 400/175	20.00
Candleholder, flat, 3½″, 400/280	13.00
Candleholder, flower, 6″, round, 400/40F . . .	15.00
Candleholder, urn, 6″, holders on cir. ctr. bead, 400/129R	37.50
Candleholder, flower, 6½″, square, 400/40S .	21.00
Candleholder, mushroom, 400/86	17.50
Candleholder, flower 9″ centerpiece, 400/196FC	55.00
Candy box, round, 5½″, 400/59	30.00
Candy box, sq., 6½″, rnd. lid, 400/245	95.00
Candy box w/cover, 7″, 400/259	45.00
Candy box w/cover, 7″ partitioned, 400/110 .	50.00
Candy box w/cover, round, 7″, 3 Sect, 400/158	60.00
Candy box w/cover, beaded, ft, 400/140	100.00
Cigarette box w/cover, 400/134	22.00
Cigarette holder, 3″, bead ft., 400/44	20.00
Cigarette set: 6 pc., (cigarette box & 4 rect. ash trays), 400/134/6	47.50
Clock, 4″, round	85.00
Coaster, 4″, 400/78	5.00
Coaster w/spoon rest, 400/226	10.00
Cocktail, seafood w/bead ft., 400/190	35.00
Cocktail set: 2 pc., plate w/indent; cocktail, 400/97	25.00
Compote, 4½″, 400/63B	12.50
Compote, 5″, 3 bead stems, 400/220	35.00
Compote, 5½″, 4 bead stem, 400/45	18.00
Compote, 5½″, low, plain stem, 400/66B	13.50
Compote, 5½″, 2 bead stem, 400/66B	15.00
Compote, 8″, bead stem, 400/48F	65.00
Compote, 10″, ftd. fruit, crimped, 40/1036 . . .	75.00
Compote, ft. oval, 400/137	95.00
Condiment set:	
4 pc., (2 squat bead ft. shakers, marmalade), 400/1786	47.50
Console sets:	
3 pc. (14″ oval bowl, two 3-lite candles), 400/1531B	225.00
3 pc. (mushroom bowl, 2 mushroom candles), 400/8692L	72.50
Creamer, domed foot, 400/1835	35.00
Creamer, 6 oz., bead handle, 400/30	7.50
Creamer, indiv. bridge, 400/122	5.00
Creamer, plain ft., 400/31	6.00
Creamer, flat, bead handle, 400/126	20.00
Cup, after dinner, 400/77	18.00
Cup, coffee, 400/37	7.50

	Crystal
Cup, punch, 400/211	6.00
Cup, tea, 400/35	7.00
Decanter w/stopper, 18 oz cordial, 400/82-2..	150.00
Decanter, hdld, with stopper, 400/82-2	225.00
Decanter w/stopper, 26 oz., 400/163	185.00
Deviled egg server, 12″, ctr. hdld	75.00
Egg cup, bead. ft., 400/19	30.00
Fork & spoon, set, 400/75	18.00
Hurricane lamp, 2 pc. candle base, 400/79 ..	35.00
Hurricane lamp, 2 pc., hold candle base, 400/76	47.50
Hurricane lamp, 3 pc. flared & crimped	
edge globe, 400/152	75.00
Ice tub, 5½″ deep, 8″ diam., 400/63	75.00
Ice tub, 7″, 2 hdld., 400/168	85.00
Icer, 2 pc., seafood/fruit cocktail, 400/53/3 . . .	45.00
Icer, 2 pc., seafood/fruit cocktail	
#3800 line, one bead stem	32.50
Jam set, 5 pc., oval tray w/2 marmalade	
jars w/ladles, 400/1589	57.50
Jar tower, 3 sect., 400/655	75.00
Knife, butter, 4000	110.00
Ladle, marmalade, 3 bead stem, 400/130	6.00
Ladle, mayonnaise, 6¼″, 400/135	6.00
Marmalade set, 3 pc., beaded ft. w/cover	
& spoon, 400/1989	24.00
Marmalade set, 3 pc. tall jar, domed bead ft., lid,	
spoon, 400/8918	37.50
Marmalade set, 4 pc., liner saucer, jar,	
lid, spoon, 400/89	30.00
Mayonnaise set, 2 pc. scoop side bowl,	
spoon, 400/23	32.50
Mayonnaise set, 3 pc. hdld. tray/hdld	
bowl/ladle, 400/52/3	32.50
Mayonnaise set, 3 pc. plate, heart bowl,	
spoon, 400/49	33.00
Mayonnaise set, 3 pc. scoop side bowl,	
spoon, tray, 400/496	40.00
Mayonnaise set, 4 pc., plate, bowl, 2	
ladles, 400/84	40.00
Mayonnaise 4 pc, plate, divided 2 ladles, 400/84	42.50
Mirror, 4½″ rnd., standing	70.00
Mustard jar w/spoon, 400/156	30.00
Oil, 4 oz. bead base, 400/164	35.00
Oil, 6 oz. bead base, 400/166	37.50
Oil, 4 oz., bulbous bottom, 400/274	35.00
Oil, 4 oz., hdld. bulbous bottom, 400/278	42.00
Oil, 6 oz., hdld. bulbous bottom, 400/279	50.00
Oil, 6 oz., bulbous bottom, 400/275	40.00
Oil w/stopper, etched "Oil", 400/121	45.00
Oil w/stopper, etched "Vinegar", 400/121 . . .	45.00
Party set, 2 pc., oval plate w/indent for cup,	
400/98	17.50
Pitcher, 14 oz., short rnd., 400/330	85.00
Pitcher, 16 oz., low ft., 400/19	125.00
Pitcher, 16 oz., no ft., 400/16	95.00
Pitcher, 20 oz., plain, 400/416	25.00
Pitcher, 40 oz., juice/cocktail, 400/19	110.00
Pitcher, 40 oz., manhattan, 400/18	150.00

	Crystal
Pitcher 40 oz., plain, 400/419	25.00
Pitcher, 64 oz., plain, 400/424	30.00
Pitcher, 80 oz., plain, 400/424	30.00
Pitcher, 80 oz., 400/16	97.50
Pitcher, 80 oz., beaded ft, 400/18	145.00
Plate, 4½″, 400/34	4.50
Plate, 5½″, 2 hdld., 400/420	6.50
Plate, 6″, bread/butter, 400/1D	6.50
Plate, 6″, canape w/off ctr. indent, 400/36 . . .	9.00
Plate, 6¾″, 2 hdld. crimped, 400/526	16.00
Plate, 7″, salad, 400/3D	8.00
Plate, 7½″, 2 hdld., 400/52D	8.00
Plate, 7½″, triangular, 400/266	35.00
Plate, 8″, oval, 400/169	12.00
Plate, 8″, salad, 400/5D	8.00
Plate, 8″ w/indent, 400/50	11.00
Plate, 8¼″, crescent salad, 400/120	37.50
Plate, 8½″, 2 hdld. crimped, 400/62C	20.00
Plate, 8½″, 2 hdld., 400/62D	12.00
Plate, 8½″, salad, 400/5D	9.00
Plate, 8½″, 2 hdld. (sides upturned), 400/62E . .	20.00
Plate, 9″, luncheon, 400/7D	12.50
Plate, 9″, oval salad, 400/38	15.00
Plate 9″, w/indent, oval, 400/98	10.50
Plate, 10″, 2 hdld., sides upturned, 400/72E .	22.50
Plate, 10″, 2 hdld. crimped, 400/72C	25.00
Plate, 10″, dinner, 400/10D	22.50
Plate, 10″, 2 hdld., 400/72D	15.00
Plate, 12″, 2 hdld., 400/145D	22.50
Plate, 12″, 2 hdld. crimp., 400/145C	32.50
Plate, 12″, service, 400/13D	22.00
Plate, 12½″, cupped edge, torte, 400/75V	27.50
Plate, 12½″, oval, 400/124	35.00
Plate, 13½″, cupped edge serving, 400/92V ..	35.00
Plate, 14″ birthday cake (holes for 72 candles),	
400/16D	265.00
Plate, 14″, 2 hdld., sides upturned, 400/113E	30.00
Plate, 14″, 2 hdld. torte, 400/113D	25.00
Plate, 14″, service, 400/92D	27.50
Plate, 14″, torte, 400/17D	30.00
Plate, 17″, cupped edge, 400/20V	42.50
Plate, 17″, torte, 400/20D	42.50
Platter, 13″, 400/124D	55.00
Platter, 16″, 400/131D	95.00
Punch ladle, 400/91	20.00
Punch set, family, 8 demi cups, ladle, lid,	
400/139/77	245.00
Punch set, 15 pc. bowl on base, 12 cups,	
ladle, 400/20	200.00
Relish & dressing set, 4 pc. (10½″ 4 pt.	
relish w/marmalade), 400/1112	57.50
Salad fork & spoon set, 400/75	18.00
Salad set, 4 pc., buffet; lg. rnd. tray, div.	
bowl, 2 spoons, 400/17	75.00
Salad set, 4 pc. (rnd. plate, flared bowl, fork,	
spoon), 400/75B	60.00
Salt & pepper, bead ft., straight side,	
chrome top, 400/247	16.00

	Crystal		Crystal
Salt & pepper, bead ft., bulbous, chrome top, 400/96	12.50	Tid bit server, 2 tier, cupped, 400/2701	40.00
Salt & pepper, bulbous w/bead stem, plastic top, 400/116	25.00	Tid bit set, 3 pc., 400/18TB	60.00
Salt & pepper, pr., indiv., 400/109	10.00	Toast w/cover, set, 7¾", 400/123	80.00
Salt & pepper, pr., ftd bead base, 400/190	25.00	Tray, 5½", hdld., upturned handles, 400/42E	18.00
Salt dip, 2", 400/61	6.00	Tray, 5½", lemon, ctr. hdld., 400/221	13.50
Salt dip, 2¼", 400/19	6.50	Tray, 5¼" x 9¼", condiment, 400/148	50.00
Salt spoon, 3, 400/616	3.50	Tray, 6½", 400/29	15.00
Salt spoon w/ribbed bowl, 4000	3.50	Tray, 6", wafer, handle bent to ctr. of dish, 400/51T	22.00
Sauce boat 400/169	65.00	Tray, 10½", ctr. hdld. fruit, 400/68F	25.00
Sauce boat liner, 400/169	30.00	Tray, 11½", ctr. hdld. party, 400/68D	30.00
Saucer, after dinner, 400/77AD	5.00	Tray, 13½", 2 hdld. celery, oval, 400/105	27.50
Saucer, tea or coffee, 400/35 or 400/37	3.00	Tray, 13", relish, 5 sections, 400/102	27.50
Set: 2 pc. hdld. cracker w/cheese compote, 400/88	35.00	Tray, 14", hdld., 400/113E	40.00
Set: 2 pc. rnd. cracker plate w/indent; cheese compote, 400/145	45.00	Tumbler, 3½ oz., cocktail, 400/18	35.00
Snack jar w/cover, bead ft., 400/139/1	85.00	Tumbler, 5 oz., juice, 400/18	32.00
Stem, 1 oz., cordial, 400/190	65.00	Tumbler, 6 oz., sherbet, 400/18	22.50
Stem, 4 oz., cocktail, 400/190	18.00	Tumbler, 7 oz., parfait, 400/18	30.00
Stem, 5 oz., tall sherbet, 400/190	14.50	Tumbler, 9 oz., water, 400/18	25.00
Stem, 5 oz., wine, 400/190	22.00	Tumbler, 12 oz., tea, 400/18	27.50
Stem, 6 oz., sherbet, 400/190	12.00	Tumbler, 3 oz. ftd cocktail, 400/19	12.00
Stem, 10 oz., water 400/190	16.00	Tumbler, 3 oz. ftd wine, 400/19	14.00
Stem, #3400, 1 oz., cordial	35.00	Tumbler, 5 oz. low sherbet, 400/19	12.00
Stem, #3400, 4 oz., cocktail	14.00	Tumbler, 5 oz., juice, 400/19	10.00
Stem, #3400, 4 oz. oyster cocktail	14.00	Tumbler, 7 oz., old fashioned, 400/19	13.50
Stem, #3400, 4 oz., wine	24.00	Tumbler, 10 oz., 400/19	10.00
Stem, #3400, 5 oz., claret	30.00	Tumbler, 12 oz., 400/19	14.00
Stem, #3400, 5 oz., low sherbet	10.00	Tumbler, 14 oz., 400/19, tea	17.00
Stem, #3400, 6 oz., parfait	35.00	Tumbler #3400, 5 oz. ft juice	15.00
Stem, #3400, 6 oz., sherbet/saucer champagne	13.00	Tumbler, #3400, 9 oz., ft.	14.00
Stem, #3400, 9 oz., goblet, water	15.00	Tumbler, #3400, 10 oz., ft.	12.50
Stem, #3800, low sherbet	14.00	Tumbler, #3400, 12 oz ft	15.00
Stem, #3800, brandy	20.00	Tumbler, #3800, 5 oz. juice	16.00
Stem, #3800, 1 oz. cordial	35.00	Tumbler, #3800, 9 oz.	14.00
Stem, #3800, 4 oz., cocktail	18.00	Tumbler, #3800, 12 oz.	18.00
Stem, #3800, 4 oz., wine	24.00	Vase, 4", bead ft. sm. neck ball, 400/25	22.00
Stem, #3800, 6 oz., champagne/sherbet	15.00	Vase, 5¾", bead ft. bud, 400/107	45.00
Stem, #3800, 9 oz. water goblet	18.00	Vase, 5¾", bead ft. mini bud, 400/107	40.00
Stem, #3800, claret	30.00	Vase, 6", flat, crimped edge, 400/287C	20.00
Stem, #4000, 1¼ oz. cordial	30.00	Vase, 6", ftd. flared rim, 400/138B	37.50
Stem, #4000, cocktail	22.00	Vase, 6" diam., 400/198	85.00
Stem, #4000, 5 oz, wine	28.00	Vase, 6" fan, 400/287 F	20.00
Stem, #4000, 6 oz. tall sherbet	14.00	Vase 7" ftd bud, 400/186	45.00
Stem, #4000, 11 oz., goblet	18.00	Vase 7" ivy bowl, 400/74J	45.00
Stem #4000, 12 oz., tea	20.00	Vase 7" rolled rim w/bead hdld., 400/87 B	45.00
Strawberry set, 2 pc. (7" plate/sugar dip bowl), 400/83	15.00	Vase 7" rose bowl, 400/142 K	65.00
Sugar, domed foot, 400/18	35.00	Vase, 7¼" ftd. rose bowl, crimped top, 400/132C	95.00
Sugar, 6 oz., bead hdld., 400/30	6.50	Vase, 7½" ftd. rose bowl, 400/132	90.00
Sugar, flat, bead handle, 400/126	20.00	Vase, 8", fan w/bead hdld., 400/87F	30.00
Sugar, indiv. bridge, 400/122	6.00	Vase, 8", flat, crimped edge, 400/143C	55.00
Sugar, plain ft., 400/31	6.50	Vase, 8", fluted rim w/bead hdlds., 400/87C	27.50
Tete-a-tete 3 pc. brandy, a.d. cup, 6½" oval tray, 400/111	47.50	Vase, 8½", bead ft. bud, 400/28C	55.00
		Vase, 8½", bead ft., flared rim, 400/21	60.00
		Vase, 8½", bead ft., inward rim, 400/27	55.00
		Vase, 8½", hdld. (pitcher shape), 400/227	100.00
		Vase, 10", bead ft., straight side, 400/22	85.00
		Vase, 10", ftd., 400/193	110.00

CAPE COD, Imperial Glass Co., 1932 - 1980's

Colors: crystal, cobalt blue, red

Were you surprised to see Cape Cod on the cover? It photographed better than Candlewick which was another consideration. Cambridge and Fostoria patterns have graced the first books, so it was Imperial's time.

I purchased a large accumulation of Fostoria, Heisey and Imperial catalogues last year. Many of these came from a collection that was eventually sold to the Corning Glass Museum. Unfortunately, it will be years, if ever, that collectors will get any knowledge from those.

I have been able to expand my listings of Cape Cod because of these catalogue purchases, but I am sure there are other pieces that have been omitted; so let me know what you find.

	Crystal		Crystal
Ash tray, 4″, 160/134/1	4.00	Cake plate, 10″, 4 toed, 160/220	65.00
Ash tray, 5½″, 160/150	7.00	Cake stand, 10½″, footed 160/67D	30.00
Basket, 9″, handled, crimped, 160/221/0	75.00	Cake stand, 11″, 160/103D	50.00
Basket, 11″ wide, 160/221/0	75.00	Candleholder, twin, 160/100	35.00
Basket, 11″ tall, handled 160/40	75.00	Candleholder, 3″, single 160/170	10.00
Bottle, bitters, 4 oz., 160/235	30.00	Candleholder, 4″, 160/81	12.00
Bottle, cologne, w/stopper, 1601	30.00	Candleholder, 4″, Aladdin style, 160/90	30.00
Bottle, condiment, 6 oz. 160/224	40.00	Candleholder, 4½″, saucer 160/175	12.00
Bottle, cordial, 18 oz., 160/256	55.00	Candleholder, 5″, 160/80	12.00
Bottle, decanter, 26 oz., 160/244	65.00	Candleholder, 5″, flower, 160/45B	27.50
Bottle, ketchup, 14 oz., 160/237	50.00	Candleholder, 5½″, flower, 160/45N	35.00
Bowl, 3″, handled mint, 160/183	6.00	Candleholder, 6″, centerpiece, 160/48BC	45.00
Bowl, 3″, jelly	3.00	Candy w/cover, 160/110	55.00
Bowl, 4″ finger, 1602	6.00	Carafe, wine, 26 oz., 160/185	95.00
Bowl, 4½″, 160/1W	4.00	Celery, 8″, 160/105	15.00
Bowl, 4½″, handled spider, 160/180	10.00	Celery, 10½″, 160/189	22.50
Bowl, 4½″, dessert, tab handled, 160/197	6.50	Cigarette box, 4½″, 160/134	20.00
Bowl, 5″, dessert, heart shape, 160/49H	8.50	Cigarette holder, ftd., 1602	12.50
Bowl, 5″, flower 1605N	7.50	Cigarette holder, small mug, 160/200	25.00
Bowl, 5½″, fruit 160/23B	3.00	Cigarette lighter, 1602	12.00
Bowl, 5½″, handled spider, 160/181	11.00	Coaster, w/spoon rest, 160/76	9.50
Bowl, 5½″, tab handled, soup 160/198	8.00	Coaster, 3″, square, 160/85	6.00
Bowl, 6″, fruit, 160/3F	5.50	Coaster, 4″, 160/78	5.00
Bowl, 6″, baked apple, 160/53X	8.00	Coaster, 4½″, 160/1R	5.00
Bowl, 6″, handled, round mint, 160/51F	13.50	Comporte, 5¼″, 160F	15.00
Bowl, 6″, handled heart 160/40H	14.50	Comporte, 5¾″, 160X	17.50
Bowl, 6″, handled mint, 160/51H	18.00	Comporte, 6″, 160/45	15.00
Bowl, 6″, handled tray, 160/51T	12.50	Comporte, 6″, w/cover, ftd, 160/140	50.00
Bowl, 6½″, handled partioned spider, 160/187	22.50	Comporte, 7″, 160/48B	25.00
Bowl, 6½″, handled spider, 160/182	20.00	Comporte, 11¼″, oval 1602	75.00
Bowl, 6½″, tab handled, 160/199	10.50	Creamer, 160/190	8.00
Bowl, 7″, nappy, 160/5F	12.50	Creamer, 160/30	8.00
Bowl, 7½″, 160/7F	13.00	Creamer, ftd., 160/31	9.00
Bowl, 7½″, 2-handled, 160/62B	22.00	Cruet, w/stopper, 4 oz., 160/119	15.00
Bowl, 8¾″, 160/10F	20.00	Cruet, w/stopper, 5 oz., 160/70	20.00
Bowl, 9″, footed fruit, 160/67F	50.00	Cruet, w/stopper, 6 oz. 160/241	35.00
Bowl, 9½″, 2-handled, 160/145B	30.00	Cup, tea, 160/35	9.00
Bowl, 9½″, crimped 160/221C	35.00	Cup, coffee, 160/37	10.00
Bowl, 9½″, float, 160/221F	32.50	Cup, bouillon, 160/250	10.00
Bowl, 10″, footed, 160/137B	55.00	Decanter, bourbon, 160/260	60.00
Bowl, 10″, oval, 160/221	37.50	Decanter, rye, 160/260	60.00
Bowl, 10″, round, 160/8A	30.00	Decanter w/stopper, 30 oz., 160/163	45.00
Bowl, 11″, oval, 160/124	37.50	Decanter w/stopper, 24 oz., 160/212	50.00
Bowl, 11″, oval divided, 160/125	40.00	Egg cup, 160/225	17.50
Bowl, 11″, salad, 160/8B	35.00	Epergne, 2 pc., plain center, 160/196	165.00
Bowl, 11¼″, oval, 1602	45.00	Fork, 160/701	7.50
Bowl, 12″, 160/75B	35.00	Gravy bowl, 18 oz., 160/202	55.00
Bowl, 12″, oval, 160/131B	45.00	Horseradish, 5 oz. jar, 160/226	60.00
Bowl, 12″, oval crimped, 160/131C	55.00	Ice bucket, 6½″, 160/63	45.00
Bowl, 12″, punch, 160/20B	42.50	Icer, 3 pc., bowl, 2 inserts, 160/53/3	30.00
Bowl, 12½″, punch, 16010B	45.00	Jar, 12 oz., hdld peanut w/lid, 160/210	50.00
Bowl, 13″, console, 160/75C	40.00	Jar, 8½″, "Pokal", 160/128	25.00
Bowl, 15″, console, 16010I	45.00	Jar, 10″, "Pokal", 160/133	30.00
Butter, 5″, w/cover, handled, 160/144	25.00	Jar, 11″, "Pokal", 160/128	45.00
Butter, w/cover, ¼ lb., 160/161	35.00	Jar, 15″, "Pokal", 160/132	85.00

CAPE COD, Imperial Glass Co., 1932 - 1980's,

	Crystal
Jar, candy w/lid, wicker hand., 5" h., 160/194	65.00
Jar, cookie w/lid, wicker hand., 6½" h. 160/195	75.00
Jar, peanut butter w/lid, wicker hand. 4" h., 160/193	50.00
Ladle, marmalade, 160/130	6.00
Ladle, mayonnaise, 160/165	6.00
Ladle, punch, 160/91	20.00
Lamp, hurricane, 2 pic., 5" base, 160/79	55.00
Lamp, hurricane, 2 pc., bowl-like base, 1604	60.00
Marmalade, 3 pc. set, 160/89/3	25.00
Marmalade, 4 pc. set, 160/89	30.00
Mayonnaise, 3 pc. set, 260/52H	25.00
Mayonnaise, 3 pc., 160/23	18.00
Mayonnaise, 12 oz., hdld, spouted, 160/205	45.00
Mug, 12 oz., handled, 160/188	35.00
Mustard, w/cover & spoon, 160/156	16.00
Nut dish, 3", hdld., 160/183	6.00
Nut dish, 4", hdld., 160/184	7.00
Pepper mill, 160/236	15.00
Pitcher, milk, 1 pt., 160/240	22.00
Pitcher, ice lipped, 40 oz., 160/19	47.50
Pitcher, martini, blown, 40 oz., 160/178	75.00
Pitcher, ice lipped, 2 qt., 160/239	55.00
Pitcher, 2 qt., 160/24	65.00
Pitcher, 48 oz. ftd., 16152	65.00
Pitcher, blown, 5 pt., 160/176	95.00
Plate, 4½" butter, 160/34	3.00
Plate, 6", cupped, (liner for 160/208 salad dressing), 160/209	12.00
Plate, 6½", bread & butter, 160/1D	2.50
Plate, 7", 160/3D	4.00
Plate, 7", cupped (liner for 160/205 Mayo), 160/206	15.00
Plate, 8", center handled tray 160/149D	22.50
Plate, 8", crescent salad, 160/12	35.00
Plate, 8", cupped, (liner for gravy), 160/203	20.00
Plate, 8", salad 160/5D	6.00
Plate, 8½", 2-handled, 160/62D	18.00
Plate, 9" 160/7D	7.50
Plate, 9½" 2 hdld., 160/62D	25.00
Plate, 10", dinner, 160/10D	30.00
Plate, 11", 1608X	27.50
Plate, 11½", 2-handled 160/145D	30.00
Plate, 12½" bread, 160/222	40.00
Plate, 13", birthday, 72 candle holes, 160/72	165.00
Plate, 13", cupped torte, 160/8V	27.50
Plate, 13", torte, 160/8F	30.00
Plate, 14", cupped, 160/75V	30.00
Plate, 14", flat 160/75D	30.00
Plate, 16", cupped, 160/20V	35.00
Plate, 17", 2 styles 160/10D or 20D	35.00
Platter, 13½", oval, 160/124D	45.00
Puff Box, w/cover, 1601	30.00
Relish, 8", hdld, 2 part. 160/223	25.00
Relish, 9½", 4 pt., 160/56	30.00
Relish, 9½", oval, 3 part, 160/55	30.00

	Crystal
Relish, 11", 5 part, 160/102	40.00
Relish, 11¼", 3 part, oval, 1602	40.00
Salad dressing, 6 oz., hdld., spouted, 160/208	35.00
Salad set, 14" plate, 12" bowl, fork & spoon, 160/75	90.00
Salt & pepper, individual, 160/251	12.00
Salt & pepper, pr., ftd., 160/116	10.00
Salt & pepper pr., ftd., stemmed, 160/243	22.50
Salt & pepper pr., 160/96	9.00
Salt & pepper, pr. square, 160/109	18.00
Salt dip, 160/61	8.00
Salt spoon, 1600	3.00
Saucer, tea, 160/35	1.50
Saucer, coffee, 160/37	1.50
Server, 12", ftd or turned over, 160/93	55.00
Spoon, 160/701	7.50
Stem, 1½ oz. cordial, 1602	10.00
Stem, 3 oz. wine, 1602	7.00
Stem, 3½ oz. cocktail, 1602	7.00
Stem, 5 oz. claret, 1602	10.00
Stem, 6 oz. low sundae, 1602	7.00
Stem, 6 oz. parfait, 1602	12.00
Stem, 6 oz. sherbet, 1600	7.50
Stem, 6 oz. tall sherbet, 1602	8.50
Stem, 9 oz. water, 1602	9.50
Stem, 10 oz. water, 1600	10.00
Stem, 11 oz. dinner goblet, 1602	10.00
Stem, 14 oz goblet, 160	22.50
Stem, oyster cocktail, 1602	7.50
Sugar, 160/190	8.00
Sugar, 160/30	7.00
Sugar, ftd., 160/31	7.00
Toast, w/cover, 160/123	45.00
Tray, 7" for creamer/sugar, 160/29	8.00
Tray, 11", pastry, center handle, 160/68D	32.50
Tumbler, 2½ oz. whiskey, 160	9.50
Tumbler, 6 oz. ftd. juice, 1602	6.00
Tumbler, 6 oz. juice, 1600	7.00
Tumbler, 7 oz. old fashion, 160	9.00
Tumbler, 10 oz. ftd, water, 1602	8.00
Tumbler, 10 oz. water, 160	9.00
Tumbler, 12 oz. ftd. ice tea, 1602	11.00
Tumbler, 12 oz. ftd. tea, 1600	11.00
Tumbler, 12 oz. ice tea, 160	12.50
Tumbler, 14 oz. double old fashion, 160	17.50
Tumbler, 16 oz., 160	15.00
Vase, 6¼", ftd., 160/22	20.00
Vase, 6½", ftd., 160/110B	35.00
Vase, 7", bud, 160/27	22.50
Vase, 7½", ftd., 160/22	27.50
Vase, 8", fan, 160/87F	45.00
Vase, 8½", flip, 160/143	40.00
Vase, 8½", ftd, 160/28	32.50
Vase, 10", cylinder, 160/192	45.00
Vase, 10½", hdld urn, 160/186	85.00
Vase, 11", ftd., 160/21	50.00

CAPRICE, Cambridge Glass Company, 1940's - Early 1950's

Colors: crystal, blue, white, amber, amethyst, pink, emerald green, pink, cobalt blue, moonlight blue, white

Moulds for items with an asterisk in the price list below are presently owned by Summit Art Glass Company. This information was obtained from Barbara Schaeffer of the "Glass Review". Many of these pieces have already been reproduced and others will surely follow. It is unlikely that these moulds were purchased for any other reason than to use them again. Most reproduced items have a small dot on the bottom, but this is not true for all. This dot can easily be removed. The blue color on most of the reproductions has been slightly off and the weight of the glass has been a little heavier. You need to know your dealer and know your glass before you spend your money.

Remarkably, there has been little hesitation by collectors in buying Caprice even with the newly made pieces on the market! It has slowed down beginning collectors until they learn how to distinguish this newly made Caprice.

There have been some dramatic price increases since the last book; so be aware of that as you shop. This is a truly beautiful pattern.

	Crystal	Blue
Ash tray, 2¾″, 3 ftd. shell, #213	6.00	10.00
*Ash tray, 3″, #214	6.00	12.00
*Ash tray, 4″ #215	7.00	
*Ash tray, 5″ #216		17.50
Bonbon, 6″, oval, ftd., #155	15.00	30.00
Bonbon, 6″ sq., 2 hdld., #154	12.00	30.00
Bonbon, 6″ sq., ftd., #133	14.00	35.00
Bottle, 7 oz., bitters, #186	65.00	150.00
*Bowl, 5″, 2 hdld., jelly, #151	13.00	27.50
*Bowl, 6½″, hdld., 2 pt. relish, #120	15.00	30.00
Bowl, 8″, 4 ftd., #49	30.00	50.00
*Bowl, 8″, 3 pt. relish, #124	17.50	32.50
Bowl, 9½″, crimped, 4 ftd., #52	27.50	50.00
Bowl, 9″, pickle, #102	15.00	32.50
Bowl, 10″, salad, 4 ftd., #57	32.50	60.00
Bowl, 10″, sq., 4 ftd., #58	30.00	52.50
Bowl, 10½″, crimped, 4 ftd., #53	30.00	65.00
Bowl, 11″, crimped, 4 ftd., #60	32.00	70.00
*Bowl, 11″, 2 hdld., oval, 4 ftd., #65	30.00	60.00
*Bowl, 12″, 4 pt. relish, oval, #126	60.00	125.00
*Bowl, 12″, relish, 3 pt., rectangular, #125	40.00	90.00
Bowl, 12½″, belled, 4 ftd., #62	30.00	65.00
Bowl, 12½″, crimped, 4 ftd., #61	32.50	65.00
Bowl, 13″, crimped, 4 ftd., #66	32.50	70.00
Bowl, 13½″, 4 ftd., shallow cupped #82	35.00	72.50
Bridge set:		
*Cloverleaf, 6½″, #173	20.00	37.50
*Club, 6½″, #170	20.00	37.50
Diamond, 6½″, #171	20.00	37.50
*Heart, 6½″, #169	20.00	37.50
*Spade, 6½″, #172	20.00	37.50
*Butterdish, ¼ lb., #52	195.00	----
Cake plate, 13″ ftd., #36	125.00	250.00
Candle reflector	125.00	-----
Candlestick, 2½″, ea., #67	12.00	20.00
Candlestick, 2-lite, keyhole, 5″, #646	14.00	32.00
Candlestick, 3-lite, #74	25.00	42.50
Candlestick, 5″, ea., keyhole, #647	17.50	35.00
Candlestick, 7″, ea. w/prism, #70	15.00	32.50
Candy, 6″, 3 ftd. w/cover, #165	40.00	85.00
Candy, 6″, w/cover (divided), #168	50.00	95.00
Celery & relish, 8½″, 3 pt., #124	17.50	35.00
Cigarette box w/cover, 3½″ x 2¼″, #207	15.00	27.50
Cigarette box w/cover, 4½″ x 3½″, #208	22.00	50.00
Cigarette holder, 2″ x 2¼″, triangular, #205	12.00	22.50
Cigarette holder, 3″ x 3″, triangular, #204	20.00	40.00
Coaster, 3½″, #13	12.00	20.00
Comport, 6″, #130	22.00	50.00
Comport, 7″ low ftd., #130	17.50	50.00
Comport, 7″, #136	35.00	70.00
Cracker jar & cover, #202	100.00	225.00
*Creamer, large, #41	10.00	17.50
*Creamer, medium, #38	8.00	15.00
*Creamer, ind., #40	10.00	16.00
Cup, #17	12.00	30.00
Decanter w/stopper, 35 oz., #187	100.00	200.00
Finger bowl & liner, #16	25.00	55.00
Ice bucket, #201	45.00	125.00
Marmalade w/cover, 6 oz., #89	45.00	120.00
*Mayonnaise, 6½″, 3 pc. set, #129	25.00	67.50
*Mayonnaise, 8″, 3 pc. set, #106	40.00	77.50
Mustard w/cover, 2 oz., #87	35.00	95.00
*Oil, 3 oz., w/stopper, #101	22.00	45.00
*Oil, 5 oz., w/stopper, #100	65.00	115.00
Pitcher, 32 oz., ball shape, # 179	75.00	265.00

*Moulds owned by Summit Art Glass

	Crystal	Blue
Pitcher, 80 oz., ball shape, #183	90.00	250.00
Pitcher, 90 oz., tall Doulton style, #178	700.00	1,350.00
Plate, 6½″, bread/butter, #21	10.00	15.00
Plate, 6½″, hdld., lemon, #152	11.00	20.00
Plate, 7½″, salad, #23	12.50	18.00
Plate, 8½″, #22	14.00	30.00
*Plate, 9½″, dinner, #24	37.50	115.00
Plate, 11″, cabaret, 4 ftd., #32	22.00	40.00
Plate, 11½″, cabaret, –26	25.00	42.50
Plate, 14″ cabaret, 4 ftd., #33	27.50	52.50
Plate, 14″, 4 ftd, #28	27.50	55.00
Plate, 16″, #30	35.00	65.00
Punch bowl, ftd.	1,500.00	----
*Salad dressing, 3 pc., ftd. & hdld., 2 spoons, #112	135.00	325.00
Saucer, #17	2.50	5.50
Salt & pepper, pr., ball, #91	37.50	75.00
*Salt & pepper, pr., flat, #96	22.00	40.00
Salt & pepper, indiv., ball, pr., #90	30.00	75.00
Salt & pepper, indiv., flat, pr., #92	30.00	80.00
Salver, 13″, 2 pc. (cake atop pedestal), #31	100.00	200.00
Stem, #300, blown, 1 oz. cordial	32.00	110.00
Stem, #300, blown, 2½ oz., wine	25.00	55.00
Stem, #300, blown, 3 oz., cocktail	22.00	40.00
Stem, #300, blown, 4½ oz., claret	30.00	65.00
Stem, #300, blown, 4½ oz., low oyster cocktail	18.00	35.00
Stem, #300, blown, 5 oz. parfait	60.00	150.00
Stem, #300, blown, 6 oz., low sherbet	10.00	14.00
Stem, #300, blown, 6 oz. tall sherbet	12.00	21.50
Stem, #300, blown, 9 oz. water	16.00	35.00
Stem, #301, blown, 1 oz., cordial	30.00	---
Stem, #301, blown, 2½ oz., wine	25.00	---
Stem, #301, blown, 3 oz., cocktail	20.00	---
Stem, #301, blown, 4½ oz., claret	25.00	---
Stem, #301, blown, 6 oz., sherbet	13.00	---
Stem, #301, blown, 9 oz., water	16.00	---
*Stem, 3 oz., wine, #6	27.50	55.00
*Stem, 3½ oz., cocktail, #3	24.00	45.00
*Stem, 4½ oz., claret, #5	25.00	60.00
Stem, 4½ oz., fruit cocktail, #7	27.50	60.00
Stem, 5 oz., low sherbet, #4	17.50	27.50
*Stem, 7 oz., tall sherbet, #2	17.50	30.00
Stem, 10 oz., water, #1	26.00	40.00
*Sugar large, #41	10.00	15.00
*Sugar, medium, #38	8.00	15.00
*Sugar, indiv., #40	10.00	16.00
*Tray, for sugar & creamer, #37	12.50	27.50
Tray, 9″ oval, #42	18.00	35.00
*Tumbler, 2 oz., flat, #188	18.00	40.00
Tumbler, 3 oz., ftd. #12	18.00	40.00
Tumbler, 5 oz., ftd., #11	20.00	42.50
Tumbler, 5 oz., flat, #180	18.00	40.00
Tumbler, #300, 2½ oz.	15.00	32.50
Tumbler, #300, 5 oz., ftd. juice	16.00	30.00
Tumbler, #300, 10 oz.	18.00	36.00
Tumbler, #300, 12 oz.	18.00	35.00
Tumbler, #301, blown, 4½ oz., low oyster cocktail	15.00	---
Tumbler, #301, blown, 5 oz., juice	13.00	---
Tumbler, #301, blown, 12 oz., tea	17.00	---
*Tumbler, 9 oz., straight side, #14	30.00	55.00
*Tumbler, 10 oz., ftd., #10	18.00	33.00
Tumbler, 12 oz., ftd., #9	22.00	40.00
*Tumbler, 12 oz., straight side, #15	35.00	65.00
Tumbler, #310, 502, flat, juice	15.00	35.00
Tumbler, #310, 702, flat, old fashion	22.00	55.00
Tumbler, #310, 10 oz., flat, table	15.00	30.00
Tumbler, #310, 10 oz., flat, tall	16.00	40.00
Tumbler, #310, 12 oz., flat tea	27.50	52.50
Vase, 3½″ #249	45.00	100.00
Vase, 4″, #252	45.00	100.00
Vase, 4½″, #344	35.00	65.00
Vase, 5″, ivy bowl, #232	40.00	85.00
Vase, 5½″, #345	40.00	85.00
Vase, 6″, #254	50.00	100.00
Vase, 6″, #342	45.00	85.00
Vase, 6½″, #338	45.00	85.00
Vase, 7½″, #346	45.00	90.00
Vase, 8½″, #339	45.00	100.00
Vase, 8½″, #343	50.00	107.50
Vase, 9½″, #340	60.00	135.00

*Moulds owned by Summit Art Glass

CARIBBEAN, Line #112, Duncan Miller Glass Company, 1936 - 1955

Colors: blue, crystal, amber, red

No other pattern had as many new collectors searching for it shortly after the last book's unveiling as did Caribbean! I did not realize how adding this Duncan pattern to the book would create one giant collector demand. Check out the price escalation! Pitchers and other scarce items have had dramatic price increases!

(One of the more entertaining aspects to me about the pattern was the pronunciation and spellings for CARIBBEAN. It seems that the accent on the second or the third syllable and whether to double r's or b's drove several people to arguments over which was correct.)

The syrup pitcher, now listed, and cup and saucers are the items that collectors have asked me about more than any others.

	Blue
Ash tray, 6″, 4 indent.	22.50
Bowl, 3¾″ x 5″, folded side, hdld.	22.00
Bowl, 4½″ finger	17.00
Bowl, 5″, fruit nappy (takes liner), hdld.	15.00
Bowl, 5″ x 7″, folded side, hdld.	22.00
Bowl, 6½″, soup (takes liner)	22.00
Bowl, 7″, hdld.	30.00
Bowl, 7¼″, ftd., hdld. grapefruit	25.00
Bowl, 8½″	40.00
Bowl, 9″, salad	45.00
Bowl, 9¼″, veg., flared edge	40.00
Bowl, 9¼″, veg., hdld.	40.00
Bowl, 9½″, epergne, flared edge	45.00
Bowl, 10″, 6¼ qt. punch	150.00
Bowl, 10″, 6¼ qt. punch, flared top	165.00
Bowl, 10¾″, oval flower, hdld.	45.00
Bowl, 12″, console, flared edge	50.00
Candelabrum, 4¾″, 2-lite	45.00
Candlestick, 7¼″, 1-lite, w/bl. prisms	85.00
Candy dish w/cover, 4″ x 7″	65.00
Cheese/cracker, compote, 3½″ h., plate 11″, hdld.	55.00
Cigarette holder, (stack ashtray top)	60.00
Cocktail shaker, 9″, 33 oz.	125.00
Creamer	15.00
Cruet	55.00
Cup, tea	32.50
Cup, punch	12.50
Epergne, 4 pt., flower (12″ bowl; 9½″ bowl; 7¾″ vase, 14″ plate)	195.00
Ice bucket, 6½″, hdld.	80.00
Ladle, punch	50.00
Mayonnaise w/liner, 5¾″, 2 pt., 2 spoons, hdld.	45.00
Mayonnaise w/liner, 5¾″, hdld., 1 spoon	40.00
Mustard, 4″, w/slotted cover	55.00
Pitcher, 4¼″, 9 oz., syrup	75.00
Pitcher, 4¾″, 16 oz., milk	100.00
Pitcher w/ice lip, 9″, 72 oz., water	300.00
Plate, 6″, hdld. fruit nappy liner	9.00
Plate, 6¼″, bread/butter	6.00
Plate, 7¼″, rolled edge soup liner	10.00
Plate, 7½″, salad	14.00
Plate, 8″, hdld. mayonnaise liner	10.00
Plate, 8½″, luncheon	20.00
Plate, 10½″, dinner	65.00
Plate, 11″, hdld. cheese/cracker liner	32.00
Plate, 12″, salad liner, rolled edge	35.00
Plate, 16″, torte	50.00
Plate, 18″, punch underliner	60.00
Relish, 6″, round, 2 pt.	17.00

	Blue
Relish, 9½″, 4 pt., oblong	45.00
Relish, 9½″, oblong	42.00
Relish, 12¾″, 5 pt., rnd.	50.00
Relish, 12¾″, 7 pt., rnd.	50.00
Salt dip, 2½″	11.00
Salt & pepper, 3″, metal tops	45.00
Salt & pepper, 5″, metal tops	55.00
Saucer	5.00
Server, 5¾″, ctr. hdld.	37.00
Server, 6½″, ctr. hdld.	45.00
Stem, 3″, 1 oz., cordial	95.00
Stem, 3½″, 3½ oz., ftd., ball stem wine	27.00
Stem, 3⅝″, 2½ oz., wine (egg cup shape)	25.00
Stem, 4″, 6 oz., ftd., ball stem champagne	21.00
Stem, 4¼″, ftd. sherbet	13.00
Stem, 4¾″, 3 oz., ftd. ball stem wine	37.00
Stem, 5¾″, 8 oz., ftd., ball stem	27.00
Sugar	14.00
Syrup, metal cut off top	125.00
Tray, 6¼″, hand., mint, div.	17.00
Tray, 12¾″, rnd.	30.00
Tumbler, 2¼″, 2 oz., shot glass	37.00
Tumbler, 3½″, 5 oz. flat	20.00
Tumbler, 5¼″, 11½ oz., flat	25.00
Tumbler, 5½″, 8½ oz., ftd.	27.50
Tumbler, 6½″, 11 oz., ftd. iced tea	30.00
Vase, 5¾″, ftd., ruffled edge	30.00
Vase, 7¼″, ftd., flared edge, ball	32.00
Vase, 7½″, ftd., flared edge, bulbous	35.00
Vase, 7¾″, flared edge epergne	40.00
Vase, 8″, ftd., straight side	45.00
Vase, 9″, ftd., ruffled top	55.00
Vase, 10″, ftd.	60.00

41

CENTURY, Line #2630, Fostoria Glass Company

Colors: crystal

I have included Century as a Fostoria blank just as we include Fairfax. Fairfax is collected for its many colors, but Century comes only in crystal. Many of Fostoria's later patterns are etched on this #2630 line. If you will notice in the photo, there are several pieces that have various etched patterns. They were included for the shapes and not the patterns. As time goes by, more and more collectors will start looking for these patterns that were made in the 1950's and 1960's. For now, we are only looking at the basic blank.

The oval piece in the back is not an ice bucket but a vase which measures 8½". It is pushed in on the sides and is one of the more unusual pieces in Century. The preserve with cover is shown in front of the covered candy on the right. There is only an inch difference in the heights of these pieces, but the candy looks much bigger.

You will learn to recognize this pattern by the scalloped edges and the odd-shaped handles. See the relish in the pattern shot which illustrates that.

	Crystal
Ash tray, 2¾"	5.00
Basket, 10¼" x 6½", wicker hdld	55.00
Bowl, 4½", hdld	8.00
Bowl, 5", fruit	8.00
Bowl, 6", cereal	10.00
Bowl, 6¼", snack, ftd.	12.50
Bowl, 7⅛", 3 ftd., triangular	14.00
Bowl, 7¼", bon bon, 3 ftd	15.00
Bowl, 8", flared	20.00
Bowl, 8½", salad	20.00
bowl, 9", lily pond	22.50
Bowl, 9½", hdld. serving bowl	22.50
Bowl, 9½", oval serving bowl	22.50
Bowl, 10", oval, hdld	23.50
Bowl, 10½", salad	23.50
Bowl, 10¾", ftd., flared	25.00
Bowl, 11", ftd., rolled edge	27.50
Bowl, 11¼", lily pond	27.50
Bowl, 12", flared	27.50
butter w/cover, ¼ lb.	25.00
Candy w/cover, 7"	27.50
Candlestick, 4½"	12.00
Candlestick, 7", double	17.50
Candlestick, 7¾", triple	22.50
comport, 2¾", cheese	12.00
Comport, 4⅜"	13.50
Cracker plate, 10¾"	20.00
Creamer, 4¼"	6.00
Creamer, individual	4.00
Cup, 6 oz., ftd	8.50
Ice Bucket	45.00
Mayonnaise, 3 piece	25.00
Mayonnaise, 4 pc., div. w/2 ladles	30.00
Mustard, w/spoon, cover	25.00
Oil w/stopper, 5 oz.	35.00
Pickle, 8¾"	13.50
Pitcher, 6⅛", 16 oz.	40.00

	Crystal
Pitcher, 7⅛", 48 oz.	60.00
Plate, 6" bread/butter	3.00
Plate, 7½", salad	4.00
Plate, 7½", crescent salad	22.50
Plate, 8½" luncheon	6.50
Plate, 8", party, w/indent for cup	12.00
Plate, 9½", dinner	17.50
Plate, 10", hdld., cake	18.00
Plate, 14", torte	18.00
Platter, 12"	25.00
Preserve w/cover, 6"	20.00
Relish, 7⅜", 2 part	13.50
Relish, 11⅛" 3 part	20.00
Salt and pepper, 2⅜", individual, pr	10.00
Salt and pepper, 3⅛", pr	13.50
Salver, 12¼", ftd. (like cake stand)	32.50
Saucer	1.50
Stem, 3½ oz., cocktail, 4⅛"	10.00
Stem, 3½ oz., wine, 4½"	11.50
Stem, 4½ oz., oyster cocktail, 3¾"	10.00
Stem, 5½ oz., sherbet, 4½"	7.00
Stem, 10 oz., goblet, 5¾"	14.00
Sugar, 4", ftd	6.00
Sugar, individual	4.00
Tid bit, 8⅛", 3 ftd., upturned edge	14.00
Tid bit, 10¼", 2 tier, metal hdld.	22.50
Tray, 4¼", for ind. salt/pepper	12.00
Tray, 7⅛", for ind. sug/cr.	12.00
Tray , 9⅛", hdld. utility	20.00
Tray, 9½", hdld. muffin	22.00
Tray, 11½", center hdld	18.00
Tumbler, 5 oz., ftd., juice, 4¾"	10.00
Tumbler, 12 oz., ftd. tea, 5⅞"	12.50
Vase, 6", bud	15.00
Vase, 7½", hdld	27.50
Vase, 8½", oval	40.00

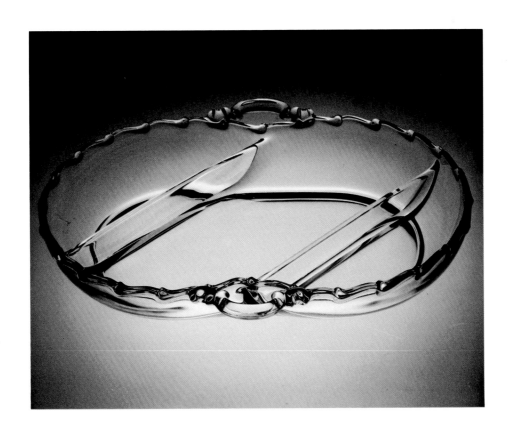

CHANTILLY, Cambridge Glass Company, late 1940's - Early 1950's

Colors: crystal

Chantilly is a Cambridge pattern that competed with Rosepoint for sales. It lost at that time and is still losing with collectors today! It's an attractive pattern! Chantilly prices are reasonable for most all pieces when compared to the prices of Rosepoint. Yet few collectors have succumbed to Chantilly's mystique. I believe it *may be one* of Cambridge's patterns that is underpriced in today's market.

The only problem encountered in collecting Chantilly is confusing it with a sister pattern, Elaine. Once you look at both closely, that will be remedied!

	Crystal		Crystal
Bowl, 7″, bonbon, 2 hdld. ftd.	16.00	Stem, #3600, 4½ oz., low oyster cocktail	15.00
Bowl, 7″, relish/pickle, 2 pt.	18.00	Stem, #3600, 7 oz. tall sherbet	17.50
Bowl, 7″, relish or pickle	18.00	Stem, #3600, 7 oz., low sherbet	15.00
Bowl, 9″, celery/relish, 3 pt.	22.00	Stem, #3600, 10 oz., water	19.50
Bowl, 10″, 4 ftd. flared	30.00	Stem, #3625, 1 oz., cordial	42.50
Bowl, 11″, tab hdld.	27.00	Stem, #3625, 3 oz., cocktail	24.00
Bowl, 11½″, tab hdld. ftd.	30.00	Stem, #3625, 4½ oz. claret	22.50
Bowl, 12″, celery/relish, 3 pt.	30.00	Stem, #3625, 4½ oz., low oyster cocktail	15.00
Bowl, 12″, 4 ftd. flared	30.00	Stem, #3625, 7 oz., low sherbet	15.00
Bowl, 12″, 4 ftd. oval	32.50	Stem, #3625, 7 oz., tall sherbet	17.50
Bowl, 12″, celery/relish, 5 pt.	30.00	Stem, #3625, 10 oz., water	22.50
Butter w/cover	125.00	Stem, #3775, 1 oz., cordial	42.50
Candlestick, 5″	17.50	Stem, #3775, 2½ oz., wine	27.00
Candlestick, 6″, 2-lite, "fleur de lis"	26.00	Stem, #3775, 3 oz., cocktail	25.00
Candlestick, 6″, 3-lite	32.00	Stem, #3775, 4½ oz., claret	22.50
Candy box w/cover, ftd.	110.00	Stem, #3775, 4½ oz., oyster cocktail	15.00
Candy box w/cover, rnd.	52.50	Stem, #3775, 6 oz., low sherbet	15.00
Cocktail icer, 2 pc.	32.00	Stem, #3775, 6 oz., tall sherbet	17.50
Comport, 5½″	30.00	Stem, #3779, 1 oz., cordial	50.00
Comport, 5⅜″, blown	35.00	Stem, #3779, 2½ oz., wine	27.50
Creamer	14.50	Stem, #3779, 3 oz., cocktail	25.00
Creamer, indiv. #3900 scalloped edge	11.00	Stem, #3779, 4½ oz., claret	25.00
Cup	12.50	Stem, #3779, 4½ oz., low oyster cocktail	15.00
Decanter, ftd.	140.00	Stem, #3779, 6 oz. tall sherbet	17.50
Hurricane lamp, candlestick base	75.00	Stem, #3779, 6 oz. low sherbet	15.00
Hurricane lamp, keyhole base w/prisms	110.00	Stem, #3779, 9 oz., water	20.00
Ice bucket w/chrome handle	60.00	Sugar	13.50
Mayonnaise, (sherbet type bowl w/ladle)	25.00	Sugar, indiv. #3900, scalloped edge	11.00
Mayonnaise div. w/liner & 2 ladles	38.00	Tumbler, #3600, 5 oz., ftd. juice	14.00
Mayonnaise w/liner & ladle	35.00	Tumbler, #3600, 12 oz., ftd. tea	18.00
Oil, 6 oz., hdld. w/stopper	45.00	Tumbler, #3625, 5 oz., ftd. juice	13.50
Pitcher, ball	110.00	Tumbler, #3625, 10 oz., ftd. water	15.00
Pitcher, Doulton	190.00	Tumbler, #3625, 12 oz., ftd tea	18 00
Pitcher, upright	155.00	Tumbler, #3775, 5 oz., ftd. juice	14.00
Plate, 6½″, bread/butter	6.50	Tumbler, #3775, 10 oz., ftd. water	15.00
Plate, 8″, salad	12.50	Tumbler, #3775, 12 oz., ftd. tea	18.00
Plate, 8″, tab hdld., ftd. bonbon	15.00	Tumbler, #3779, 5 oz., ftd. juice	15.00
Plate, 10½″, dinner	42.00	Tumbler, #3779, 12 oz., ftd. tea	18.00
Plate, 12″, 4 ftd. service	23.00	Tumbler, 13 oz.	20.00
Plate, 13″, 4 ftd.	30.00	Vase, 5″, globe	27.00
Plate, 13½″, tab hdld. cake	31.50	Vase, 6″, high ftd. flower	18.00
Plate, 14″, torte	32.00	Vase, 8″, high ftd. flower	22.00
Salt & pepper, pr.	27.50	Vase, 9″, keyhole base	27.50
Saucer	2.50	Vase, 10″, bud	25.00
Stem, #3600, 1 oz., cordial	42.50	Vase, 11″, ftd. flower	35.00
Stem, #3600, 2½ oz., cocktail	24.00	Vase, 11″, ped. ftd. flower	37.50
Stem, #3600, 2½ oz., wine	29.00	Vase, 12″, keyhole base	35.00
Stem, #3600, 4½ oz., claret	23.00	Vase, 13″, ftd. flower	45.00

Note: See Pages 166-167 for stem identification.

CHEROKEE ROSE, Tiffin Glass Company, 1940's - 1950's

Colors: crystal

Several collectors asked me to point out that Cherokee Rose comes on two different stems. One is No. 17399 and the other is No. 17403. I don't know which is the most collected; all I ever find is the No. 17399. This tear drop stem (17399) is shown clearly on the cordial on the right and most other stems in the photo. The cordial on the left (behind the fruit bowl) is on stem #17403. Many collectors, having difficulty finding stems, are buying both even though they are so dissimilar! One lady told my wife that as long as she could serve wine in it, she didn't care what kind of stem it had!

I still wonder how much more collectible Cherokee Rose would be if there were cup and saucers! In fact, there would be more Tiffin collectors if any of the patterns had an adequate supply of these essential items. Just as in Depression Glass collecting, the lack of a cup and saucer causes some collectors to shy away from the pattern.

This pattern is still confused with the Rose Point pattern by Cambridge. In fact, I bought a large set of Rosepoint that had six pieces of Cherokee Rose mixed in with it. I wondered if friends had mistakenly purchased gifts of the wrong pattern or if the owners had bought pieces to go with the Rose Point on purpose? Sometimes, I wish the glass could talk!

You may find other pieces that I do not have listed in this pattern. Please let me know if you do!

	Crystal		Crystal
Bowl, 5″, finger	12.00	Stem, 2 oz., sherry	20.00
Bowl, 6″, fruit or nut	14.00	Stem, 3½ oz. cocktail	16.00
Bowl, 7″, salad	20.00	Stem, 3½ oz., wine	27.00
Bowl, 10″, deep salad	30.00	Stem, 4 oz., claret	23.00
Bowl, 10½″, celery, oblong	23.00	Stem, 4½ oz. parfait	24.00
Bowl, 12″, crimped	30.00	Stem, 5½ oz., sherbet/champagne	15.00
Bowl, 12½″, centerpiece, flared	32.50	Stem, 9 oz., water	22.00
Bowl, 13″, centerpiece	35.00	Sugar	12.00
Cake plate, 12½″, center hdld.	30.00	Table bell	40.00
Candlesticks, pr. double branch	40.00	Tumbler, 4½ oz., oyster cocktail	12.00
Comport, 6″	20.00	Tumbler, 5 oz., ftd. juice	14.00
Creamer	13.50	Tumbler, 8 oz., ftd. water	16.00
Mayonnaise, liner and ladle	35.00	Tumbler, 10½ oz., ftd. iced tea	20.00
Pitcher	125.00	Vase, 6″, bud	20.00
Plate, 6″, sherbet	5.00	Vase, 8″, bud	25.00
Plate, 8″, luncheon	12.00	Vase, 8½″, tear drop	35.00
Plate, 13½″, turned-up edge, lily	35.00	Vase, 9¼″, tub	45.00
Plate, 14″, sandwich	25.00	Vase, 10″, bud	30.00
Relish, 6½″, 3 part	20.00	Vase, 11″, bud	35.00
Relish, 12½″, 3 pt.	27.00	Vase, 11″, urn	40.00
Stem, 1 oz., cordial	40.00	Vase, 12″ flared	50.00

CHINTZ, (Plate Etching #338), Fostoria Glass Company

Colors: crystal

Chintz is a Fostoria pattern that is rapidly becoming noticed by both novice collectors and those of us who have ignored it in the past. Many pieces are found on the #2496 blank which most of us know as Baroque. It is this fleur-de-lis that many collectors see first on the #2496 blank. There are several Fostoria etchings that are found on this blank so you need to learn to recognize each of them. Look at Navarre which is also made on this blank.

The small vase (5", #4108) is not commonly found. It is shown in the center back, in front of the plate. There has not been enough collecting of this pattern to be able to say exactly which pieces are rare. Time and more collecting will tell us that.

Prices for Chintz are reasonable when compared to many other Fostoria patterns. This pattern only comes in crystal, and that is a deterrent to some collectors who look for only colored glass.

You may find additional pieces in this pattern; so let me know if you do.

	Crystal		Crystal
Bowl, #2496, 4⅝", tri-cornered	10.00	Plate, #2496, 7½", salad	6.50
Bowl, #869, 4½", finger	18.00	Plate, #2496, 8½", luncheon	10.00
Bowl, #2496, cream soup	17.50	Plate, #2496, 9½", dinner	22.50
Bowl, #2496, 5", fruit	11.00	Plate, #2496, 10", hdld., cake	25.00
Bowl, #2496, 5", hdld.	12.00	Plate, #2496, 14", upturned edge	32.50
Bowl, #2496, 7⅜", bon bon	20.00	Plate, #2496, 16", torte, plain edge	37.50
Bowl, #2496, 8½", hdld.	30.00	Relish, #2496, 6", 2 part, square	20.00
Bowl, #2496, 9½", vegetable	27.50	Relish, #2496, 10" x 7½", 3 part	25.00
Bowl, #2484, 10", hdld.	32.50	Salad dressing bottle, #2083, 6½"	110.00
Bowl, #2496, 10½", hdld.	35.00	Salt and pepper, #2496, 2¾", flat, pr.	55.00
Bowl, #2496, 12", flared	37.50	Saucer, #2496	3.50
Candlestick, #2496, 4"	10.00	Stem #6026, 1 oz., cordial, 3⅞"	35.00
Candlestick, #2496, 3½", double	20.00	Stem, #6026, 4 oz., cocktail, 5"	19.00
Candlestick, #2496, 5½"	17.50	Stem, #6026, 4 oz., oyster cocktail, 3⅜"	15.00
Candlestick, #2496, 6", triple	30.00	Stem, #6026, 4½ oz., claret-wine, 5⅜"	22.00
Candy w/cover, #2496, 3 part	65.00	Stem, #6026, 6 oz., low sherbet, 4⅜"	13.50
Celery, #2496, 11"	20.00	Stem, #6026, 6 oz., saucer champagne, 5½"	15.00
Comport, #2496, 3¼", cheese	20.00	Stem, #6026, 9 oz., water goblet, 7⅝"	20.00
Comport, #2496, 4¾"	22.50	Sugar, #2496, 3½", ftd	8.00
Cracker, #2496, 11" plate	35.00	Sugar, #2496 ½, individual	10.00
Creamer, #2496, 3¾", ftd	9.00	Syrup, metal cut-off top	75.00
Creamer, #2496 ½, individual	10.00	Tid bit, #2496, 8¼", 3 ftd., upturned edge	18.00
Cup, #2496, ftd	15.00	Tray, #2496 ½, 6½", for ind. sugar/creamer	12.00
Ice bucket, #2496	50.00	Tray, #2375, 11", center hdld	23.50
Jelly, w/cover #2496, 7½"	50.00	Tumbler, #6026, 5 oz., juice, ftd	13.00
Mayonnaise, #2496 ½, 3 piece	40.00	Tumbler, #6026, 9 oz., water or low goblet	14.00
Oil, w/stopper, #2496, 3½ oz	50.00	Tumbler, #6026, 13 oz., tea, ftd	17.50
Pickle, #2496, 8"	20.00	Vase, #4108, 5"	42.50
Pitcher, #5000, 48 oz., ftd	165.00	Vase, #4143, 6", ftd	45.00
Plate, #249, 6", bread/butter	4.50	Vase, #4143, 7½", ftd	65.00

CHINTZ, #1401 (Empress Blank) and CHINTZ #3389 (Duquesne Blank) A.H. Heisey Co., 1931-1938

Colors: crystal; "Sahara" yellow; "Moongleam" green; "Flamingo" pink, and "Alexandrite" orchid

Chintz was a popular name for patterns of this era. With the listing of Fostoria's Chintz in this book, collectors will have to remember to add the COMPANY name to want lists or advertisements. Remember that the butterflies are on the Heisey pattern and that Fostoria's Chintz only comes in crystal.

	Crystal	Sahara
Bowl, finger, #4107	8.00	15.00
Bowl, 5½", ftd. preserve, hdld.	15.00	27.00
Bowl, 6", ftd. mint	18.00	30.00
Bowl, 6", ftd., 2 hdld, jelly	15.00	30.00
Bowl, 7", triplex relish	16.00	33.00
Bowl, 7½", Nasturtium	16.00	30.00
Bowl, 8½", ftd., 2 hdld. floral	32.00	65.00
Bowl, 11", dolp. ft. floral	35.00	75.00
Bowl, 13", 2 pt., pickle & olive	15.00	25.00
Comport, 7", oval	40.00	75.00
Creamer, 3 dolp. ftd.	20.00	42.50
Grapefruit, ftd. #3389, Duquesne	25.00	45.00
Ice bucket, ftd.	65.00	100.00
Mayonnaise, 5½", dolp. ft.	35.00	65.00
Oil, 4 oz.	50.00	110.00
Pitcher, 3 pint, dolp. ft.	110.00	185.00
Plate, 6", square bread	6.00	15.00
Plate, 7", square salad	8.00	18.00
Plate, 8", square luncheon	10.00	22.00
Plate, 10½", square dinner	30.00	65.00
Platter, 14", oval	25.00	45.00
Stem, #3389, Duquesne, 1 oz., cordial	90.00	165.00
Stem, #3389, 2½ oz., wine	17.50	42.50
Stem, #3389, 3 oz., cocktail	15.00	35.00
Stem, #3389, 4 oz., claret	17.50	40.00
Stem, #3389, 4 oz., oyster cocktail	10.00	20.00
Stem, #3389, 5 oz., parfait	14.00	30.00
Stem, #3389, 5 oz., saucer champagne	11.00	22.50
Stem, #3389, 5 oz., sherbet	8.00	17.50
Stem, #3389, 9 oz., water	15.00	30.00
Sugar, 3 dolp. ft.	20.00	42.50
Tray, 10", celery	14.00	27.50
Tray, 12", sq., ctr. hdld. sandwich	35.00	65.00
Tray, 13", celery	18.00	26.00
Tumbler, #3389, 5 oz., ftd. juice	11.00	22.00
Tumbler, #3389, 8 oz., soda	12.00	24.00
Tumbler, #3389, 10 oz., ftd. water	13.00	25.00
Tumbler, #3389, 12 ., iced tea	14.00	27.50
Vase, 9"dolp. ft.	75.00	150.00

CLEO, Cambridge Glass Company, Introduced 1930

Colors: amber, blue, crystal, green, pink, yellow

Cleo is a pattern that I enjoy finding because I often wonder what unusual item will turn up next! The big amber bowl was found in an antique mall in Columbus, Ohio. The owner knew only that the piece was Cambridge and had circled the "C" in a triangle with a marker.

No one has been able to explain the center-handled tray which is etched in the center with Cleo and around the edge with the Apple-Blossom pattern. It is now in a California collection. Another amber tobacco humidor was found in Michigan. Maybe one will be found in another color?

As you can see by the blue photo, Cleo etching can be found on several different blanks, but the Decagon is the predominately found blank. Keep looking for unusual pieces!

	All Colors*		All Colors*
Basket, 7", 2 hdld. (upturned sides) DECAGON	17.50	Pitcher w/cover, 62 oz. #955	225.00
Basket, 11", 2 hdld. (upturned sides) DECAGON	30.00	Pitcher w/cover, 63 oz. #3077	210.00
Bouillon cup w/saucer, 2 hdld. DECAGON ..	25.00	Pitcher w/cover, 68 oz. #937	230.00
Bowl, 2 pt. relish	20.00	Plate, 7"	11.50
Bowl, 5½", fruit	15.00	Plate, 7", 2 hdld DECAGON	14.00
Bowl, 5½", 2 hdld., bonbon DECAGON	20.00	Plate, 9½", dinner DECAGON	40.00
Bowl, 6", 4 ft., comport	35.00	Plate, 11", 2 hdld. DECAGON	24.00
Bowl, 6", cereal, DECAGON	20.00	Platter, 12"	37.50
Bowl, 6½", 2 hdld., bonbon DECAGON	22.00	Platter, 15"	55.00
Bowl, 6½", cranberry	20.00	Platter w/cover	150.00
Bowl, 7½", tab hdld. soup	30.00	Platter, indented w/sauce & spoon	250.00
Bowl, 8", miniature console	90.00	Saucer, DECAGON	3.00
Bowl, 8½"	40.00	Server, 12", ctr. hand.	35.00
Bowl, 8½", 2 hdld. DECAGON	40.00	Stem, #3077, 1 oz., cordial	95.00
Bowl, 9", covered vegetable	100.00	Stem, #3077, 2½ oz., cocktail	27.50
Bowl, 9½", oval veg., DECAGON	40.00	Stem, #3077, 3½ oz. wine	60.00
Bowl, 9", pickle, DECAGON	25.00	Stem, #3077, 6 oz, low sherbet	12.50
Bowl, 10", 2 hdld DECAGON	30.00	Stem, #3077, 6 oz., tall sherbet	15.00
Bowl, 11", oval	35.00	Stem, #3115, 9 oz.	27.00
Bowl, 11½", oval	37.50	Stem, #3115, 3½ oz., cocktail	25.00
Bowl, 12", console	35.00	Stem, #3115, 6 oz., fruit	14.00
Bowl, cream soup w/saucer, 2 hdld. DECAGON	25.00	Stem, #3115, 6 oz., low sherbet	13.00
Bowl, finger w/liner #3077	22.00	Stem, #3115, 6 oz., tall sherbet	15.00
Bowl, finger w/liner #3115	22.00	Stem, #3115, 9 oz.	30.00
Candlestick, 1-lite, 2 styles	22.50	Sugar, DECAGON	17.50
Candlestick, 2-lite	35.00	Sugar, ftd.	15.00
Candy box	65.00	Tobacco humidor	250.00
Comport, 7", tall #3115	40.00	Tray, 12", oval service DECAGON	25.00
Creamer, DECAGON	17.50	Tumbler, #3077, 2½ oz., ftd.	20.00
Creamer, ftd.	15.00	Tumbler, #3077 5 oz., ftd.	16.50
Cup, DECAGON	15.00	Tumbler, #3077, 8 oz., ftd.	22.00
Decanter and stopper	100.00	Tumbler, #3077, 10 oz., ftd.	22.50
Gravy boat w/liner plate DECAGON	110.00	Tumbler, #3077, 12 oz., ftd.	27.00
Ice pail	57.50	Tumbler, #3115, 2½ oz., ftd.	22.00
Ice tub	42.50	Tumbler, #3115, 5 oz., ftd.	20.00
Mayonnaise w/liner and ladle, DECAGON ..	40.00	Tumbler, #3115, 8 oz., ftd.	22.00
Mayonnaise, ftd.	30.00	Tumbler, #3115, 10 oz., ftd.	22.50
Oil, 6 oz., w/stopper DECAGON	95.00	Tumbler, #3115, 12 oz., ftd.	27.00
Pitcher, 3½ pt. #38	150.00	Tumbler, 12 oz., flat	30.00
Pitcher w/cover, 22 oz.	125.00	Vase, 5½"	50.00
Pitcher w/cover 60 oz., #804	210.00	Vase, 9½"	80.00
		Vase, 11"	100.00

*Blue add 25% to 35%.

53

COLONY, Line #2412, Fostoria Glass Company, 1920's - 1970's

Colors: crystal; some yellow, blue, green, white, amber

There has been a growing interest in collecting Colony. New pieces are being found regularly. There are two styles of ice buckets. The one normally found has the usual Colony scalloped edge. The unusual ice bucket is in front of the candy on the right. It has a straight, plain edge extending upward from a flattened, scalloped edge. This was shown in a 1941 Fostoria catalogue.

Cream soups seem to be few and far between. The 12″ tall vase (shown in the center at the back) was often used in making lamps. Serving pieces are harder to find than they should be. The dinner plate is only 9″ and not 10″.

You may find additional pieces. Do not be surprised if you do; but please let me know what you find.

	Crystal
Ash tray, 3″, round	7.00
Ash tray, 3½″	10.00
Ash tray, 4½″ round	12.50
Ash tray, 6″, round	15.00
Bowl, 2¾″ ftd., almond	10.00
Bowl, 4½″, rnd.	6.50
Bowl, 4¾″, finger	9.00
Bowl, 4¾″, hdld	7.50
Bowl, 5″, bonbon	9.00
Bowl, 5″, cream soup	35.00
Bowl, 5″, hdld	7.50
Bowl, 5½″, sq.	10.00
Bowl, 5¾″, hi ft.	12.00
Bowl, 5″, rnd.	7.50
Bowl, 6″, rose	25.00
Bowl, 7″, bonbon, 3 ftd	10.00
Bowl, 7″, olive, oblong	10.00
Bowl, 7¾″, salad	20.00
Bowl, 8″, cupped	30.0C
Bowl, 8″, hdld	30.00
Bowl, 9″, rolled console	30.00
Bowl, 9½″, pickle	10.00
Bowl, 9¾″, salad	30.00
Bowl, 10″, fruit	27.50
Bowl, 10½″, low ft	65.00
Bowl, 10½″, hi ft.	75.00
Bowl, 10½″, oval	26.00
Bowl, 10½″, oval, 2 part	30.00
Bowl, 11″, oval, fd	32.50
Bowl, 11″, flared	32.50
Bowl, 11½″, celery	15.00
Bowl, 13″, console	32.50
Bowl, 13¼″, punch, ftd	275.00
Bowl, 14″, fruit	35.00
Candlestick, 3½″	10.00
Candlestick, 6½″, double	20.00
Candlestick, 7″	15.00
Candlestick, 7½″ w/8 prisms	50.00
Candlestick, 9″	25.00
Candlestick, 9¾″, w/prisms	60.00
Candlestick, 14½″ w/10 prisms	100.00
Candy w/cover, 6½″	30.00
Cheese & cracker	35.00
Comport, 4″	15.00
Comport, cover, 6½″	30.00

	Crystal
Creamer, 3¼″ indiv.	5.50
Creamer, 3¾″	5.00
Cup, 6 oz., ftd.	6.00
Cup, punch	10.00
Ice bucket	45.00
Ice bucket, plain edge	75.00
Mayonnaise, 3 pc.	32.50
Oil w/stopper, 4½ oz.	35.00
Pitcher, 16 oz., milk	37.50
Pitcher, 48 oz., ice lip	75.00
Pitcher, 2 qt., ice lip	85.00
Plate, ctr. hand sand	22.50
Plate, 6″, bread & butter	4.00
Plate, 6½″, lemon, hdld	12.00
Plate, 7″ salad	7.00
Plate, 8″ luncheon	9.00
Plate, 9″ dinner	17.50
Plate, 10″, hdld cake	20.00
Plate, 12″, ftd. salver	42.50
Plate, 13″, torte	25.00
Plate, 15″, torte	35.00
Plate, 18″, torte	50.00
Platter, 12″	35.00
Relish, 10½″, hdld, 3 part	20.00
Salt, 2½″ indiv	12.00
Salt & pepper pr., 3⅝″	12.50
Saucer	2.00
Stem, 3⅜″, oyster cocktail (4 oz.)	10.00
Stem, 3⅝″, sherbet (5 oz.)	9.00
Stem, 4″ cocktail (3½ oz)	12.00
Stem, 4¼″, wine (3¼ oz)	22.00
Stem, 5¼″, (9 oz) goblet	14.00
Sugar, 2¾″, indiv	5.00
Sugar, 3½″	4.50
Tray for indiv. sug/cream	10.00
Tumbler, 5 oz., 3⅝″, juice	14.00
Tumbler, 9 oz., 3 ⅞″, water	12.00
Tumbler, 12 oz., 4⅞″, tea	17.50
Tumbler, 4½″, 5 oz., ftd	12.50
Tumbler, 5¾″, 12 oz., ftd	17.50
Vase, 6″, bud, flared	14.00
Vase, 7″, cupped	35.00
Vase, 7½″, flared	35.00
Vase, 9″, cornucopia	50.00
Vase, 12″, straight	145.00

CRYSTOLITE, Blank #1503, A. H. Heisey & Co.

Colors: crystal, Zircon/Limelight, Sahara and rare in amber

	Crystal
Ash tray, 3½″, square	4.00
Ash tray, 4½″, square	4.50
Ash tray, 5″, w/book match	25.00
Ash tray (coaster), 4″, rnd.	5.00
Basket, 6″, hdld.	365.00
Bonbon, 7″, shell	17.00
Bonbon, 7½″, 2 hdld.	15.00
Bottle, 1 qt. rye, #107 stopper	160.00
Bottle, 4 oz. bitters w/short tube	75.00
Bottle, 4 oz. cologne w/#108 stopper	60.00
w/drip stop	145.00
Bottle, syrup w/drip & cut top	55.00
Bowl, 7½ quart punch	95.00
Bowl, 2″, indiv. swan nut (or ash tray)	15.00
Bowl, 3″, indiv. nut, hdld.	15.00
Bowl, 4½″, dessert (or nappy)	6.00
Bowl, 5″, preserve	12.00
Bowl, 5″, thousand island dressing, ruffled top	18.00
Bowl, 5½″, dessert	8.00
Bowl, 6″, oval jelly, 4 ft.	13.00
Bowl, 6″, preserve, 2 hdld.	13.00
Bowl, 7″, shell praline	27.00
Bowl, 8″, dessert (sauce)	15.00
Bowl, 8″, 2 pt. conserve, hdld.	16.00
Bowl, 9″, leaf pickle	17.00
Bowl, 10″, salad, rnd.	23.00
Bowl, 11″, w/attached mayonnaise (chip 'n dip)	55.00
Bowl, 12″, gardenia, shallow	30.00
Bowl, 13″, oval floral, deep	30.00
Candle block, 1-lite, sq.	12.00
Candle block, 1-lite, swirl	12.00
Candlestick, 1-lite, ftd.	12.00
Candlestick, 1-lite, w/#4233 5″, vase	25.00
Candlestick, 2-lite	20.00
Candlestick, 2-lite, bobeche & 10 "D" prisms	50.00
Candlestick sans vase, 3-lite	17.00
Candlestick w/#4233 5″, vase, 3-lite	30.00
Candy, 6½″, swan	35.00
Candy box w/cover, 5½″	50.00
Candy box w/cover, 7″	55.00
Cheese, 5½″, ftd.	9.00
Cigarette box w/cover, 4″	15.00
Cigarette box w/cover, 4½″	17.00
Cigarette holder, ftd.	17.50
Cigarette holder, oval	12.00
Cigarette holder, rnd.	10.00
Cigarette lighter	10.00
Coaster, 4″	6.00
Cocktail shaker, 1 qt. w/#1 strainer; #86 stopper	150.00
Comport, 5″, ftd., deep	25.00
Creamer, indiv.	12.00
Cup	10.00

	Crystal
Cup, punch or custard	8.00
Hurricane block, 1-lite, sq.	25.00
Hurricane block w/#4061, 10″ plain globe, 1-lite, sq.	55.00
Ice tub w/silver plate handle	75.00
Jam jar w/cover	50.00
Ladle, glass, punch	25.00
Ladle, plastic	7.50
Mayonnaise, 5½″, shell, 3 ft.	32.00
Mayonnaise, 6″, oval, hdld.	22.00
Mayonnaise ladle	7.00
Mustard & cover	37.00
Oil bottle, 3 oz.	36.00
Oil bottle w/stopper, 2 oz.	26.00
Oval creamer, sugar w/tray, set	47.50
Pitcher, ½ gallon, ice, blown	75.00
Pitcher, 2 quart swan, ice lip	750.00
Plate, 7″, salad	8.00
Plate, 7″, shell	12.00
Plate, 7″, underliner for 1000 island dressing bowl	7.00
Plate, 7½″, coupe	30.00
Plate, 8″, oval, mayonnaise liner	9.00
Plate, 8½″, salad	15.00
Plate, 10½″, service	50.00
Plate, 11″, ftd. cake salver	300.00
Plate, 11″, torte	24.00
Plate, 12″, sand.	24.00
Plate, 14″, sand.	30.00
Plate, 14″, torte	30.00
Plate, 20″, buffet or punch liner	42.00
Puff box w/cover, 4¾″	50.00
Salad dressing set, 3 pc.	38.00
Salt & pepper, pr.	30.00
Saucer	5.00
Stem, 1 oz., cordial, wide optic, blown	85.00
Stem, 3½ oz., cocktail, w.o., blown	22.00
Stem, 3½ oz., claret, w.o., blown	25.00
Stem, 3½ oz., oyster cocktail, w.o. blown	20.00
Stem, 6 oz., sherbet/saucer champagne	12.00
Stem, 10 oz., w.o., blown	20.00
Sugar, indiv.	12.00
Tray, 5½″, oval, liner indiv. creamer/sugar	35.00
Tray, 9″, 4 pt. leaf relish	22.50
Tray, 10″, 5 pt., rnd. relish	35.00
Tray, 12″, 3 pt. relish	25.00
Tray, 12″, rect., celery	35.00
Tray, 12″, rect., celery/olive	35.00
Tumbler, 5 oz., ftd., juice, w.o., blown	15.00
Tumbler, 10 oz., pressed	15.00
Tumbler, 10 oz., iced tea, w.o., blown	20.00
Tumbler, 12 oz., ftd., iced tea, w.o., blown	18.00
Urn, 7″, flower	17.50
Vase, 3″, short stem	17.50
Vase, 6″, ftd.	17.50

DANCING GIRL, Morgantown Glass Works, Late 1920's, Early 1930's

Colors: pink, green, blue

Several collectors have written about buying SETS of this pattern in blue! Sets were found in the far West in Oregon and Washington and another was found in Alabama. There seems to be a big discrepancy in measurements according to these collectors. I have no catalogue listing for this pattern so I can only report what is being found. Write me!

Oyster cocktails vary from 2⅜" to 2½"; sherbets vary from 4¾" to 4⅞" and banquet wines from 7¾" to 8". Most reports concern variances occurring in stems. That was brought about by two stem styles. Notice in the photo that some stems are plain while others are twisted.

Variations in measurements naturally occur more in the handmade glass than in those that were moulded.

I had two reports of cordials being found in Dancing Girl, but a confirming picture was never received. (Collecting cordials is one way of saving space if you already live in a "glass" house. They take up so little room, unless you have several hundred, as I do).

The 10" bud vase is the only piece I have seen in green! Has anyone seen this vase in blue? Although this is rarely found, there is ready made collector interest due to its unusual color and entrancing design.

Sugar and creamer collectors are still surprised by their shape. The ones shown here were bought several years ago at Washington Court House, Ohio. That particular lot of Dancing girl was the only time I ever saw the pattern for sale outside a Depression Glass or antique show.

Due to addition of new patterns and many new pictures, I have very little space for commentary in this book, so I hope those of you who are looking for many tidbits of information on each pattern will forgive those ommisions. I have only a few patterns where space will permit observation about the glassware market in general.

	All Colors
Creamer	45.00
Pitcher	225.00
Plate, 5⅞", sherbet	10.00
Plate, 7½"	17.00
Stem, 2½", 3½ oz., oyster cocktail	22.50
Stem, 4¾", 7 oz., sherbet	27.50
Stem, 6⅛", cocktail	30.00
Stem, 7¾", 9 oz. banquet wine	40.00
Sugar	40.00
Tumbler, 4¼"	30.00
Tumbler, 4¾", 9 oz.	30.00
Tumbler, 5½", 11 oz.	32.50
Vase, 10", slender bud	40.00

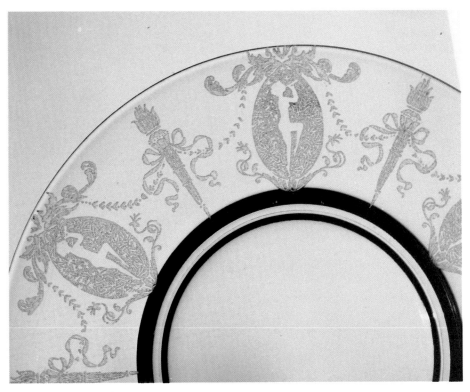

61

DECAGON, Cambridge Glass Company, 1930's

Colors: green, pink, red, cobalt blue, amber, Moonlight blue

Stemware pictured here is etched with Hunt Scene or Cleo. It was easier to use that which was already purchased on the Decagon blank than find other pieces without an etching. I still need a blue relish insert if anyone has a spare. Speaking of blue, both the "Moonlight" (light) and the "Royal" (cobalt) are THE colors to find. There are few collectors of green, pink and amber at the present; now might be a good time to start those.

	Pastel Colors	Red Blue
Basket, 7″, 2 hdld. (upturned sides)	12.00	20.00
Bowl, bouillon w/liner	7.50	12.50
Bowl, cream soup w/liner	10.00	22.00
Bowl, 2½″, indiv. almond	16.00	27.50
Bowl, 3¾″, flat rim cranberry	10.00	14.00
Bowl, 3½″, belled cranberry	9.00	14.00
Bowl, 5½″, 2 hdld. bonbon	10.00	17.00
Bowl, 5½″, belled fruit	5.50	10.00
Bowl, 5¾″, flat rim fruit	6.00	11.00
Bowl, 6″, belled cereal	7.00	12.50
Bowl, 6″, flat rim cereal	8.00	12.00
Bowl, 6″, ftd. almond	20.00	35.00
Bowl, 6¼″, 2 hdld., bonbon	10.00	17.00
Bowl, 8½″, flat rim soup "plate"	8.00	15.00
Bowl, 9″, rnd. veg.	14.00	24.00
Bowl, 9″, 2 pt. relish	9.00	15.00
Bowl, 9½″, oval veg.	12.00	22.00
Bowl, 10″, berry	12.00	20.00
Bowl, 10½″, oval veg.	16.00	27.50
Bowl, 11″, rnd. veg.	17.00	30.00
Bowl, 11″, 2 pt. relish	10.00	17.50
Comport, 5¾″	12.50	20.00
Comport, 6½″, low ft.	15.00	25.00
Comport, 7″, tall	20.00	30.00
Creamer, ftd.	9.00	20.00
Creamer, scalloped edge	8.00	18.00
Creamer, lightning bolt handles	7.00	12.00
Creamer, tall, lg. ft.	10.00	22.00
Cup	6.00	10.00
French dressing bottle, "Oil/Vinegar"	45.00	75.00
Gravy boat w/2 hdld. liner (like spouted cream soup)	55.00	85.00
Mayonnaise, 2 hdld. w/2 hdld. liner and ladle	25.00	40.00
Mayonnaise w/liner & ladle	18.00	30.00
Oil, 6 oz., tall, w/hdld. & stopper	40.00	65.00
Plate, 6¼″, bread/butter	3.00	5.00
Plate, 7″, 2 hdld.	9.00	15.00
Plate, 7½″	4.00	10.00
Plate, 8½″, salad	6.00	10.00
Plate, 9½″, dinner	15.00	25.00
Plate, 10″, grill	8.00	14.00
Plate, 10″, service	8.50	16.00
Plate, 12½″, service	9.00	17.50
Relish, 6 inserts	70.00	100.00
Salt dip, 1½″, ftd.	11.00	20.00
Sauce boat & plate	45.00	65.00
Saucer	1.00	2.50
Server, center hdld.	12.00	20.00
Stem, 1 oz., cordial	25.00	50.00
Stem, 3½ oz., cocktail	12.00	20.00
Stem, 6 oz., low sherbet	9.00	15.00
Stem, 6 oz., high sherbet	10.00	20.00
Stem, 9 oz., water	15.00	30.00
Sugar, lightning bolt handles	7.00	12.00
Sugar, ftd.	9.00	20.00
Sugar, scalloped edge	9.00	20.00
Sugar, tall, lg. ft.	8.00	18.00
Tray, 8″, 2 hdld., flat pickle	10.00	17.00
Tray, 9″, pickle	10.00	17.50
Tray, 11″, oval service	8.00	15.00
Tray, 11″, celery	10.00	20.00
Tray, 12″, oval service	10.00	20.00
Tray, 13″, 2 hdld. service	20.00	30.00
Tray, 15″, oval service	15.00	25.00
Tumbler, 2½ oz., ftd.	8.00	13.00
Tumbler, 5 oz., ftd.	8.00	15.00
Tumbler, 8 oz., ftd.	10.00	20.00
Tumbler, 10 oz., ftd.	12.00	22.00
Tumbler, 12 oz., ftd.	15.00	30.00

"DEERWOOD" or "BIRCH TREE", U.S. Glass Company, late 1920's/early 1930's

Colors: light amber, green, pink

If you came from Black Forest to Deerwood, there is a simple explanation. There was no room to write about Black Forest on the pages allowed, so I will cover both patterns here. A special thanks to Lottie and Bill Porter for driving to Paducah from Michigan to bring these two patterns for use in the book. Lottie not only furnished her glass but most of the information on these patterns! With collectors like these willing to share their glass, my task of writing and photographing becomes easier. It is very difficult to continue to find new patterns and material which interest more than a small number of people.

I believe the pattern shots will show the differences in Deerwood and Black Forest sufficiently; so I will not try to explain that. The maker of Black Forest is unknown, but there are many characteristics of Paden City which stand out. Catalogues show Deerwood made by United States Glass Company, but the flat pink candy dish on the left is typical of Paden City also. It makes one wonder if blanks were used from more than a single company to etch these patterns.

The dark green and blue comports as well as the red goblet shown with Black Forest were made in the middle 1970's and reported in *The Depression Glass Daze* by Nora Koch. These are easily detected by the squared knob on the stem! I'm sure you will find additional pieces in these patterns; so let me know what you have or see!

	Amber	Green	Pink
Bowl, 10″, straight edge			30.00
Bowl, 12″, console		50.00	50.00
Cake plate, low pedestal			45.00
Candlestick, 2½″		35.00	
Candlestick, 4″			40.00
Candy dish w/cover, 3 part, flat			70.00
Candy jar w/cover, ftd. cone			80.00
Celery, 12″		45.00	45.00
Cheese and cracker		65.00	
Comport, 10″, low, ftd., flared			35.00
Creamer, 2 styles		35.00	35.00
Cup		50.00	50.00
Plate, 5½″		12.00	12.00
Plate, 7½″, salad			20.00
Plate, 9½″, dinner			35.00
Saucer		15.00	15.00
Server, center hdld		40.00	40.00
Stem, 6 oz., sherbet, 4¾″		22.00	
Stem, 6 oz., cocktail, 5″		25.00	
Stem, 9 oz., water, 7″		30.00	
Sugar, 2 styles		35.00	35.00
Tumbler, 9 oz	30.00	28.00	28.00
Tumbler, 12 oz., tea, 5½″	35.00		
Vase, 7″, sweet pea, rolled edge			50.00
Vase, 10″, ruffled top		85.00	75.00
Whipped cream pail w/ladle		40.00	40.00

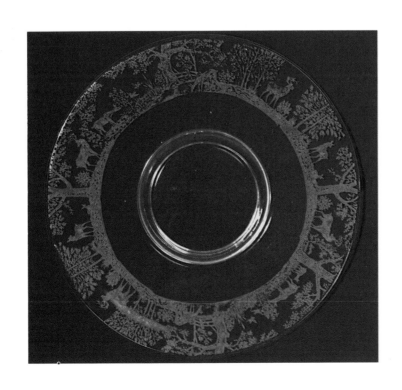

65

DIANE, Cambridge Glass Company, 1934 - Early 1950's

Colors: crystal, some pink, yellow, blue, heatherbloom

Few pieces of the "Moonlight" blue and Heatherbloom Diane are being found. Sets in any color would be difficult to collect since only a piece or two are found at a time. Yellow (Gold Krystol) is the color I see most often. The dark Emerald Green candy lid has needed a bottom for three years. However, I haven't found any other pieces in that color - let alone the bottom!

Add 30% to 50% for colors.

	Crystal
Basket, 6", 2 hdld, ftd.	16.00
Bowl, #3106, finger w/liner	25.00
Bowl, #3122, finger w/liner	25.00
Bowl, #3400, cream soup w/liner	23.00
Bowl, 5", berry	20.00
Bowl, 5¼", 2 hdld. bonbon	18.00
Bowl, 6", 2 hdld. ftd. bonbon	17.00
Bowl, 6", 2 pt. relish	18.00
Bowl, 6", cereal	23.00
Bowl, 6½", 3 pt. relish	20.00
Bowl, 7", 2 hdld. ftd. bonbon	22.00
Bowl, 7", 2 pt. relish	20.00
Bowl, 7", relish or pickle	22.00
Bowl, 9", 3 pt. celery & relish	30.00
Bowl, 9½", pickle (like corn)	22.00
Bowl, 10", 4 ft. flared	40.00
Bowl, 10", baker	35.00
Bowl, 11", 2 hdld.	35.00
Bowl, 11", 4 ftd.	40.00
Bowl, 11½", tab hdld., ftd.	40.00
Bowl, 12", 3 pt. celery & relish	32.50
Bowl, 12", 4 ft.	40.00
Bowl, 12", 4 ft. flared	40.00
Bowl, 12", 4 ft. oval	42.00
Bowl, 12", 4 ft. oval w/"ears" hdl.	47.00
Bowl, 12", 5 pt. celery & relish	32.50
Butter, rnd.	100.00
Cabinet flask	150.00
Candelabrum, 2-lite, keyhole	22.50
Candelabrum, 3-lite, keyhole	30.00
Candlestick, 1-lite, keyhole	17.50
Candlestick, 5"	17.50
Candlestick, 6", 2-lite "fleur-de-lis"	30.00
Candlestick, 6", 3-lite	35.00
Candy box w/cover, rnd.	70.00
Cigarette urn	35.00
Cocktail shaker, glass top	100.00
Cocktail shaker, metal top	70.00
Cocktail icer, 2 pc.	35.00
Comport, 5½"	25.00
Comport, 5⅜", blown	35.00
Creamer	14.00
Creamer, indiv. #3500 (pie crust edge)	14.00
Creamer, indiv. #3900, scalloped edge	14.00
Creamer, scroll handle #3400	14.00
Cup	15.00
Decanter, lg. ftd.	135.00
Decanter, short ft. cordial	165.00
Hurricane lamp, candlestick base	90.00
Hurricane lamp, keyhole base w/prisms	150.00
Ice bucket w/chrome hand.	60.00
Mayonnaise, div., w/liner & ladles	38.00
Mayonnaise (sherbet type w/ladle)	27.50
Mayonnaise w/liner, ladle	25.00
Oil, 6 oz., w/stopper	45.00
Pitcher, ball	100.00
Pitcher, Doulton	200.00
Pitcher, upright	135.00

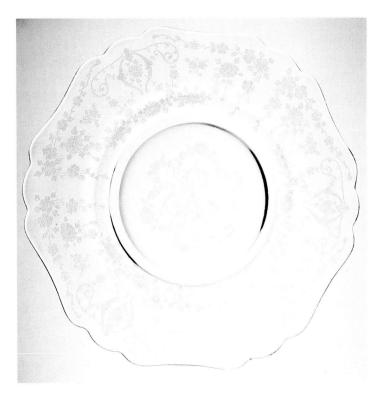

	Crystal
Plate, 6″, 2 hdld. plate	7.00
Plate, 6″, sq. bread/butter	5.00
Plate, 6½″, bread/butter	5.00
Plate, 8″, 2 hdld. ftd. bonbon	11.00
Plate, 8″, salad	10.00
Plate, 8½″	11.00
Plate, 10½″, dinner	47.50
Plate, 12″, 4 ft. service	35.00
Plate, 13″, 4 ft. torte	35.00
Plate, 13½″, 2 hdld.	30.00
Plate, 14″, torte	40.00
Platter, 13½″	45.00
Salt & pepper, ftd. w/glass tops, pr.	32.00
Salt & pepper, pr., flat	28.00
Saucer	5.00
Stem, #1066, 1 oz. cordial	45.00
Stem, #1066, 3 oz. cocktail	16.00
Stem, #1066, 3 oz. wine	22.00
Stem, #1066, 3½ oz. tall cocktail	17.50
Stem, #1066, 4½ oz. claret	17.50
Stem, #1066, 5 oz. oyster/cocktail	12.00
Stem, #1066, 7 oz. low sherbet	11.50
Stem, #1066, 7 oz. tall sherbet	13.50
Stem, #1066, 11 oz. water	15.00
Stem, #3122, 1 oz. cordial	47.00
Stem, #3122, 2½ oz., wine	22.00
Stem, #3122, 3 oz., cocktail	14.00
Stem, #3122, 4½ oz., claret	19.00
Stem, #3122, 4½ oz., oyster/cocktail	15.00
Stem, #3122, 7 oz., low sherbet	11.00
Stem, #3122, 7 oz., tall sherbet	15.00
Stem, #3122, 9 oz., water goblet	18.00
Sugar, indiv., #3500 (pie crust edge)	13.00
Sugar, indiv., #3900, scalloped edge	13.00
Sugar, scroll handle #3400	14.00
Tumbler, 2½ oz., sham bottom	27.00
Tumbler, 5 oz. ft. juice	27.00
Tumbler, 5 oz., sham bottom	27.00
Tumbler, 7 oz., old fashioned w/sham bottom	29.00
Tumbler, 8 oz. ft.	22.00
Tumbler, 10 oz. sham bottom	27.00
Tumbler, 12 oz. sham bottom	30.00
Tumbler, 13 oz.	30.00
Tumbler, 14 oz. sham bottom	35.00
Tumbler, #1066, 3 oz.	16.00
Tumbler, #1066, 5 oz., juice	11.00
Tumbler, #1066, 9 oz., water	12.00
Tumbler, #1066, 12 oz., tea	14.00
Tumbler, #3106, 3 oz., ftd.	15.00
Tumbler, #3106, 5 oz., ftd., juice	13.00
Tumbler, #3106, 9 oz., ftd. water	11.00
Tumbler, #3106, 12 oz., ftd. tea	14.00
Tumbler, #3122, 2½ oz.	14.00
Tumbler, #3122, 5 oz., juice	13.00
Tumbler, #3122, 9 oz., water	15.00
Tumbler, #3122, 12 oz., tea	17.00
Tumbler, #3135, 2½ oz., ft. bar	18.00
Tumbler, #3135, 10 oz. ft. tumbler	14.00
Tumbler, #3135, 12 oz. ft. tea	17.00
Vase, 5″, globe	25.00
Vase, 6″, high ft. flower	24.00
Vase, 8″, high ft. flower	28.00
Vase, 9″, keyhole base	35.00
Vase, 10″, bud	22.00
Vase, 11″, flower	35.00
Vase, 11″, ped. ft. flower	50.00
Vase, 12″, keyhole base	45.00
Vase, 13″, flower	60.00

Note: See Page 166-167 for stem identification.

69

ELAINE, Cambridge Glass Company, 1934 - 1950's

Colors: crystal

Beginning collectors often confuse Elaine with Chantilly; so, look closely at the gold encrusted console bowl in the foreground so you will easily recognize this pattern. I repeat the listing of #3104 stems in this pattern, but I still have yet to see them. They are shown in the catalogues as having been made.

	Crystal		Crystal
Basket, 6", 2 hdld. (upturned sides)........	15.00	Stem, #1402, 1 oz. cordial..................	45.00
Bowl, #3104, finger w/liner...............	20.00	Stem, #1402, 3 oz., wine	25.00
Bowl, 5¼", 2 hdld. bonbon.............	13.00	Stem, #1402, 3½ oz., cocktail.............	20.00
Bowl, 6", 2 hdld., ftd. bonbon	16.00	Stem, #1402, 5 oz., claret	20.00
Bowl, 6", 2 pt. relish	16.00	Stem, #1402, low sherbet.................	14.00
Bowl, 6½", 3 pt. relish	15.00	Stem, #1402, tall sherbet	15.00
Bowl, 7", 2 pt. pickle or relish...........	16.00	Stem, #1402, goblet	20.00
Bowl, 7", ftd. tab hdld. bonbon	27.00	Stem, #3104, (very tall stems),	
Bowl, 7", pickle or relish	18.00	¾ oz. brandy	----
Bowl, 9", 3 pt. celery & relish	20.00	Stem, #3104, 1 oz., cordial	----
Bowl, 9½", pickle (like corn dish)	22.00	Stem, #3104, 1 oz., pousse-cafe	----
Bowl, 10", 3 ftd, flared	30.00	Stem, #3104, 2 oz., sherry	----
Bowl, 11", tab hdld.....................	25.00	Stem, #3104, 2½ oz., creme de menthe	----
Bowl, 11½", ftd., tab hdld.	28.00	Stem, #3104, 3 oz., wine	----
Bowl, 12", 3 pt. celery & relish	27.50	Stem, #3104, 3½ oz., cocktail............	----
Bowl, 12", 4 ftd. flared	30.00	Stem, #3104, 4½ oz., claret	----
Bowl, 12", 4 ftd. oval, "ear" hdld..........	35.00	Stem, #3104, 5 oz., roemer	----
Bowl, 12", 5 pt. celery & relish	35.00	Stem, #3104, 5 oz., tall hock	----
Candlestick, 5"	17.50	Stem, #3104, 7 oz., tall sherbet	----
Candlestick, 6", 2-lite..................	25.00	Stem, #3104, 9 oz., goblet	----
Candlestick, 6", 3-lite..................	32.00	Stem, #3121, 1 oz., cordial	47.50
Candy box w/cover, rnd.................	60.00	Stem, #3121, 3 oz., cocktail.............	22.00
Cocktail icer, 2 pc...................	35.00	Stem, #3121, 3½ oz., wine	27.50
Comport, 5½"	30.00	Stem, #3121, 4½ oz., claret	20.00
Comport, 5⅜", #3500 stem	39.00	Stem, #3121, 4½ oz., oyster cocktail,	
Comport, 5⅜", blown.................	40.00	low stem	15.00
Creamer	11.00	Stem, #3121, 5 oz., parfait, low stem	25.00
Creamer, indiv.......................	10.00	Stem, #3121, 6 oz., low sherbet	15.00
Cup	16.00	Stem, #3121, 6 oz., tall sherbet...........	17.50
Decanter, lg., ftd....................	140.00	Stem, #3121, 10 oz., water	21.00
Hurricane lamp, candlestick base	75.00	Stem, #3500, 1 oz., cordial	47.50
Hurricane lamp, keyhole ft. w/prisms.......	130.00	Stem, #3500, 2½ oz., wine	25.00
Ice bucket w/chrome handle..............	57.50	Stem, #3500, 3 oz., cocktail.............	20.00
Mayonnaise, (cupped "sherbet" w/ladle)	22.00	Stem, #3500, 4½ oz., claret.............	20.00
Mayonnaise (div. bowl, liner, 2 ladles)	35.00	Stem, #3500, 4½ oz., oyster cocktail	
Mayonnaise, w/liner & ladle	25.00	low stem	14.00
Oil, 6 oz., hdld. w/stopper...............	45.00	Stem, #3500, 5 oz., parfait, low stem	23.00
Pitcher, ball........................	90.00	Stem, #3500, 7 oz., low sherbet	13.00
Pitcher, Doulton	200.00	Stem, #3500, 7 oz., tall sherbet.............	15.00
Pitcher, upright......................	145.00	Stem, #3500, 10 oz., water	20.00
Plate, 6", 2 hdld.	10.00	Sugar	10.00
Plate, 6½", bread/butter	6.50	Sugar, indiv.	10.00
Plate, 8", 2 hdld., ftd.	15.00	Tumbler, #1402, 9 oz., ftd. water..........	17.00
Plate, 8", salad	12.50	Tumbler, #1402, 12 oz., tea...............	20.00
Plate, 8", tab hdld. bonbon	15.00	Tumbler, #1402, 12 oz., tall ftd. tea........	20.00
Plate, 10½", dinner	45.00	Tumbler, #3121, 5 oz., ftd. juice	19.00
Plate, 11½", 2 hdld., ringed "Tally		Tumbler, #3121, 10 oz., ftd. water.........	20.00
Ho" sand.	25.00	Tumbler, #3121, 12 oz., ftd. tea	22.00
Plate, 12", 4 ftd. service	25.00	Tumbler, #3500, 5 oz., ftd. juice	17.00
Plate, 13", 4 ftd. torte	30.00	Tumbler, #3500, 10 oz., ftd. water	18.00
Plate, 13½", tab hdld. cake.............	30.00	Tumbler, #3500, 12 oz., ftd. tea	22.00
Plate, 14", torte.....................	30.00	Vase, 6", ftd.	22.00
Salt & pepper, pr....................	27.50	Vase, 8", ftd.	32.00
Saucer	3.00	Vase, 9", keyhole, ftd.	38.00

Note: See Pages 166-167 for stem identification.

EMPRESS, Blank #1401, A. H. Heisey & Co.

Colors: crystal, "Flamingo" pink, "Sahara" yellow, "Moongleam" green, cobalt and "Alexandrite"; some Tangerine

Empress is a Heisey pattern that attracts the eye because the footed items are dolphins. Flat pieces come in two shapes: round and square. I have had more success selling the rounded items than the square. Whether that holds true for all dealers I do not know.

	Crystal	Flam.	Sahara	Moon.	Cobalt	Alexan.
Ash Tray	30.00	60.00	85.00	175.00	200.00	165.00
Bonbon, 6″	10.00	20.00	25.00	30.00		
Bowl, cream soup	15.00	26.00	27.00	35.00		65.00
Bowl, cream soup w/sq. liner	20.00	25.00	30.00	45.00		165.00
Bowl, frappe w/center	20.00	35.00	50.00	65.00		
Bowl, nut, dolphin ftd., indiv.	15.00	22.00	26.00	32.00		80.00
Bowl, 4½″, nappy	5.00	8.00	10.00	12.50		
Bowl, 5″, preserve, 2 hdld.	12.00	18.00	22.00	27.50		
Bowl, 6″, ftd., jelly, 2 hdld.	12.00	17.00	23.00	27.50		
Bowl, 6″, dolp. ftd. mint	14.00	20.00	25.00	30.00		90.00
Bowl, 6″, grapefruit, sq. top, grnd. bottom	9.00	12.50	15.00	22.50		
Bowl, 6½″, oval lemon w/cover	35.00	65.00	75.00	90.00		
Bowl, 7″, 3 pt. relish, triplex	12.50	25.00	27.50	37.50		
Bowl, 7″, 3 pt. relish, ctr. hand.	20.00	45.00	50.00	75.00		
Bowl, 7½″ dolp. ftd. nappy	25.00	55.00	60.00	65.00	260.00	310.00
Bowl, 7½″, dolp. ftd. nasturtium	30.00	85.00	100.00	110.00	310.00	375.00
Bowl, 8″, nappy	22.00	30.00	35.00	40.00		
Bowl, 8½″, ftd., floral, 2 hdld.	30.00	40.00	50.00	65.00		
Bowl, 9″, floral, rolled edge	22.00	32.00	38.00	42.00		
Bowl, 9″, floral, flared	30.00	70.00	75.00	90.00		
Bowl, 10″, 2 hdld. oval dessert	30.00	45.00	60.00	65.00		
Bowl, 10″, lion head, floral	225.00	500.00	450.00	600.00		
Bowl, 10″, oval veg.	27.00	35.00	45.00	55.00		
Bowl, 10″, square salad, 2 hdld.	30.00	40.00	55.00	65.00		
Bowl, 10″, triplex relish	20.00	40.00	50.00	60.00		
Bowl, 11″, dolphin ftd. floral	32.00	65.00	75.00	90.00	350.00	400.00
Bowl, 13″, pickle/olive, 2 pt.	15.00	18.00	20.00	27.50		
Bowl, 15″, dolp. ftd. punch	350.00	650.00	700.00	850.00		
Candlestick, low, 4 ftd. w/2 hand.	15.00	35.00	40.00	45.00		
Candlestick, 6″, dolphin ftd.	50.00	75.00	85.00	125.00	225.00	
Candy w/cover, 6″, dolphin ftd.	35.00	90.00	95.00	125.00		
Comport, 6″, ftd.	25.00	40.00	55.00	65.00		
Comport, 6″, square	40.00	70.00	75.00	85.00		
Comport, 7″, oval	35.00	60.00	66.00	75.00		
Compotier, 6″, dolphin ftd.	70.00	130.00	170.00	195.00		
Creamer, dolphin ftd.	15.00	30.00	40.00	42.50		200.00
Creamer, indiv.	15.00	25.00	35.00	40.00		200.00
Cup	12.00	27.00	31.00	36.00		97.50
Cup, after dinner	15.00	33.00	40.00	50.00		
Cup, bouillon, 2 hdld.	16.00	28.00	30.00	33.00		
Cup, 4 oz. custard or punch	12.00	25.00	28.00	30.00		
Cup #1401½, has rim as demi-cup	20.00	28.00	32.00	40.00		
Grapefruit w/square liner	15.00	25.00	30.00	35.00		
Ice tub w/metal handles	40.00	95.00	100.00	130.00		
Jug, 3 pint, ftd.	70.00	165.00	190.00	200.00		
Jug, flat				165.00		
Marmalade w/cover, dolp. ftd.	40.00	70.00	80.00	95.00		
Mayonnaise, 5½″, ftd.	20.00	35.00	45.00	55.00		150.00
Mustard w/cover	30.00	60.00	65.00	75.00		
Oil bottle, 4 oz.	35.00	75.00	105.00	120.00		

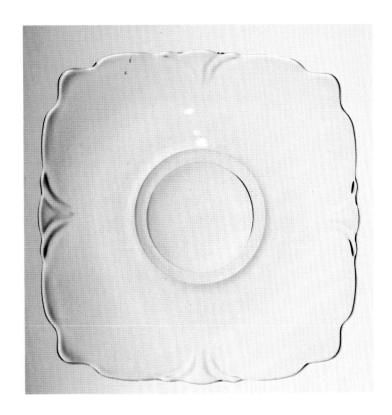

	Crystal	Flam.	Sahara	Moon.	Cobalt	Alexan.
Plate, bouillon liner	4.00	7.00	10.00	12.00		
Plate, cream soup liner	5.00	9.00	13.00	15.00		20.00
Plate, 4½″	5.00	6.00	6.00	8.00		
Plate, 6″	5.00	11.00	14.00	16.00		35.00
Plate, 6″, square	5.00	10.00	13.00	15.00		35.00
Plate, 7″	8.00	12.00	15.00	17.00		45.00
Plate, 7″, square	7.00	12.00	15.00	17.00	55.00	45.00
Plate, 8″, square	10.00	18.00	22.00	35.00	60.00	60.00
Plate, 8″	9.00	16.00	20.00	24.00	60.00	60.00
Plate, 9″	12.00	25.00	35.00	40.00		
Plate, 10½″	40.00	100.00	100.00	125.00		
Plate, 10½″, square	40.00	100.00	100.00	125.00		135.00
Plate, 12″	25.00	45.00	55.00	65.00		
Plate, 12″, muffin, sides upturned	30.00	50.00	60.00	70.00		
Plate, 12″, sandwich, 2 hdld	25.00	35.00	40.00	50.00		150.00
Plate, 13″, hors d'oeuvre, 2 hdld.	28.00	40.00	45.00	55.00		
Plate, 13″, square, 2 hdld.	28.00	40.00	45.00	55.00		
Platter, 14″	25.00	35.00	40.00	47.50		
Salt & pepper, pr.	40.00	85.00	100.00	125.00		250.00
Saucer, square	3.00	8.00	14.00	16.00		22.50
Saucer, after dinner	2.00	7.00	10.00	10.00		
Saucer	3.00	8.00	14.00	16.00		
Stem, 2½ oz., oyster cocktail	15.00	20.00	25.00	30.00		
Stem, 4 oz., saucer champagne	20.00	35.00	40.00	60.00		
Stem, 4 oz., sherbet	15.00	22.00	28.00	35.00		
Stem, 9 oz., Empress stemware, unusual	25.00	50.00	55.00	65.00		
Sugar, indiv.	15.00	25.00	35.00	40.00		200.00
Sugar, dolphin ftd. 3 hdld.	10.00	22.00	25.00	27.00		200.00
Tray, condiment & line for indiv. sugar/creamer	10.00	15.00	20.00	23.00		
Tray, 10″, 3 pt. relish	18.00	25.00	30.00	35.00		
Tray, 10″, 7 pt. hors d'oeuvre	25.00	45.00	50.00	75.00		
Tray, 10″, celery	12.00	16.00	22.00	26.00		150.00
Tray, 12″, ctr. hdld sand.	30.00	48.00	57.00	65.00		
Tray, 12″, sq. ctr. hdld. sand.	32.50	52.00	60.00	67.50		
Tray, 13″, celery	16.00	20.00	24.00	30.00		
Tray, 16″, 4 pt. buffet relish	30.00	50.00	75.00	85.00		
Tumbler, 8 oz., dolp. ftd., unusual	60.00	100.00	120.00	130.00		
Tumbler, 8 oz., grnd. bottom	15.00	30.00	35.00	39.50		
Tumbler, 12 oz., tea, grnd. bottom	16.00	31.00	36.00	40.00		
Vase, 8″, flared	45.00	80.00	90.00	105.00		
Vase, 9″, ftd.	55.00	90.00	100.00	135.00		525.00

FAIRFAX NO. 2375, Fostoria Glass Company, 1927 - 1944

Colors: blue, orchid, amber, rose, green, topaz, some ruby and black

Fairfax is the Fostoria blank on which many of the most popular Fostoria etching are found, notably June, Versailles and Trojan. Most collectors do not get as excited about this No. 2375 line without an etching. It is the Azure blue that is the most collected color even in the non-etched line.

The blue pitchers show the differences in Fostoria's blue. The light blue was called Azure while the more vivid color was called Blue. This Blue was an early color and used in only the first dinnerware lines and the popular American pattern.

Note the Azure flower vase with frog in front of the pitcher. This piece is found rarely and the frog even less often than its holder.

Due to confusion among collectors and dealers alike, I have shown the various Fostoria stems on page 79 so that differences in shapes can be seen. The claret and high sherbets are major concerns. Each is 6″ high. Note the claret is shaped like the wine; and the parfait is taller than the juice!

	Blue, Orchid	Amber, Rose	Green, Topaz		Blue, Orchid	Amber, Rose	Green, Topaz
Ash tray	20.00	13.00	17.50	Plate, 7″, salad	5.00	3.00	3.50
Baker, 9″, oval	25.00	15.00	20.00	Plate, 7″, cream soup			
Baker, 10½″, oval	32.00	20.00	22.50	liner	5.00	3.00	3.50
Bonbon	12.50	9.00	10.00	Plate, 8″, salad	9.00	4.50	5.00
Bottle, salad dressing	95.00	60.00	70.00	Plate, 9½″, luncheon	12.00	6.00	7.00
Bouillon, ftd.	11.00	7.00	8.00	Plate, 10¼″, dinner	21.00	13.00	15.00
Bowl, 9″lemon, 2 hdld.	9.00	6.00	7.00	Plate, 10¼″, grill	12.00	8.00	10.00
Bowl, whipped cream	11.00	8.00	9.00	Plate, 10″, cake	17.50	13.00	15.00
Bowl, 5″, fruit	8.50	5.00	6.00	Plate, 12″, bread	14.00	10.00	12.00
Bowl, 6″, cereal	16.00	9.00	11.00	Plate, 14″, torte	17.50	14.00	15.00
Bowl, 7″, soup	20.00	12.00	14.00	Platter, 10½″, oval	27.00	17.00	19.00
Bowl, 8″, rnd. nappy	22.00	13.00	14.00	Platter, 12″, oval	32.00	20.00	22.50
Bowl, lg., hdld. dessert	17.00	10.00	12.00	Platter, 15″, oval	50.00	27.00	32.00
Bowl, 12″	20.00	15.00	18.00	Relish, 8½″	10.00	7.00	8.00
Bowl, 12″, centerpiece.....	22.00	17.50	20.00	Relish, 11½″	15.00	10.00	12.00
Bowl, 13″, oval centerpiece	27.50	20.00	22.50	Sauce boat	30.00	20.00	25.00
Bowl, 15″, centerpeice.....	29.00	20.00	24.00	Sauce boat liner	12.00	9.00	10.00
Butter dish w/cover	125.00	80.00	90.00	Saucer, after dinner	6.00	4.00	5.00
Candlestick, flattened top ..	12.00	10.00	10.00	Saucer	4.00	2.50	3.00
Candlestick, 3″	11.50	9.00	10.00	Shaker, ftd., pr.	55.00	30.00	35.00
Celery, 11½″	16.00	12.00	14.00	Shaker, indiv., ft., pr.	----	20.00	25.00
Cheese & cracker, set......	25.00	20.00	22.50	Stem, 4″, ¾ oz., cordial....	40.00	25.00	30.00
Comport, 7″	15.00	10.00	12.00	Stem, 4¼″, 6 oz., low sherbet	12.00	11.00	11.00
Cream soup, ftd.	12.00	9.00	8.00	Stem, 5¼″, 3 oz., cocktail ..	20.00	15.00	18.00
Creamer, flat	----	10.00	12.00	Stem, 5½″, 3 oz., wine	25.00	22.50	22.50
Creamer, ftd.	11.00	7.00	9.00	Stem, 6″, 4 oz., claret	20.00	18.00	18.00
Creamer, tea	13.00	7.00	9.00	Stem, 6″, 6 oz., high sherbet	13.00	12.50	12.50
Cup, after dinner	15.00	10.00	12.50	Stem, 8¼″, 10 oz., water ...	20.00	17.50	18.00
Cup, flat	----	4.00	6.00	Sugar, flat	----	10.00	12.00
Cup, ftd.	8.00	6.00	7.00	Sugar, ftd.	10.00	6.00	8.00
Flower holder, oval	27.00	18.00	20.00	Sugar cover	30.00	20.00	22.50
Ice bucket	40.00	30.00	35.00	Sugar pail	40.00	25.00	28.00
Mayonnaise	12.00	9.00	10.00	Sugar, tea	12.50	6.00	8.00
Mayonnaise ladle	14.00	10.00	10.00	Sweetmeat	11.00	7.00	9.00
Mayonnaise liner, 7″	5.00	3.00	3.50	Tray, 11″, ctr. hand.	20.00	12.00	15.00
Oil, ftd.................	105.00	80.00	90.00	Tumbler, 4½″, 5 oz., ftd....	12.00	10.00	11.00
Pickle, 8½″	10.00	7.00	9.00	Tumbler, 5¼″, 9 oz., ftd....	13.50	12.00	12.50
Pitcher	160.00	110.00	120.00	Tumbler, 6″, 12 oz., ftd. ...	15.00	13.50	14.00
Plate, canape	5.00	3.00	4.00	Whipped cream pail	40.00	25.00	28.00
Plate, 6″, bread/butter	3.00	2.00	2.50				

See page 79 for stem identification.

76

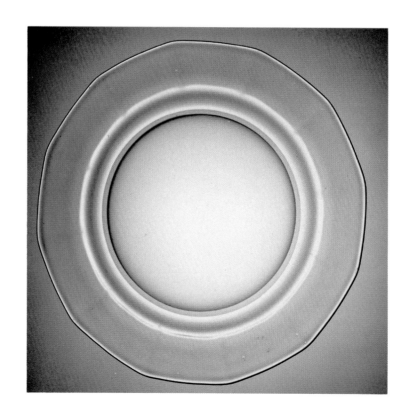

FOSTORIA STEMS AND SHAPES

Top Row: Left to Right
1. Water, 10 oz., 8¼″
2. Claret, 4 oz., 6″
3. Wine, 3 oz., 5½″
4. Cordial, ¾ oz., 4″
5. Sherbet, low, 4¼″
6. Cocktail, 3 oz., 5¼″
7. Sherbet, high, 6 oz.

Bottom Row: Left to Right
1. Grapefruit and liner
2. Ice tea tumbler, 12 oz., 6″
3. Water tumbler, 9 oz., 5¼″
4. Parfait, 6 oz., 5¼″
5. Juice tumbler, 5 oz., 4½″
6. Oyster cocktail, 5½ oz.
7. Bar tumbler, 2½ oz.

FLANDERS, Tiffin Glass Company, mid 1910's - mid 1930's

Colors: crystal, pink, yellow

Flanders was originally named Poppy before World War I according to new information released by the Tiffin Glass Collectors newsletter. After the WWI battle at Flanders, this pattern's name was changed. Thus, it is a memorial pattern.

Flanders has been a pattern that I have kept a more watchful eye on than some of the others. I have been intrigued with it since I bought a large lot of glass at an auction a few years ago. In that lot was one lonely goblet which I thought was Cambridge Gloria. Several weeks later, I realized that it was not Gloria and began a search of my bookshelf to find out what it was. That story was brought to mind in Pittsburgh by a lady who brought in the vase shown here. She had purchased it thinking it was Gloria. I tried to buy it for photographing, but it was not for sale. Thankfully, she lent it to me so it could be shown.

I have mentioned previously how difficult it is to find cups and saucers in Tiffin patterns. Flanders is no exception; amazingly, there are two different styles in this pattern. The one pictured here is damaged, but it is the only one I have been able to buy. I found it in Indianapolis at a shop that had six on the previous day. The six saucers were all there, but only a damaged cup was left. Someone walked away with five without paying for them! That is another problem that dealers face which causes prices to increase and something that new dealers have to be aware of happening when you start your business. Not everyone is *honest*.

As in most Tiffin patterns, there are two stemware lines. There are also two styles of plates and creamer and sugars. One style plate is round; the other is scalloped. The footed creamer and sugar were made later in the pattern's history. The flat style was very early and not many have been found. The ones shown here are one of two pairs I have seen in my travels.

Pink is the color most collected, but sets can be found in yellow and crystal. I have seen more yellow than crystal; so I do not know how difficult it would be to complete a set in crystal. In any case, a Flanders collection in any color will not be completed without a lot of searching.

	Pink/Yellow		Pink/Yellow
Bowl, finger w/liner	24.00	Plate, 9½", dinner	40.00
Bowl, 2 hdld., bonbon	20.00	Relish, 3 pt.	35.00
Bowl, 12", flanged rim console	35.00	Saucer	9.00
Candlestick, 2 styles	40.00	Stem, bar	50.00
Candy Jar w/cover	150.00	Stem, cordial	65.00
Celery, 11"	30.00	Stem, cocktail	25.00
Comport, 3½"	35.00	Stem, oyster cocktail	18.00
Comport, 6"	75.00	Stem, parfait	45.00
Creamer, flat	62.50	Stem, saucer, champagne	18.00
Creamer, ftd.	45.00	Stem, sherbet	15.00
Cup, 2 styles	28.00	Stem, water	25.00
Decanter	200.00	Stem, wine	40.00
Grapefruit w/liner	40.00	Sugar, flat	62.50
Mayonnaise, w/liner	50.00	Sugar, ftd.	45.00
Oil bottle & stopper	145.00	Tumbler, 9 oz., ftd. water	20.00
Pitcher & cover	275.00	Tumbler, 12 oz., ftd. tea	27.50
Plate, 6"	9.00	Vase	100.00
Plate, 7½"	12.50		

81

FUCHSIA Tiffin Glass Company, Late 1930's - early 1940's

Colors: crystal

Fuchsia is the one Tiffin pattern found today in which coridals out number all other stems except the sherbets. In all other Tiffin patterns I have had difficulty finding cordials! I have run into five or six batches of Fuchsia cordials in my travels. Either I have been lucky or they are abundant.

Fuchsia is not presently as well collected as some of the other Tiffin patterns; but newer collectors are finding it less expensive to collect than Cherokee Rose or Flanders.

I have never seen a Fuchsia cup and saucer.

Sometimes there are gremlins at work in this business. In Houston I purchased a Fuchsia icer and insert. It was packed in a box with my few other purchases and with duplicated items that we had unpacked out of the forty-five chicken boxes we had carried to the show. The insert made it home and to this day in June, the icer itself has not surfaced. To make matters worse, the dealer I bought it from called to ask me to hold it for a customer of his after I photographed it. I wish I could!

I recently found two 12″ cylinders of glass with the Fuchsia etch on them. I have no idea how they were used or even what they are. That is one of the things that keeps an author searching through stacks of books and catalogues. Sometimes it takes ages to find an answer to a question; some have no answer to be found! I get over a hundred questions in the mail each week. That is why you are restricted to questions or information about *patterns in this book*!

A letter received this week asked if something made in the middle 1970's was considered to be recently made. Time is a matter of relativity. If you are twenty, then the 1970's may not be recent; but in glass making terms that is RECENT! Glass is considered to be antique only after surviving fifty years. However, some later made glassware is considered to be collectible.

	Crystal		**Crystal**
Bowl, finger w/liner	18.00	Plate, 9½″, dinner	32.00
Bowl, 2 hdld., bonbon	15.00	Relish, 3 pt.	25.00
Bowl, 12″, flanged rim console	25.00	Saucer	7.50
Candlestick	20.00	Stem, cordial	35.00
Celery, 11″	20.00	Stem, cocktail	17.00
Comport, 6″	22.00	Stem, oyster cocktail	14.00
Creamer, ftd.	17.50	Stem, parfait	25.00
Cup	25.00	Stem, saucer champagne	15.00
Icer, with insert	45.00	Stem, sherbet	12.00
Mayonnaise, w/liner	40.00	Stem, water	25.00
Pitcher & cover	200.00	Stem, wine	30.00
Plate, 6″	6.00	Sugar, ftd.	16.50
Plate, 7½″	9.00	Tumbler, 9 oz., ftd. water	15.00
Plate, 8½″	15.00		

GLORIA, (etching 1746), Cambridge Glass 3400 Line Dinnerware Introduced 1930

Colors: crystal, yellow, pink, green, emerald green, amber, Heatherbloom

Gloria is the Cambridge pattern that is most often confused with Tiffin's Flanders. Note the similarities, but distinct differences, in the pattern shots of these two patterns.

Yellow (Gold Krystol) is the most commonly found color. Sets are available in crystal. Either shade of green or the Heatherbloom (pinkish/purple) will cause severe damage to your patience and pocketbook if you try for a full set; you might want to settle for a few pieces in these colors. The Heatherbloom wine and water goblet caught the eye of a local doctor's wife in my shop. She wanted a twelve-piece setting in that beautiful color! Grannie Bear told her they were for a picture in the book and showed her what I had paid for them. She changed her mind about a twelve place setting! She's right though; a twelve place setting would be "awesome" (to use my son's word).

Add 50% for prices in dark emerald green and 75% to 100% for Heatherbloom.

	Crystal	Colors		Crystal	Colors
Basket, 6", 2 hdld. (sides up)	13.00	20.00	Comport, 4", fruit cocktail	10.00	17.50
Bowl, 3", indiv. nut, 4 ftd.	22.00	40.00	Comport, 5", 4 ftd.	17.00	37.50
Bowl, 3½", cranberry, 4 ftd.	12.50	32.00	Comport, 6", 4 ftd.	19.00	35.00
Bowl, 5", ftd., crimped edge bonbon	14.00	22.00	Comport, 7", low	30.00	45.00
Bowl, 5", sq. fruit "saucer"	7.00	14.00	Comport, 7", tall	35.00	65.00
Bowl, 5½", bonbon, 2 hdld.	14.00	21.00	Comport, 9½", tall, 2 hdld., ftd bowl	60.00	110.00
Bowl, 5½", bonbon ftd.,	12.00	19.00	Creamer, ftd.	11.00	16.00
Bowl, 5½", flattened, ftd. bonbon	12.00	18.00	Creamer, tall, ftd.	11.00	17.50
Bowl, 5½", fruit "saucer"	7.50	14.00	Cup, rnd., or sq.	15.00	25.00
Bowl, 6", rnd. cereal	9.00	17.50	Cup, 4 ftd. sq.	17.00	40.00
Bowl, 6", sq. cereal	9.00	16.00	Cup, after dinner (demitasse), rnd. or sq.	27.00	48.00
Bowl, 8", 2 pt., 2 hdld. relish	15.00	23.00	Fruit cocktail, 6 oz., ftd. (3 styles)	9.00	15.00
Bowl, 8", 3 pt., 3 hdld. relish	20.00	34.00	Ice pail, metal handle w/tongs	37.50	65.00
Bowl, 8¾", 2 hdld., figure "8" pickle	17.50	27.00	Mayonnaise w/liner & ladle, (4 ftd. bowl)	35.00	55.00
Bowl, 8¾", 2 pt., 2 hdld. figure "8" relish	20.00	32.00	Oil w/stopper; tall, ftd., hdld.	65.00	125.00
Bowl, 9", salad, tab hdld.	20.00	40.00	Oyster cocktail, #3035, 4½ oz.	10.00	15.00
Bowl, 9½", 2 hdld., veg.	55.00	80.00	Oyster cocktail, 4½ oz., low stem	10.00	15.00
Bowl, 10", oblong, tab hdld. "baker"	25.00	35.00	Pitcher, 67 oz., middle indent	110.00	235.00
Bowl, 10", 2 hdld.	32.00	60.00	Pitcher, 80 oz., ball	100.00	175.00
Bowl, 11", 2 hdld. fruit	30.00	55.00	Pitcher w/cover, 64 oz.	95.00	165.00
Bowl, 12", 4 ftd. console	25.00	50.00	Plate, 6", 2 hdld.	8.00	13.50
Bowl, 12", 4 ftd. flared rim	22.00	45.00	Plate, 6", bread/butter	6.00	9.00
Bowl, 12", 4 ftd. oval	30.00	60.00	Plate, 7½", tea	8.00	12.00
Bowl, 12", 5 pt. celery & relish	25.00	45.00	Plate, 8½"	9.00	14.00
Bowl, 13", flared rim	25.00	45.00	Plate, 9½" dinner	35.00	55.00
Bowl, cream soup w/rnd. liner	15.00	30.00	Plate, 10", tab hdld. salad	15.00	30.00
Bowl, cream soup w/sq. saucer	15.00	30.00	Plate, 11", 2 hdld.	15.00	25.00
Bowl, finger, flared edge w/rnd. plate	14.00	26.00	Plate, 11", sq., ftd. cake	45.00	100.00
Bowl, finger, ftd.	12.00	25.00	Plate, 11½", tab hdld. sandwich	17.50	38.00
Bowl, finger w/rnd. plate	15.00	30.00	Plate, 14", chop or salad	35.00	55.00
Butter w/cover, 2 hdld.	90.00	195.00	Plate, sq. bread/butter	6.00	9.00
Candlestick, 6", ea.	17.50	32.50	Plate, sq. dinner	35.00	55.00
Candy box w/cover, 4 ftd. w/tab hdld.	40.00	75.00	Plate, sq. salad	7.00	12.00
Cheese compote w/11½" cracker plate, tab hdld.	25.00	45.00	Plate, sq. service	22.00	45.00
			Platter, 11½"	30.00	60.00
Cocktail shaker, grnd. stopper, spout (like pitcher)	70.00	175.00	Salt & pepper, pr., short	25.00	55.00
			Salt & pepper, pr., w/glass top, tall	27.50	70.00

GLORIA, (etching 1746), Cambridge Glass 3400 Line Dinnerware Introduced 1930, (continued)

	Crystal	Colors
Salt & pepper, ftd., metal tops	32.50	62.50
Saucer, rnd.	2.00	4.00
Saucer, rnd. after dinner	4.00	5.00
Saucer, sq., after dinner (demitasse)	4.00	5.00
Saucer, sq.	2.00	3.00
Stem, #3035, 2½ oz., wine	17.50	30.00
Stem, #3035, 3 oz., cocktail	17.50	28.00
Stem, #3035, 3½ oz., cocktail	17.00	27.00
Stem, #3035, 4½ oz., claret	17.50	30.00
Stem, #3035, 6 oz., low sherbet	10.00	15.00
Stem, #3035, 6 oz., tall sherbet	11.00	17.50
Stem, #3035, 9 oz., water	15.00	26.00
Stem, #3035, 3½ oz., cocktail	17.00	28.00
Stem, #3115, 9 oz., goblet	13.00	26.00
Stem, #3120, 1 oz., cordial	43.00	75.00
Stem, #3120, 4½ oz., claret	16.00	30.00
Stem, #3120, 6 oz., low sherbet	10.00	15.00
Stem, #3120, 6 oz., tall sherbet	11.00	16.00
Stem, #3120, 9 oz., water	15.00	25.00
Stem, #3130, 2½ oz., wine	16.00	30.00
Stem, #3130, 6 oz., low sherbet	10.00	15.00
Stem, #3130, 6 oz., tall sherbet	11.00	16.00
Stem, #3130, 8 oz., water	15.00	25.00
Stem, #3135, 1 oz., cordial	35.00	70.00
Stem, #3135, 6 oz., low sherbet	11.00	15.00
Stem, #3135, 6 oz., tall sherbet	12.00	16.00
Stem, #3135, 8 oz., water	15.00	26.00
Sugar, ftd.	11.00	18.00
Sugar, tall, ftd.	11.00	19.00
Sugar shaker w/glass top	75.00	175.00
Syrup, tall, ftd.	40.00	65.00
Tray, 11", ctr. hdld. sandwich	20.00	30.00

	Crystal	Colors
Tray, 2 pt. ctr. hdld. relish	22.00	35.00
Tray, 4 pt. ctr. hdld. relish	30.00	45.00
Tray, 9", pickle, tab hdld.	15.00	25.00
Tumbler, #3035, 5 oz., high ftd.	11.00	20.00
Tumbler, #3035, 10 oz., high ftd.	12.00	22.00
Tumbler, #3035, 12 oz., high ftd.	15.00	23.00
Tumbler, #3115, 5 oz., ftd. juice	12.00	20.00
Tumbler, #3115, 8 oz., ftd.	12.00	20.00
Tumbler, #3115, 10 oz., ftd.	13.00	21.00
Tumbler, #3115, 12 oz., ftd.	15.00	22.00
Tumbler, #3120, 2½ oz., ftd. (used w/cocktail shaker	12.00	20.00
Tumbler, #3120, 5 oz., ftd.	12.00	20.00
Tumbler, #3120, 10 oz., ftd.	12.00	20.00
Tumbler, #3120, 12 oz., ftd.	15.00	22.00
Tumbler, #3120, 2½ oz., ftd. (used w/shaker)	12.00	21.00
Tumbler, #3130, 5 oz., ftd.	12.00	20.00
Tumbler, #3130, 10 oz., ftd.	13.00	20.00
Tumbler, #3130, 12 oz., ftd.	15.00	21.00
Tumbler, #3135, 5 oz., juice	12.00	20.00
Tumbler, #3135, 10 oz., water	12.00	20.00
Tumbler, #3135, 12 oz., tea	15.00	22.00
Tumbler, 12 oz., flat, (2 styles)-one w/indent side to match, 67 oz. pitcher	14.00	25.00
Vase, 9", oval, 4 indent	45.00	90.00
Vase, 10", keyhole base	37.50	75.00
Vase, 10", squarish top	35.00	70.00
Vase, 11"	40.00	80.00
Vase, 11", neck indent	42.50	85.00
Vase, 12", keyhole base, flared rim	42.50	85.00
Vase, 12", squarish top	40.00	80.00
Vase, 14", keyhole base, flared rim	47.50	90.00

Note: See Pages 166-167 for stem identification.

GREEK KEY, A. H. Heisey & Co.

Colors: crystal, "Flamingo" pink punch bowl and cups only

	Crystal		Crystal
Bowl, finger	15.00	Pitcher, 1 pint	60.00
Bowl, Jelly w/cover, 2 hdld. ftd.	135.00	Pitcher, 1 quart	65.00
Bowl, indiv. ftd. almond	25.00	Pitcher, 3 pint	85.00
Bowl, 4″, nappy	10.00	Pitcher, ½ gal.	95.00
Bowl, 4″, shallow, low ft., jelly	15.00	Oil bottle, 2 oz., squat w/#8 stopper	60.00
Bowl, 4½″, nappy	15.00	Oil bottle, 2 oz., w/#6 stopper	65.00
Bowl, 4½″, scalloped nappy	17.50	Oil bottle, 4 oz., squat w/#8 stopper	70.00
Bowl, 4½″, shallow, low ft., jelly	14.00	Oil bottle, 4 oz., w/#6 stopper	75.00
Bowl, 5″, ftd. almond	35.00	Oil bottle, 6 oz., w/#6 stopper	85.00
Bowl, 5″, ftd. almond w/cover	90.00	Oil bottle, 6 oz., squat w/#8 stopper	85.00
Bowl, 5″, hdld. jelly	35.00	Plate, 4½″	10.00
Bowl, 5″, low ft. jelly w/cover	40.00	Plate, 5″	11.00
Bowl, 5″, nappy	22.50	Plate, 5½″	11.00
Bowl, 5½″, nappy	25.00	Plate, 6″	12.00
Bowl, 5½″, shallow nappy, ftd.	55.00	Plate, 6½″	12.00
Bowl, 6″, nappy	25.00	Plate, 7″	13.00
Bowl, 6″, shallow nappy	27.50	Plate, 8″	15.00
Bowl, 6½″, nappy	30.00	Plate, 9″	20.00
Bowl, 7″, low ft., straight side	35.00	Plate, 10″	45.00
Bowl, 7″, nappy	32.00	Plate, 16″, orange bowl liner	50.00
Bowl, 8″, low ft., straight side	40.00	Puff box, #1 w/cover	65.00
Bowl, 8″, nappy	37.50	Puff box, #3 w/cover	75.00
Bowl, 8″, scalloped nappy	42.00	Salt & pepper, pr.	65.00
Bowl, 8″, shallow, low ft.	45.00	Sherbet, 4½ oz., ftd., straight rim	12.50
Bowl, 8½″, shallow nappy	45.00	Sherbet, 4½ oz., ftd., flared rim	12.50
Bowl, 9″, flat banana split	21.00	Sherbet, 4½ oz., hi. ft., shallow	12.50
Bowl, 9″, ftd. banana split	20.00	Sherbet, 4½ oz., ftd., shallow	12.50
Bowl, 9″, low ft., straight side	45.00	Sherbet, 4½ oz., ftd., cupped rim	12.50
Bowl, 9″, nappy	40.00	Sherbet, 6 oz., low ft.	13.00
Bowl, 9″, shallow, low ft.	45.00	Spooner, lg.	65.00
Bowl, 9½″, shallow nappy	45.00	Spooner, 4½″, (or straw jar)	75.00
Bowl, 10″, shallow, low ft.	50.00	Stem, ¾ oz., cordial	165.00
Bowl, 11″, shallow nappy	50.00	Stem, 2 oz., wine	135.00
Bowl, 12″, orange bowl	55.00	Stem, 2 oz., sherry	125.00
Bowl, 12″, punch, ftd.	175.00	Stem, 3 oz., cocktail	22.00
(Flamingo)	725.00	Stem, 3½ oz., burgundy	95.00
Bowl, 14″, orange, flared rim	65.00	Stem, 4½ oz., saucer champagne	22.00
Bowl, 14½″, orange, flared rim	67.50	Stem, 4½ oz., claret	90.00
Bowl, 15″, punch, ftd.	140.00	Stem, 7 oz.	65.00
Bowl, 18″, punch, shallow	150.00	Stem, 9 oz.	75.00
Butter, indiv. (plate)	15.00	Stem, 9 oz., low ft.	65.00
Butter/jelly, 2 hdld. w/cover	175.00	Straw jar w/cover	250.00
Candy w/cover, ½ lb.	120.00	Sugar	25.00
Candy w/cover, 1 lb.	130.00	Sugar, oval, hotel	30.00
Candy w/cover, 2 lb.	175.00	Sugar, rnd., hotel	27.50
Cheese & cracker set, 10″	60.00	Sugar & creamer, oval, individual	67.50
Compote, 5″	50.00	Tray, 9″, oval celery	17.50
Compote, 5″, w/cover	75.00	Tray, 12″, oval celery	20.00
Creamer	25.00	Tray, 12½″, French roll	55.00
Creamer, oval, hotel	30.00	Tray, 13″, oblong	60.00
Creamer, rnd., hotel	27.50	Tray, 15″, oblong	62.50
Cup, 4½ oz., punch	18.00	Tumbler, 2½ oz., (or toothpick)	265.00
(Flamingo)	30.00	Tumbler, 5 oz., flared rim	18.00
Egg cup, 5 oz.	50.00	Tumbler, 5 oz., straight side	18.00
Hair receiver	65.00	Tumbler, 5½ oz., water	19.00
Ice tub, lg., tab hdld.	75.00	Tumbler, 7 oz., flared rim	21.00
Ice tub, sm., tab hdld.	60.00	Tumbler, 7 oz., straight side	22.50
Ice tub w/cover, hotel	85.00	Tumbler, 8 oz., w/straight, flared, cupped, shallow	27.50
Ice tub w/cover, 5″, individual w/5″ plate	85.00	Tumbler, 10 oz., flared rim	30.00
Jar, 1 qt., crushed fruit w/cover	185.00	Tumbler, 10 oz., staight wide	30.00
Jar, 2 qt., crushed cruit w/cover	235.00	Tumbler, 12 oz., flared rim	32.00
Jar, lg. cover horseradish	67.50	Tumbler, 12 oz., straight side	32.00
Jar, sm. cover horseradish	57.50	Tumbler, 13 oz., straight side	33.00
Jar, tall celery	62.00	Tumbler, 13 oz., flared rim	35.00
Jar w/knob cover, pickle	95.00	Water bottle	100.00

89

IMPERIAL HUNT SCENE, #718, Cambridge Glass Company, Late 1920's - 1930's

Colors: amber, black, crystal, Emerald green; green, pink

I finally found a cordial in this pattern! It took the help of a friend and several months of work to put it in my collection. Hunt Scene remains very popular but very elusive in many colors.

Hunt Scene is mostly found on the 1402 Cambridge line called Tally-Ho and the Decagon Blank. Tally-Ho remains an appropriate name for a scene with running dogs and horses jumping over fences and hedges.

Prices for the dark, emerald green and the black will fetch 25% to 30% higher than the prices listed.

	All Colors
Bowl, 6″, cereal	17.50
Bowl, 8″	37.50
Bowl, 8½″, 3 pt.	40.00
Candlestick, 2-lite, keyhole	27.50
Candlestick, 3-lite, keyhole	40.00
Creamer, ftd.	27.50
Ice bucket	57.50
Ice tub	55.00
Mayonnaise, w/liner	50.00
Pitcher, w/cover, 63 oz., #3077	195.00
Pitcher, w/cover, 76 oz., #711	175.00
Plate, 8″	22.00
Stem, 1 oz., cordial #1402	95.00
Stem, 2½ oz., wine #1402	55.00
Stem, 3 oz., cocktail #1402	30.00
Stem, 6 oz., tomato #1402	20.00
Stem, 6½ oz., sherbet #1402	15.00
Stem, 7½ oz., sherbet #1402	20.00
Stem, 10 oz., water #1402	25.00
Stem, 14 oz., #1402	30.00
Stem, 18 oz., #1402	45.00
Stem, 1 oz., cordial #3077	95.00
Stem, 2½ oz., cocktail #3077	30.00
Stem, 6 oz., low sherbet #3077	17.50
Stem, 6 oz., high sherbet #3077	20.00
Stem, 9 oz., water #3077	27.00
Sugar, ftd.	24.00
Tumbler, 2½ oz., flat, #1402	17.00
Tumbler, 5 oz., flat, #1402	16.00
Tumbler, 7 oz., flat, #1402	20.00
Tumbler, 10 oz., flat, #1402	22.50
Tumbler, 10 oz., flat, tall, #1402	25.00
Tumbler, 15 oz., flat, #1402	35.00
Tumbler, 2½ oz., ftd., #3077	18.00
Tumbler, 5 oz., ftd., #3077	17.50
Tumbler, 8 oz., ftd., #3077	22.00
Tumbler, 10 oz., ftd., #3077	25.00
Tumbler, 12 oz., ftd., #3077	27.00

IPSWICH, Blank #1405, A. H. Heisey & Co.

Colors: crystal, "Flamingo" pink, "Sahara" yellow, "Moongleam" green, cobalt and "Alexandrite"

Only the Ipswich goblet was made in Alexandrite. If you find a purple colored piece of Ipswich, it will be Imperial's Heather which was made from Heisey's moulds from 1961-1965. Other colors made in this pattern include Imperial's amber, Antique Blue and Verde (green). The tumbler was fitted with a plain lid to make a candy in Moonlight blue and Mandarin gold (yellow).

The pink, yellow and green (shown here) were made only by Heisey. The Imperial Verde is a more yellow-green when compared to Heisey's Moongleam.

The Moongleam shown is from the collection of Dick and Pat Spencer (except for the pitcher which he has been trying to buy since 1981 when we did the first book). He found it this time in Beverly Hine's box and put a cheap price sticker on it telling her he had finally found one. He had to fess up when hers was no where to be found! We do have a little fun in these marathon photography sessions.

	Crystal	Pink	Sahara	Green	Cobalt	Alexan.
Bowl, finger w/underplate	20.00	45.00	40.00	45.00		
Bowl, 11", ft. floral	35.00				300.00	
Candlestick, 6", 1-lite	75.00	205.00	160.00	200.00	325.00	
Candlestick centerpiece, ft., vase, "A" prisms	95.00	260.00	250.00	325.00	450.00	
Candy jar, ½ lb., w/cover	45.00	175.00	235.00	285.00		
Cocktail shaker, 1 quart, strainer #86 stopper	160.00	275.00	275.00	500.00		
Creamer.........................	17.00	32.00	35.00	40.00		
Stem, 4 oz., oyster cocktail..........	8.00					
Stem, 5 oz., saucer champagne	12.50					
Stem, 10 oz., goblet	18.00					700.00
Stem, 12 oz., schoppen	27.50					
Pitcher, ½ gal.	125.00	225.00	325.00	600.00		
Oil bottle, 2 oz., ft. #86 stopper	65.00	175.00	135.00	175.00		
Plate, 7", square	15.00	20.00	22.00	26.00		
Plate, 8", square	16.00	22.00	24.00	29.00		
Sherbet, 4 oz.	7.00	17.50	22.50	30.00		
Sugar	17.00	40.00	35.00	40.00		
Tumbler, 5 oz., ft.	9.00	32.00	27.00	32.00		
Tumbler, 8 oz., ft.	10.00	34.00	30.00	35.00		
Tumbler, 10 oz., cupped rim	12.50	37.00	32.00	37.00		
Tumbler, 10 oz., straight rim	12.50	37.00	32.00	37.00		
Tumbler, 12 oz., ft.	14.00	47.00	42.00	47.00		

JUNE, Fostoria Glass Company, 1928 - 1944

Colors: crystal; "Azure" blue, "Topaz" yellow, "Rose" pink

Blue is the most desirable color in this pattern! Prices are always moving in one direction—UP! A few new collectors who like the pattern, but do not like the price in blue, have begun looking seriously at yellow and pink. I have had a few requests for crystal in my shop; but I rarely find that color.

You can tell the desirable pieces from the prices shown! I only record what is happening; so, I warn you, now is the time if you are ever going to get this set completed.

	Crystal	Blue	Rose, Topaz		Crystal	Blue	Rose, Topaz
Ash tray	23.00	45.00	32.00	Ice bucket	47.50	90.00	75.00
Bottle, salad dressing,				Ice dish	21.00	42.50	37.50
sterling top	165.00	325.00	265.00	Ice dish liner (tomato,			
Bowl, baker, 9″, oval	31.50	65.00	47.00	crab, fruit)	5.00	10.00	7.50
Bowl, bonbon	12.50	25.00	20.00	Mayonnaise w/liner	22.50	45.00	37.50
Bowl, bouillon, ftd.	12.00	25.00	20.00	Oil, ftd.	165.00	375.00	250.00
Bowl, finger w/liner	32.50	35.00	45.00	Oyster cocktail, 5½ oz.	16.00	30.00	23.00
Bowl, lemon	14.00	25.00	18.00	Parfait, 5¼″	22.50	60.00	47.50
Bowl, mint	10.00	20.00	15.00	Pitcher	195.00	400.00	300.00
Bowl, 5″, fruit	11.00	22.00	18.00	Plate, canape	10.00	18.00	15.00
Bowl, 6″, cereal	15.00	29.00	23.50	Plate, 6″, bread/butter	4.50	6.00	5.00
Bowl, 6″, nappy, ftd.	10.00	23.00	18.00	Plate, 6″, finger bowl			
Bowl, 7″, soup	17.50	37.50	25.00	liner	4.50	6.00	5.00
Bowl, lg., dessert, hdld.	20.00	65.00	35.00	Plate, 7½″, salad	5.00	10.00	8.00
Bowl, 10″	20.00	47.50	35.00	Plate, 7½″, cream soup	4.00	9.00	7.50
Bowl, 10″, Grecian	30.00	60.00	50.00	Plate, 8¾″, luncheon	6.00	12.00	10.00
Bowl, 11″, centerpiece	20.00	50.00	35.00	Plate, 9½″, sm. dinner	8.00	18.00	15.00
Bowl, 12″, centerpiece,				Plate, 10″, grill	16.00	35.00	27.50
several types	25.00	60.00	42.50	Plate, 10″, cake, hdld.	20.00	45.00	35.00
Bowl, 13″, oval				Plate, 10¼″, dinner	22.00	50.00	39.50
centerpiece w/flower frog	30.00	67.50	47.50	Plate, 13″, chop	20.00	44.00	35.00
Candlestick, 2″	10.00	20.00	15.00	Platter, 12″	22.00	50.00	40.00
Candlestick, 3″	12.00	22.00	18.00	Platter, 15″	30.00	115.00	75.00
Candlestick, 3″, Grecian	15.00	25.00	25.00	Relish, 8½″	14.00	22.00	20.00
Candlestick, 5″	15.00	30.00	22.50	Sauce boat	35.00	110.00	75.00
Candy w/cover, 3 pt.	50.00	155.00	90.00	Sauce boat liner	12.00	40.00	25.00
Candy w/cover, ½ lb.	50.00	145.00	110.00	Saucer, after dinner	6.00	10.00	8.00
Celery, 11½″	25.00	40.00	35.00	Saucer	4.00	7.50	5.00
Cheese & cracker, set	25.00	57.50	40.00	Shaker, ftd. pr.	60.00	130.00	92.50
Comport, 5″	18.00	32.50	27.50	Sherbet, high, 6″, 6 oz.	17.50	29.00	25.00
Comport, 6″	20.00	55.00	30.00	Sherbet, low, 4¼″, 6 oz.	15.00	25.00	20.00
Comport, 7″	22.00	65.00	35.00	Sugar, ftd.	12.00	25.00	20.00
Cream soup, ftd.	12.00	35.00	30.00	Sugar cover	45.00	165.00	115.00
Creamer, ftd.	12.00	20.00	16.00	Sugar pail	65.00	150.00	125.00
Creamer, tea	15.00	35.00	30.00	Sugar, tea	15.00	35.00	30.00
Cup, after dinner	20.00	45.00	35.00	Tray, 11″, ctr. hdld.	20.00	45.00	35.00
Cup, ftd.	15.00	27.50	22.00	Tumbler, 2½ oz., ftd.	20.00	40.00	35.00
Decanter	150.00		350.00	Tumbler, 5 oz., 4½″, ftd.	15.00	27.50	22.50
Goblet, claret, 6″, 4 oz.	30.00	55.00	50.00	Tumbler, 9 oz., 5¼″, ftd.	15.00	27.50	21.50
Goblet, cocktail, 5¼″, 3 oz.	20.00	40.00	32.50	Tumbler, 12 oz., 6″, ftd.	17.50	30.00	27.50
Goblet, cordial, 4″, ¾ oz.	40.00	77.50	65.00	Vase, 8″	60.00	165.00	135.00
Goblet, water, 8¼″ 10 oz.	21.00	33.00	28.00	Vase, 8½″, fan ftd.	60.00	135.00	100.00
Goblet, wine, 5½″, 3 oz.	22.00	52.50	45.00	Whipped cream bowl	10.00	17.50	14.00
Grapefruit	25.00	60.00	50.00	Whipped cream pail	65.00	145.00	115.00
Grapefruit liner	20.00	50.00	40.00				

Note: See page 79 for stem identification.

KASHMIR, Fostoria Glass Company, 1930 - 1934

Colors: "Topaz" yellow, green; some blue

On a recent trip, I saw a large set of yellow Kashmir for sale; however, I saw few people paying much attention to it. The blue is rarely seen, but there seem to be more collectors searching for that color.

The pieces listed with blank prices have not been found today, although, they are listed in catalogues. I will remove them from the listings next time if they do not make an appearance by then.

Note that there are two separate styles of regular cups and saucers as well as after dinner cups and saucers.

	Yellow, Green		Yellow, Green
Ash tray	25.00	Plate, 9″, luncheon	9.00
Bowl, cream soup	22.00	Plate, 10″, dinner	35.00
Bowl, finger	15.00	Plate, 10″, grill	22.00
Bowl, 5″, fruit	13.00	Plate, cake, 10″	-----
Bowl, 6″, cereal	22.00	Salt and pepper	90.00
Bowl, 7″, soup	25.00	Sandwich, center hdld.	35.00
Bowl, 8½″, pickle	20.00	Sauce boat w/liner	75.00
Bowl, 9″, baker	37.50	Saucer, rnd.	5.00
Bowl, 10″	40.00	Saucer, sq.	5.00
Bowl, 12″, centerpiece	40.00	Saucer, after dinner, rnd.	6.00
Candlestick, 2″	15.00	Stem, ¾ oz., cordial	85.00
Candlestick, 3″	20.00	Stem, 2½ oz., ftd.	25.00
Candlestick, 5″	22.50	Stem, 2 oz., ftd. whiskey	25.00
Candlestick, 9½″	40.00	Stem, 2½ oz., wine	32.00
Candy w/cover	65.00	Stem, 3 oz., cocktail	22.00
Cheese and cracker set	65.00	Stem, 3½ oz., ftd. cocktail	22.00
Comport, 6″	35.00	Stem, 4 oz., claret	28.00
Creamer, ftd.	17.50	Stem, 4½ oz., oyster cocktail	16.00
Cup	15.00	Stem, 5½ oz., parfait	-----
Cup, after dinner, flat	25.00	Stem, 5 oz., ftd. juice	15.00
Cup, after dinner, ftd.	25.00	Stem, 5 oz., low sherbet	13.00
Grapefruit	37.50	Stem, 6 oz., high sherbet	17.50
Grapefruit liner	27.50	Stem, 9 oz., water	-----
Ice bucket	65.00	Stem, 10 oz., ftd. water	-----
Oil, ftd.	250.00	Stem, 11 oz.	-----
Pitcher, ftd.	350.00	Stem, 12 oz., ftd.	-----
Plate, 6″, bread and butter	5.00	Stem, 13 oz., ftd. tea	-----
Plate, 7″, salad, rnd.	6.00	Stem, 16 oz., ftd. tea	-----
Plate, 7″, salad, sq.	6.00	Sugar, ftd.	15.00
Plate, 8″, salad	8.00	Vase, 8″	85.00

Note: See stemware identification on page 79.

97

LARIAT, Blank #1540, A. H. Heisey & Co.

Colors: crystal; rare in black

	Crystal		Crystal
Ash tray, 4″	8.00	Oil bottle, 4 oz., hdld. w/#133 stopper	67.50
Basket, 7½″, bonbon	85.00	Oil bottle, 6 oz., oval	50.00
Basket, 8½″, ftd.	150.00	Plate, 6″, finger bowl liner	5.00
Basket, 10″, ftd.	175.00	Plate, 7″, salad	7.00
Bowl, 7 quart punch	100.00	Plate, 8″, salad	9.00
Bowl, 4″, nut	14.00	Plate, 11″, cookie	22.00
Bowl, 7″, 2 pt. relish	17.00	Plate, 12″, demi-torte, rolled edge	22.50
Bowl, 7″, nappy	13.00	Plate, 13″, deviled egg	125.00
Bowl, 8″, flat nougat	13.00	Plate, 14″, 2 hdld. sandwich	35.00
Bowl, 9½″, camellia	20.00	Plate, 21″, buffet	60.00
Bowl, 10″, hdld. celery	27.00	Platter, 15″, oval	30.00
Bowl, 10½″, 2 hdld. salad	27.50	Salt & pepper, pr.	175.00
Bowl, 10½″, salad	27.50	Saucer	5.00
Bowl, 11″, 2 hdld., oblong relish	20.00	Stem, 1 oz., cordial, double loop	160.00
Bowl, 12″, floral or fruit	16.00	Stem, 1 oz., cordial blown	135.00
Bowl, 13″, celery	18.00	Stem, 2½ oz., wine, blown	21.00
Bowl, 13″, gardenia	22.00	Stem, 3½ oz., cocktail, pressed	11.00
Bowl, 13″, oval floral	27.00	Stem, 3½ oz., cocktail, blown	11.00
Candlestick, 1-lite	10.00	Stem, 3½ oz., wine, pressed	11.00
Candlestick, 2-lite	17.50	Stem, 4 oz., claret, blown	17.00
Candlestick, 3-lite	27.50	Stem, 4¼ oz., oyster cocktail or fruit	11.00
Candy box w/cover	35.00	Stem, 4½ oz., oyster cocktail, blown	11.00
Candy w/cover, 7″	42.00	Stem, 5½ oz., sherbet/saucer champagne	
Cheese, 5″, ftd. w/cover	30.00	blown	12.00
Cheese dish w/cover 8″	42.00	Stem, 6 oz., low sherbet	7.50
Cigarette box	22.50	Stem, 6 oz., sherbet/saucer champagne,	
Coaster, 4″	7.50	pressed	10.00
Compote, 10″, w/cover	60.00	Stem, 9 oz., pressed	16.00
Creamer	12.50	Stem, 10 oz., blown	16.00
Creamer & sugar w/tray, indiv.	37.50	Sugar	12.00
Cup	12.00	Tray for sugar & creamer	15.00
Cup, punch	5.25	Tumbler, 5 oz., ftd. juice	11.00
Ice tub	65.00	Tumbler, 5 oz., ftd., juice, blown	11.00
Jar w/cover, 12″, urn	135.00	Tumbler, 12 oz., ftd. iced tea	16.00
Lamp & globe, 7″, black-out	85.00	Tumbler, 12 oz., ftd. iced tea, blown	16.00
Lamp & globe, 8″, candle	75.00	Vase, 7″, ftd. fan	29.00
Mayonnaise, 5″ bowl, 7″ plate	32.50		

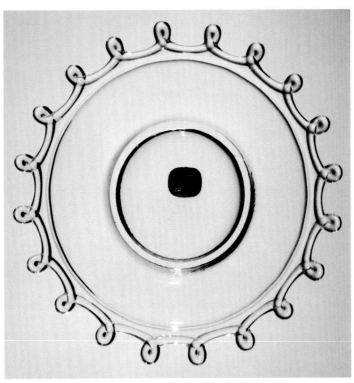

MINUET, Etch 1530, QUEEN ANN Blank, #1509; TOUJOURS Blank, #1511; SYMPHONE Blank, #5010, et. al.; 1939 - 1950's

Colors: crystal

I have encountered a number of collectors of Minuet in Newark, Ohio. This pattern sells well each year at the National Heisey show. The design, as well as the Toujours shape, makes this pattern attractive to people who collect certain pieces such as sugar and creamers or candlesticks.

I am particularly fond of the cordial and the centerpiece vase with prisms.

	Crystal
Bell, dinner	47.50
Bowl, finger, #3309	16.00
Bowl, 6″, ftd. mint	14.00
Bowl, 6″, ftd., 2 hdld. jelly	18.00
Bowl, 6½″, salad dressings	25.00
Bowl, 7″, salad dressings	27.50
Bowl, 7″, triplex relish	25.00
Bowl, 7½″, sauce, ftd.	25.00
Bowl, 9½″, 3 pt., "5 o'clock" relish	35.00
Bowl, 10″, salad, #1511, TOUJOURS	39.00
Bowl, 11″, 3 pt., "5 o'clock" relish	45.00
Bowl, 11″, ftd. floral	45.00
Bowl, 12″, oval floral, #1511 TOUJOURS	45.00
Bowl, 12″, oval, #1514	45.00
Bowl, 13″, floral, #1511 TOUJOURS	42.50
Bowl, 13″, pickle & olive	27.50
Bowl, 13½″, shallow salad	35.00
Candelabrum, 1-lite w/prisms	110.00
Candelabrum, 2-lite, bobeche & prisms	100.00
Candlestick, 1-lite, #112	22.50
Candlestick, 3-lite, #142 CASCADE	65.00
Candlestick, 5″, 2-lite, #134 TRIDENT	50.00
Centerpiece vase & prisms #1511 TOUJOURS	350.00
Cocktail icer w/liner #3304 UNIVERSAL	40.00
Comport, 5½″, #5010	35.00
Comport, 7½″, #1511 TOUJOURS	75.00
Creamer, #1511	35.00
Creamer, dolp. ft.	40.00
Creamer, indiv. #1509 QUEEN ANNE	27.50
Creamer, indiv. #1511 TOUJOURS	32.50
Cup	30.00
Ice bucket, dolp. ft.	125.00
Marmalade w/cover, #1511 TOUJOURS (apple shape)	75.00
Mayonnaise, 5½″, dolp. ft.	35.00
Mayonnaise, ftd. #1511 TOUJOURS	37.50
Pitcher, 73 oz., #4164	175.00
Plate, 7″, mayonnaise liner	12.00

	Crystal
Plate, 7″, salad	12.00
Plate, 7″, salad #1511 TOUJOURS	14.00
Plate, 8″, luncheon	18.00
Plate, 8″, luncheon #1511 TOUJOURS	20.00
Plate, 10½″, service	45.00
Plate, 12″, rnd., 2 hdld. sandwich	45.00
Plate, 13″, floral salver #1511 TOUJOURS	40.00
Plate, 14″, torte, #1511 TOUJOURS	40.00
Plate, 15″, sand., #1511 TOUJOURS	45.00
Plate, 16″, Snack rack w/1477 2-lite candle	75.00
Salt & pepper, pr. (#10)	60.00
Saucer	5.00
Stem, #5010, SYMPHONE, 1 oz., cordial	140.00
Stem, #5010, 2½ oz., wine	65.00
Stem, #5010, 3½ oz., cocktail	40.00
Stem, #5010, 4 oz., claret	40.00
Stem, #5010, 4½ oz., oyster cockail	30.00
Stem, #5010, 6 oz., saucer champagne	30.00
Stem, #5010, 6 oz., sherbet	18.00
Stem, #5010, 9 oz., water	32.00
Sugar, indiv. #1511 TOUJOURS	30.00
Sugar, indiv. #1509 QUEEN ANN	25.00
Sugar, dolp. ft. #1509 QUEEN ANN	40.00
Sugar, #1511 TOUJOURS	35.00
Tray, 12″, celery #1511 TOUJOURS	30.00
Tray, 15″, social hour	45.00
Tray for indiv. sugar & creamer	17.50
Tumbler, #5010, 5 oz., fruit juice	25.00
Tumbler, #5010, 9 oz., low ftd. water	30.00
Tumbler, #5010, 12 oz., tea	35.00
Tumbler, #2351, 12 oz., tea	35.00
Vase, 5″, #5013	27.50
Vase, 5½″, ftd. #1511 TOUJOURS	45.00
Vase, 6″, urn #5012	40.00
Vase, 7½″, urn #5012	50.00
Vase, 8″, #4196	50.00
Vase, 9″, urn #5012	60.00
Vase, 10″, #4192	65.00
Vase, 10″, #4192, SATURN optic	80.00

MT. VERNON, Cambridge Glass Company, late 1920's - 1940's

Colors: amber, crystal, red, blue, Heatherbloom, emerald green (light and dark), rare in violet

The range of colors in Mt. Vernon gives collectors a wide choice. Large sets can be accumulated in only amber and crystal. Carmen, Royal Blue and Heatherbloom are eagerly acquired, but are difficult to assemble as sets. Note the Violet sherbet shown as it is seldom seen!

	Amber/ Crystal		Amber/ Crystal
Ash tray, 3½", #63	7.50	Decanter, 40 oz., w/stopper, #52	60.00
Ashtray, 4", #68	11.00	Honey jar w/cover (marmalade), #74	25.00
Ash tray, 6" x 4½", oval, #71	11.00	Ice bucket, w/tongs, #92	30.00
Bon bon, 7", ftd., #10	12.50	Lamp, 9" hurricane, #1607	60.00
Bottle, bitters, 2½ oz., #62	50.00	Mayonnaise, divided, 2 spoons, #107	25.00
Bottle, 7 oz., sq. toilet, #18	60.00	Mug, 14 oz., stein, #84	25.00
Bowl, finger, #23	10.00	Mustard, w/cover, 2½ oz., #28	22.00
Bowl, 4½", fruit, #31	6.00	Pickle, 6", 1 hdld., #78	12.00
Bowl, 4½", ivy ball or rose, ftd., #12	27.50	Pitcher, 50 oz., #90	75.00
Bowl, 5¼", fruit, #6	10.00	Pitcher, 66 oz., #13	80.00
Bowl, 6", cereal, #32	12.00	Pitcher, 80 oz., ball, #95	90.00
Bowl, 6", preserve, #76	12.00	Pitcher, 86 oz., #91	100.00
Bowl, 6½", rose, #106	18.00	Plate, finger bowl liner, #23	4.00
Bowl, 8", pickle, #65	15.00	Plate, 6", bread & butter, #4	3.00
Bowl, 8½", 4 pt., 2 hdld. sweetmeat, #105	27.50	Plate, 6⅜", bread & butter, #19	4.00
Bowl, 10", 2 hdld., #39	20.00	Plate, 8½", salad, #5	7.00
Bowl, 10½", deep, #43	25.00	Plate, 10½", dinner, #40	20.00
Bowl, 10½", salad, #120	25.00	Plate, 11½", tab hdld., #37	20.00
Bowl, 11", oval, 4 ftd., #136	27.50	Relish, 6", 2 pt., 2 hdld., 6"106	12.00
Bowl, 11", oval, #135	25.00	Relish, 8", 2 pt., hdld., #101	17.50
Bowl, 11½", belled, #128	25.00	Relish, 8", 3 pt., 3 hdld., #103	20.00
Bowl, 11½", belled, #68	25.00	Relish, 11", 3 part, #200	22.50
Bowl, 11½", shallow, #126	25.00	Relish, 12", 2 part, #80	25.00
Bowl, 11½", shallow cupped, #61	25.00	Relish, 12", 5 part, #104	25.00
Bowl, 12", flanged, rolled edge, #129	30.00	Salt, indiv., #24	7.00
Bowl, 12", oblong, crimped, #118	30.00	Salt, oval, 2 hdld., #102	12.00
Bowl, 12", rolled edge, crimped, #117	30.00	Salt & pepper, pr., #28	22.50
Bowl, 12½", flanged, rolled edge, #45	30.00	Salt & pepper, pr., short, #88	20.00
Bowl, 12½", flared, #121	32.00	Salt & pepper, tall, #89	25.00
Bowl, 12½", flared, #44	32.00	Salt dip, #24	8.50
Bowl, 13", shallow, crimped, #116	35.00	Sauce boat & ladle, tab hdld., #30-445	55.00
Box, 3", w/cover, round, #16	22.00	Saucer, #7	7.50
Box, 4", w/cover, sq., #17	25.00	Stem, 3 oz., wine, #27	12.50
Box, 4½", w/cover, ftd., round, #15	30.00	Stem, 3½ oz., cocktail, #26	9.00
Butter tub, w/cover, #73	60.00	Stem, 4 oz., oyster cocktail, #41	9.00
Cake stand, 10½", ftd., #150	35.00	Stem, 4½ oz., claret, #25	12.50
Candelabrum, 13½", #38	40.00	Stem, 4½ oz., low sherbet, #42	7.50
Candlestick, 4", #130	10.00	Stem, 6½ oz., tall sherbet, #2	9.00
Candlestick, 5", 2-lite, #110	15.00	Stem, 10 oz., water, #1	12.50
Candlestick, 8", #35	20.00	Sugar, ftd., #8	10.00
Candy, w/cover, 1 lb., ftd., #9	40.00	Sugar, indiv., #4	10.00
Celery, 10½", #79	15.00	Sugar, #86	10.00
Celery, 11", #98	17.50	Tray, for indiv., sugar and creamer, #4	10.00
Celery, 12", #79	20.00	Tumbler, 1 oz., ftd. cordial, #87	20.00
Cigarette box, 6", w/cover, oval, #69	25.00	Tumbler, 2 oz., whiskey, #55	10.00
Cigarette holder, #66	15.00	Tumbler, 3 oz., ftd. juice, #22	9.00
Coaster, 3", plain, #60	5.00	Tumbler, 5 oz., #56	12.00
Coaster, 3", ribbed, #70	5.00	Tumbler, 5 oz., ftd., #21	12.00
Cocktail icer, 2 pc., #85	22.50	Tumbler, 7 oz., old fashion, #57	14.00
Cologne, 2½ oz., w/stopper, #1340	30.00	Tumbler, 10 oz., ftd. water, #3	15.00
Comport, 4½", #33	12.00	Tumbler, 10 oz., table, #51	12.00
Comport, 5½", 2 hdld., #77	15.00	Tumbler, 10 oz., tall, #58	12.00
Comport, 6", #34	15.00	Tumbler, 12 oz., barrel shape, #13	15.00
Comport, 6½", #97	17.50	Tumbler, 12 oz., ftd. tea, #20	16.00
Comport, 6½", belled, #96	20.00	Tumbler, 14 oz., barrel shape, #14	20.00
Comport, 7½", #11	25.00	Tumbler, 14 oz., tall, #59	20.00
Comport, 8", #81	25.00	Urn w/cover (same as candy), #9	40.00
Comport, 9", oval, 2 hdld., #100	27.50	Vase, 5", #42	15.00
Comport, 9½", #99	27.50	Vase, 6", crimped, #119	20.00
Creamer, ftd., #8	10.00	Vase, 6", ftd., #50	25.00
Creamer, indiv., #4	10.00	Vase, 6½", squat, #107	27.50
Creamer, #86	10.00	Vase, 7", #58	30.00
Cup, #7	6.50	Vase, 7", ftd., #54	35.00
Decanter, 11 oz., #47	40.00	Vase, 10", ftd., #46	50.00

NAVARRE, (Plate Etching #327) Fostoria Glass Company, 1937-1980

Colors: crystal

Navarre was introduced in 1937 and was made into the early 1980's. Some of the latter-made items were in color, but for now we will only explore the crystal.

One of the things about Navarre is that it is a transitional pattern. Many pieces are shaped like those of the popular patterns of June or Versailles and many pieces are on the Baroque blank #2496. Other pieces take on the more modernistic shapes of the 1950's. Some items occur in two shapes. This makes for a dilemma when you have to decide which mayonnaise to buy. Some collectors decide on one; others settle for the first one found. You could splurge and get both the flat and the footed styles!

I would like to thank Ralph Leslie for his help in compiling this listing from a large collection.

	Crystal		Crystal
Bowl, #2496, 4″, square, hdld.,	8.50	Plate, #2440, 7½″, salad	7.50
Bowl, #2496, 4⅜″, hdld	9.50	Plate, #2440, 8½″, luncheon	10.00
Bowl, #869, 4½″, finger	18.00	Plate, #2440, 9½″, dinner	27.50
Bowl, #2496, 4⅝″. tri-cornered	12.00	Plate, #2496, 10″, hdld., cake	30.00
Bowl, #2496, 5″, hdld., ftd.	12.00	Plate, #2440, 10½″ oval cake	32.00
Bowl, #2496, 6″, square, sweet meat	15.00	Plate, #2496, 14″, torte	35.00
Bowl, #2496, 6¼″, 3 ftd., nut	17.50	Plate, #2364, 16″, torte	45.00
Bowl, #2496, 7⅜″, ftd., bon bon	20.00	Relish, #2496, 6″, 2 part, square	17.50
Bowl, #2496, 10″, oval, floating garden	35.00	Relish, #2496, 10″ x 7½″, 3 part	30.00
Bowl, #2496, 10½″, hdld., ftd.	35.00	Relish, #2496, 10″, 4 part	30.00
Bowl, #2470 ½, 10½″, ftd.	37.50	Relish, #2419, 13¼″, 5 part	35.00
Bowl, #2496, 12″, flared	40.00	Salt and pepper, #2364, 3¼″, flat, pr.	40.00
Bowl, #2545, 12½″, oval, "Flame"	40.00	Salt and pepper, #2375, 3½″, ftd., pr	55.00
Candlestick, #2496, 4″	13.50	Salad dressing bottle, #2083, 6½″	95.00
Candlestick, #2496, 4½″, double	20.00	Sauce dish, #2496, div. mayo., 6½″	25.00
Candlestick, #2472, 5″, double	30.00	Sauce dish, #2496, 6½″x5¼″	35.00
Candlestick, #2496, 5½″	20.00	Sauce dish liner, #2496, 8″ oval	12.50
Candlestick, #2496, 6″, triple	30.00	Saucer, #2440	3.50
Candlestick, #2545, 6¾″, double, "Flame"	30.00	Syrup, #2586, metal cut-off top, 5½″	75.00
Candlestick, #2482, 6¾″, triple	30.00	Stem, #6106, 1 oz., cordial, 3⅞″	28.00
Candy w/cover, #2496, 3 part	65.00	Stem, #6106, 3¼ oz., wine, 5½″	25.00
Celery, #2440, 9″	18.00	Stem, #6106, 3½ oz., cocktail, 6″	20.00
Celery, #2496, 11″	20.00	Stem, #6106, 4 oz., oyster cocktail, 3⅝″	14.00
Comport, #2496, 3¼″, cheese	25.00	Stem, #6106, 4½ oz., claret, 6½″	22.50
Comport, #2400, 4½″	22.50	Stem, #6106, 6 oz., low sherbet, 4⅜″	10.00
Comport, #2496, 4¾″	25.00	Stem, #6106, 6 oz., saucer champagne, 5⅝″	13.00
Cracker, #2496, 11″ plate	40.00	Stem, #6106, 10 oz., water, 7⅝″	17.50
Creamr, #2440, 4¼″, ftd	9.00	Sugar, #2440, 3⅝″, ftd.	8.00
Creamer, #2496, individual	10.00	Sugar, #2496, individual	10.00
Cup, #2440	15.00	Tid bit, #2496, 8¼″, 3 ftd., turned up edge	18.00
Ice bucket, #2496, 4⅜″ high	65.00	Tray, #2496½″, for ind. sugar/creamer	12.00
Ice bucket, #2375, 6″ high	65.00	Tumbler, #6106, 5 oz., ftd. juice, 4⅝″	17.50
Mayonnaise, #2375, 3 piece	45.00	Tumbler, #6106, 10 oz., ftd water, 5⅜″	13.50
Mayonnaise, #2496½″, 3 piece	45.00	Tumbler, #6106, 13 oz., ftd. tea, 5⅞″	18.00
Pickle, #2496, 8″	20.00	Vase, #4108, 5″,	45.00
Pickle, #2440, 8½″	22.00	Vase, #4121, 5″	45.00
Pitcher, #5000, 48 oz., ftd	195.00	Vase, #4128, 5″	40.00
Plate, #2440, 6″, bread/butter	5.00	Vase, #2470, 10″, ftd.	60.00

OCTAGON, Blank #1231 - Ribbed; also Blank 500 and Blank 1229, A. H. Heisey & Co.

Colors: crystal, "Flamingo" pink, "Sahara" yellow, "Moongleam" green; "Hawthorne" orchid; "Marigold", a deep, amber/yellow, and "Dawn"

The twelve-inch four-part tray (shown in Moongleam in the photo) is a rarely found piece in the Dawn color. It is appropos that the last one found was purchased at sunrise at the Courthouse Square flea market sponsored by the Heisey Collectors. Avid collectors start shopping this market by flashlight and accomodating dealers start setting up as early as 3:00 A.M.!

	Crystal	Flam.	Sahara	Moon.	Hawth.	Marigold
Basket, 5", #500	60.00	85.00	97.50	95.00	135.00	
Bonbon, 6", sides up, #1229	5.00	8.00	10.00	12.00	15.00	
Bowl, cream soup, 2 hdld.	10.00	18.00	22.50	30.00	35.00	
Bowl, 5½", jelly, #1229	5.00	8.00	10.00	12.00	15.00	
Bowl, 6", mint, #1229	5.00	8.00	10.00	12.00	15.00	
Bowl, 6", #500	12.00	17.00	19.00	20.00	25.00	
Bowl, 6½", grapefruit	9.00	15.00	17.50	16.00	27.50	
Bowl, 8", ftd., #1229	12.00	17.00	20.00	24.00	28.00	
Bowl, 9", vegetable	10.00	18.00	20.00	25.00	45.00	
Bowl, 12½", salad	12.00	20.00	24.00	28.00	45.00	
Candlestick, 3", 1-lite	7.00	17.50	22.00	26.00	37.50	
Cheese dish, 6", 2 hdld., #1229	5.00	8.00	10.00	12.00	15.00	
Creamer #500	5.00	12.50	16.00	17.00	22.00	
Creamer, hotel	7.00	13.00	15.00	19.00	25.00	
Cup, after dinner	6.00	12.50	18.00	22.50	30.00	
Dish, frozen dessert #500	7.00	10.00	14.00	12.00	22.00	40.00
Ice tub, #500	26.00	55.00	75.00	80.00	90.00	120.00
Mayonnaise, 5½", ftd. #1229	10.00	14.00	16.00	18.00	22.50	
Plate, cream soup liner	3.00	5.00	7.00	9.00	12.00	
Plate, 6"	4.00	6.00	8.00	10.00	12.00	
Plate, 7", bread	5.00	7.00	9.00	11.00	13.00	
Plate, 8", luncheon	6.00	8.00	10.00	12.00	14.00	
Plate, 9", soup	10.00	14.00	19.00	27.50	27.00	
Plate, 10", sand., #1229	13.00	18.00	22.00	25.00	30.00	
Plate, 10", muffin, #1229	15.00	20.00	24.00	30.00	32.00	
Plate, 10½"	16.00	22.00	27.00	30.00	32.00	
Plate, 10½", ctr. hdld. sandwich	21.00	30.00	37.50	45.00	55.00	
Plate, 12", muffin, #1229	18.00	25.00	29.00	30.00	35.00	
Plate, 13", hors d'oeuvre #1229	15.00	22.00	26.00	32.00	40.00	
Plate, 14"	22.00	25.00	30.00	30.00	35.00	
Platter, 12¾"	22.00	32.00	37.50	42.50	52.50	
Saucer, after dinner	2.00	5.00	6.00	6.00	12.00	
Sugar #500	5.00	12.00	16.00	17.00	22.00	
Sugar, hotel	7.00	12.00	15.00	18.00	27.50	
Tray, 6", oblong, #500	5.00	12.00	16.00	17.00	22.00	
Tray, 9", celery	7.00	15.00	18.00	20.00	25.00	
Tray, 12", celery	10.00	20.00	25.00	27.00	32.00	(Dawn)
Tray, 12", 4 pt., #500	22.00	55.00	65.00	75.00	80.00	250.00

OLD COLONY, Empress Blank #1401; Caracassone Blank #3390; and Old Dominion Blank #3380, A. H. Heisey & Co., 1930 - 1939

Colors: crystal, "Flamingo" pink, "Sahara" yellow, "Moongleam" green; "Marigold", a deep, amber/yellow; cobalt

	Crystal	Flam.	Sahara	Moon.	Marigold
Bouillion cup, 2 hdld., ftd.	12.50	18.00	20.00	24.00	
Bowl, finger, #4075	5.50	10.00	11.00	14.00	16.00
Bowl, ftd. finger, #3390	5.50	16.00	21.00	27.50	
Bowl, 4½", nappy	7.00	10.00	12.50	15.00	
Bowl, 5", ftd., 2 hdld.	12.50	17.50	22.50	27.50	
Bowl, 6", ftd., 2 hdld. jelly	15.00	20.00	25.00	32.50	
Bowl, 6", dolp. ftd. mint	16.00	22.00	27.50	35.00	
Bowl, 7", triplex relish	15.00	22.00	25.00	28.00	
Bowl, 7½", dolp. ftd. nappy	22.00	60.00	65.00	75.00	
Bowl, 8", nappy	25.00	35.00	40.00	42.50	
Bowl, 8½", ftd. floral, 2 hdld.	32.00	47.00	57.50	67.50	
Bowl, 9", 3 hdld.	36.00	72.50	85.00	90.00	
Bowl, 10", rnd., 2 hdld. salad	32.00	47.50	57.50	65.00	
Bowl, 10", sq. salad, 2 hdld.	30.00	45.00	55.00	65.00	
Bowl, 10", oval dessert, 2 hdld.	30.00	40.00	50.00	62.50	
Bowl, 10", oval veg.	30.00	34.00	42.00	50.00	
Bowl, 11", floral, dolp. ft.	32.00	67.50	75.00	85.00	
Bowl, 13", ftd. flared	30.00	35.00	40.00	45.00	
Bowl, 13", 2 pt. pickle & olive	12.50	20.00	22.50	27.50	
Cigarette holder #3390, (Cobalt $100.00)	16.00	47.50	42.50	55.00	
Comport, 7", oval, ftd.	36.00	70.00	75.00	80.00	
Comport, 7", ftd. #3368	30.00	57.50	62.50	85.00	85.00
Cream soup, 2 hdld.	12.00	20.00	22.00	27.00	
Creamer, dolp. ft.	17.50	32.00	45.00	50.00	
Creamer, indiv.	12.50	27.50	37.50	35.00	
Cup, after dinner	12.00	25.00	35.00	50.00	
Cup	10.00	26.00	32.00	38.00	
Decanter, 1 pt.	135.00	275.00	250.00	500.00	
Flagon, 12 oz., #3390	25.00	50.00	50.00	75.00	
Grapefruit, 6"	15.00	23.00	30.00	35.00	
Grapefruit, ftd. #3380	10.00	16.00	18.00	20.00	25.00
Ice tub, dolp. ft.	42.50	95.00	105.00	125.00	
Mayonnaise, 5½", dolp. ft.	36.00	55.00	70.00	80.00	
Oil, 4 oz., ftd.	42.50	70.00	105.00	120.00	
Pitcher, 3 pt., #3390	80.00	235.00	185.00	375.00	
Pitcher, 3 pt., dolp. ft.	75.00	155.00	175.00	185.00	
Plate, bouillon	5.00	8.00	12.00	15.00	
Plate, cream soup	5.00	8.00	12.00	15.00	
Plate, 4½", rnd.	3.00	6.00	7.00	8.00	
Plate, 6", rnd.	6.00	12.00	15.00	18.00	
Plate, 6", sq.	6.00	12.00	15.00	18.00	
Plate, 7", rnd.	8.00	14.00	18.00	20.00	
Plate, 7", sq.	8.00	14.00	18.00	20.00	
Plate, 8", rnd.	10.00	17.00	22.00	27.00	
Plate, 8", sq.	10.00	17.00	22.00	27.00	
Plate, 9", rnd.	15.00	22.00	25.00	28.00	
Plate, 10½", rnd.	28.50	55.00	65.00	70.00	
Plate, 10½", sq.	27.50	50.00	60.00	65.00	
Plate, 12", rnd.	31.00	57.50	67.50	72.50	
Plate, 12", 2 hdld. rnd. muffin	31.00	57.50	67.50	72.50	
Plate, 12", 2 hdld., rnd. sand.	31.00	57.50	67.50	72.50	
Plate, 13", 2 hdld., sq. sand.	35.00	40.00	45.00	50.00	
Plate, 13", 2 hdld., muffin, sq.	35.00	40.00	45.00	50.00	
Platter, 14", oval	25.00	35.00	40.00	45.00	
Salt & pepper, pr.	52.50	75.00	100.00	120.00	
Saucer, sq.	4.00	8.00	10.00	10.00	
Saucer, rnd.	4.00	8.00	10.00	10.00	
Stem, #3380, 1 oz., cordial	65.00	120.00	120.00	145.00	325.00
Stem, #3380, 2½ oz., wine	18.00	40.00	35.00	50.00	60.00
Stem, #3380, 3 oz., cocktail	13.00	34.00	25.00	40.00	50.00
Stem, #3380, 4 oz., oyster/cocktail	8.00	13.00	15.00	17.00	20.00
Stem, #3380, 4 oz., claret	17.00	40.00	30.00	45.00	55.00
Stem, #3380, 5 oz., parfait	10.00	15.00	15.00	17.00	35.00
Stem, #3380, 6 oz., champagne	8.00	13.00	15.00	17.00	20.00
Stem, #3380, 6 oz., sherbet	6.00	11.00	13.00	15.00	20.00
Stem, #3380, 10 oz., short soda	7.00	18.00	15.00	22.00	30.00

	Crystal	Flam.	Sahara	Moon.	Marigold
Stem, #3380, 10 oz., tall soda	-----	21.00	18.00	25.00	32.50
Stem, #3390, 1 oz., cordial	50.00	120.00	115.00	145.00	
Stem, #3390, 2½ oz., wine	12.00	20.00	27.50	35.00	
Stem, #3390, 3 oz., cocktail	7.00	15.00	20.00	25.00	
Stem, #3390, 3 oz., oyster/cocktail	7.00	15.00	20.00	25.00	
Stem, #3390, 4 oz., claret	12.00	22.50	27.50	32.50	
Stem, #3390, 6 oz., champagne	10.00	20.00	25.00	30.00	
Stem, #3390, 6 oz., sherbet	10.00	20.00	25.00	30.00	
Stem, #3390, 11 oz., low water	8.00	20.00	25.00	30.00	
Stem, #3390, 11 oz., tall water	10.00	22.00	27.00	32.00	
Sugar, dolp. ft.	17.50	30.00	45.00	50.00	
Sugar, indiv.	12.50	27.50	32.50	35.00	
Tray, 10″, celery	14.00	20.00	25.00	30.00	
Tray, 12″, ctr. hdld. sand.	35.00	65.00	75.00	85.00	
Tray, 12″, ctr. hdld. sq.	35.00	65.00	75.00	85.00	
Tray, 13″, celery	17.00	20.00	26.00	30.00	
Tray, 13″, 2 hdld. hors d'oeuvre	30.00	36.00	45.00	55.00	
Tumbler, dolp. ft.	80.00	110.00	145.00	160.00	
Tumbler, #3380, 1 oz., ftd. bar	22.00	37.50	42.50	52.50	55.00
Tumbler, #3380, 2 oz., ftd. bar	12.00	20.00	20.00	25.00	35.00
Tumbler, #3380, 5 oz., ftd. bar	7.00	12.00	12.00	17.00	25.00
Tumbler, #3380, 8 oz., ftd. soda	10.00	21.00	18.00	25.00	32.50
Tumbler, #3380, 10 oz., ftd. soda	12.00	23.00	20.00	25.00	32.50
Tumbler, #3380, 12 oz., ftd. tea	13.00	25.00	22.00	27.00	35.00
Tumbler, #3390, 2 oz., ftd.	7.00	18.00	22.50	28.00	
Tumbler, #3390, 5 oz., ftd. juice	7.00	15.00	20.00	25.00	
Tumbler, #3390, 8 oz., ftd. soda	10.00	22.00	25.00	30.00	
Tumbler, #3390, 12 oz., ftd. tea	12.00	24.00	27.00	30.00	
Vase, 9″, ftd.	75.00	120.00	135.00	160.00	

OLD SANDWICH, Blank #1404, A. H. Heisey & Co.

Colors: crystal, "Flamingo" pink, "Sahara" yellow, "Moongleam" green; cobalt

	Crystal	Flam.	Sahara	Moon.	Cobalt
Ash tray, individual	5.00	25.00	23.00	26.00	32.00
Beer mug, 12 oz.	30.00	200.00	210.00	400.00	300.00
Beer mug, 14 oz.	35.00	200.00	225.00	425.00	325.00
Beer mug, 18 oz.	40.00	225.00	250.00	450.00	375.00
Bottle, catsup w/#3 stopper (like lg. cruet)	30.00	65.00	80.00	85.00	
Bowl, finger	9.00	12.00	15.00	18.00	
Bowl, ftd. popped corn, cupped	35.00	50.00	60.00	67.50	
Bowl, 11″, rnd. ftd., floral	25.00	40.00	50.00	60.00	
Bowl, 12″, oval, ftd., floral	27.00	50.00	60.00	70.00	
Candlestick, 6″	30.00	55.00	65.00	75.00	220.00
Cigarette holder	27.50	35.00	40.00	45.00	
Comport, 6″	37.50	80.00	85.00	90.00	
Creamer, oval	7.00	20.00	22.00	25.00	
Creamer, 12 oz.	32.00	165.00	170.00	175.00	275.00
Creamer, 14 oz.	35.00	175.00	180.00	185.00	
Creamer, 18 oz.	40.00	185.00	190.00	195.00	
Cup	40.00	65.00	65.00	65.00	
Decanter, 1 pint w/#98 stopper	75.00	175.00	185.00	195.00	400.00
Floral block #22	15.00	25.00	30.00	35.00	
Oil bottle, 2½ oz., #85 stopper	65.00	85.00	90.00	95.00	
Parfait, 4½ oz.	10.00	15.00	20.00	25.00	
Pilsner, 8 oz.	14.00	28.00	32.00	38.00	
Pilsner, 10 oz.	16.00	32.00	37.00	42.00	
Pitcher, ½ gallon, ice	75.00	145.00	155.00	165.00	
Pitcher, ½ gallon, reg.	70.00	140.00	150.00	160.00	
Plate, 6″, sq., grnd. bottom	4.00	8.00	10.00	13.00	
Plate, 7″, sq.	5.00	10.00	13.00	15.00	
Plate, 8″, sq.	7.00	12.00	15.00	17.00	
Salt & pepper, pr.	40.00	60.00	70.00	80.00	
Saucer	10.00	15.00	15.00	15.00	
Stem, 2½ oz., wine	12.00	24.00	32.00	38.00	
Stem, 3 oz., cocktail	9.00	15.00	18.00	20.00	
Stem, 4 oz., claret	10.00	18.00	20.00	25.00	135.00
Stem, 4 oz., oyster cocktail	5.00	10.00	12.00	15.00	
Stem, 4 oz., sherbet	6.00	12.00	15.00	18.00	
Stem, 5 oz., saucer champagne	9.00	27.50	28.00	32.00	
Stem, 10 oz., low ft.	9.00	25.00	30.00	35.00	
Sugar, oval	8.00	20.00	22.00	25.00	
Sundae, 6 oz.	5.00	10.00	15.00	20.00	
Tumbler, 1½ oz., bar, grnd. bottom	12.00	30.00	35.00	45.00	
Tumbler, 5 oz., juice	5.00	13.00	17.50	22.00	
Tumbler, 6½ oz., toddy	8.00	15.00	18.00	20.00	
Tumbler, 8 oz., grnd. bottom, cupped and straight rim	9.00	17.00	22.00	27.50	
Tumbler, 10 oz.	10.00	17.00	22.00	27.50	
Tumbler, 10 oz., low ft.	10.00	17.00	22.00	27.50	
Tumbler, 12 oz., ftd. iced tea	11.00	20.00	27.50	35.00	
Tumbler, 12 oz., iced tea	11.00	20.00	27.50	35.00	

ORCHID (Etching 1507) ON WAVERLY BLANK 11519, A.H. Heisey & Co. 1940-1957

Colors: crystal

Orchid is one of the Heisey patterns that is universally recognized by anyone who knows the word Heisey. Sometimes it seems that Orchid has become synonymous with Heisey, but that is only a small part of the Heisey world to insiders.

One of the blessings for collectors who know this pattern is that many pieces are not marked with the "Diamond H". Unknowing dealers and some "collectors" will not buy unmarked pieces! In fact, I was able to sell a Cabochon quarter pound butter to a lady for $225.00 instead of the commonly found Waverly for $155.00 because the Cabochon was marked and the Waverly was not. Some people cannot be convinced unless they see that mark no matter what you tell them. Orchid was a later pattern; most pieces carried stickers proclaiming it was Heisey! Do not let a bargain escape you for lack of a trademark! Learn to recognize the pattern and not just the mark!

	Crystal
Ash tray, 3″	25.00
Basket, 8½″, LARIAT, ftd.	350.00
Bell, dinner, #5022 or #5025	120.00
Bottle, 8 oz., French dressings	135.00
Bowl, finger, #3309 or #5022 or #5025	50.00
Bowl, 4½″, nappy QUEEN ANN	37.50
Bowl, 5½″, ftd. mint	32.00
Bowl, 6″, jelly, 2 hdld.	30.00
Bowl, 6″, oval lemon w/cover QUEEN ANN	185.00
Bowl, 6½″, ftd. honey; cheese QUEEN ANN	32.50
Bowl, 6½″, ftd. jelly	30.00
Bowl, 6½″, 2 pt. oval dressings	47.50
Bowl, 7″, lily	40.00
Bowl, 7″ salad	42.50
Bowl, 7″, 3 pt., rnd, relish	42.50
Bowl, 7″, ftd. honey; cheese	47.50
Bowl, 7″, ftd. jelly	40.00
Bowl, 7″, ftd. oval nut	50.00
Bowl, 8″, mint, ftd. QUEEN ANN	57.50
Bowl, 8″, nappy, QUEEN ANN	47.50
Bowl, 8″, 2 pt. oval dressings	47.50
Bowl, 8″, pt., rnd. relish	57.50
Bowl, 8½″, flared, QUEEN ANN	50.00
Bowl, 8½″, floral, 2 hdld., ftd. QUEEN ANN	57.50
Bowl, 9″, 4 pt., rnd. relish	60.00
Bowl, 9″, ft. fruit or salad	75.00
Bowl, 9″, gardenia QUEEN ANN	50.00
Bowl, 9″, salad	57.50
Bowl, 9½″, crimped floral	47.50
Bowl, 9½″, epergne	350.00
Bowl, 10″, crimped	60.00
Bowl, 10″, gardenia	65.00
Bowl, 10½″, ftd. floral	80.00
Bowl, 11″, shallow, rolled edge	67.50
Bowl, 11″, 3 ftd. floral, seahorse ft.	120.00
Bowl, 11″, 3 pt., oblong relish	67.50
Bowl, 11″, 4 ftd., oval	75.00
Bowl, 11″, flared	55.00
Bowl, 11″, floral	55.00

	Crystal
Bowl, 11″, ftd. floral	75.00
Bowl, 12″, crimped floral	60.00
Bowl, 13″, floral	65.00
Bowl, 13″, crimped floral	60.00
Bowl, 13, gardenia	65.00
Butter w/cover, ¼ lb. CABOCHON	225.00
Butter w/cover, 6″,	155.00
Candleholder, 6″, deep epernette	150.00
Candlestick, 1-lite MERCURY	30.00
Candlestick, 1-lite QUEEN ANN w/prisms	110.00
Candlestick 2-lite FLAME	125.00
Candlestick, 2 lite 5″, TRIDENT	55.00
Candlestick 3 lite CASCADE	72.50
Candlestick, 3 lite WAVERLY	87.50
Candy box w/cover, 6″, low ft.	140.00
Candy w/cover, 5″, high ft.	155.00
Candy w/cover, 6″, bow knot finial	155.00
Cheese (comport) & cracker (11½″) plate	100.00
Cheese & cracker, 14″ plate	130.00
Chocolate w/cover, 5″	165.00
Cigarette box w/cover, 4″ PURITAN	110.00
Cigarette holder #4035	57.50
Cigarette holder w/cover	125.00
Cocktail icer w/liner UNIVERSAL #3304	90.00
Cocktail shaker, pt., #4225	150.00
Cocktail shaker, qt. #4036 or #4225	195.00
Comport, 5½″ blown	87.50
Comport, 6″, low ft.	40.00
Comport, 6½″, low ft	42.50
Comport, 7″, ftd. oval	100.00
Creamer, indiv.	30.00
Creamer, ftd.	27.50
Cup, Waverly or QUEEN ANN	45.00
Decanter, oval sherry, pt.	160.00
Decanter, pt., ftd. #4036	275.00
Decanter, pt. #4036½	200.00
Ice bucket, ftd. QUEEN ANN	185.00
Ice bucket, 2 hand.	165.00
Marmalade w/cover	90.00

ORCHID, (Etching 1507) on Waverly Blank 11519, A.H. Heisey & Co., 1940-1957

	Crystal
Mayonnaise, 5½", 1 hand.	40.00
Mayonnaise, 5½", ftd.	40.00
Mayonnaise, 5½", 1 hand., div.	42.50
Mayonnaise, 6½", 1 hand.	50.00
Mayonnaise, 6½", 1 hand., div	52.50
Mustard w/cover QUEEN ANN	125.00
Oil, 3 oz., ftd.	155.00
Pitcher, 73 oz.	350.00
Pitcher, 64 oz. ice tankard	450.00
Plate, 6"	12.50
Plate, 7", mayonnaise	15.00
Plate, 7", salad	15.50
Plate, 8", salad	22.00
Plate, 10½", dinner	90.00
Plate, 11", demi-torte	50.00
Plate, 11", sandwich	50.00
Plate, 12", ftd. salver	210.00
Plate, 13½", ftd. cake or salver	250.00
Plate, 14", torte, rolled edge	52.50
Plate, 14", torte	50.00
Plate, 14", sandwich	80.00
Salt & pepper, pr.	60.00
Salt & pepper, ft., pr.	65.00
Saucer, WAVERLY OR QUEEN ANN	9.00
Stem, #5022 or #5025, 1 oz., cordial	135.00

	Crystal
Stem, #5022 or #5025, 2 oz., sherry	85.00
Stem, #5022 or #5025, 3 oz., wine	65.00
Stem, #5022 or #5025, 4 oz., oyster cocktail	37.50
Stem, #5022 or #5025, 4 oz., cocktail	40.00
Stem, #5022 or #5025, 4½ oz., claret	50.00
Stem, #5022 or #5025, 6 oz., saucer champagne	30.00
Stem, #5022 or #5025, 6 oz., sherbet	25.00
Stem, #5022 or #5025, 10 oz., low water goblet	35.00
Stem, #5022 or #5025, 10 oz., water goblet	40.00
Sugar, indiv.	30.00
Sugar, ftd.	25.00
Toast w/dome	200.00
Tray, 12", celery	45.00
Tray, 13", celery	47.50
Tumbler, #5022 or #5025, 5 oz. fruit	45.00
Tumbler, #5022 or #5025, 12 oz., iced tea	60.00
Vase, 4", ftd. violet	67.50
Vase, 6", crimped top	95.00
Vase, 7", ftd. fan	75.00
Vase, 7", ftd.	72.50
Vase, 8", ftd. bud	135.00
Vase, 8", sq. ftd. bud	135.00
Vase, 10". sq. ftd. bud	125.00

PLANTATION, Blank # 1567, A. H. Heisey & Co.

Colors: crystal; rare in amber

	Crystal		Crystal
Ash tray, 3½″	17.50	Marmadale w/cover	55.00
Bowl, 9 qt. Dr. Johnson punch	275.00	Mayonnaise, 4½″, rolled ft.	45.00
Bowl, 5″, nappy	13.00	Mayonnaise, 5¼″, w/liner	22.00
Bowl, 5½″, nappy	14.00	Oil bottle, 3 oz., w/#125 stopper	65.00
Bowl, 6½″, 2 hdld. jelly	17.50	Pitcher, ½ gallon, ice lip, blown	100.00
Bowl, 6½″, flared jelly	18.00	Plate, coupe (rare)	200.00
Bowl, 6½″, ftd. honey, cupped	27.50	Plate, 7″, salad	10.00
Bowl, 8″, 4 pt., rnd. relish	25.00	Plate, 8″, salad	12.00
Bowl, 8½″, 2 pt., dressing	18.00	Plate, 10½″, demi-torte	20.00
Bowl, 9″, salad	25.00	Plate, 13″, ftd. cake salver	85.00
Bowl, 9½″, crimped, fruit or flower	25.00	Plate, 14″, sandwich	35.00
Bowl, 9½″, gardenia	25.00	Plate, 18″, buffet	45.00
Bowl, 11″, 3 part relish	22.50	Plate, 18″, punch bowl liner	85.00
Bowl, 11½″, ftd. gardenia	30.00	Salt & pepper, pr	35.00
Bowl, 12″, crimped, fruit or flower	35.00	Saucer	5.00
Bowl, 13″, celery	20.00	Stem, 1 oz., cordial	85.00
Bowl, 13″, 2 part celery	25.00	Stem, 3 oz., wine, blown	35.00
Bowl, 13″, 5 part oval relish	35.00	Stem, 3½ oz., cocktail, pressed	20.00
Bowl, 13″, gardenia	30.00	Stem, 4 oz., fruit/oyster cocktail	15.00
Butter, ¼ lb., oblong w/cover	60.00	Stem, 4½ oz., claret, blown	20.00
Butter, 5″, rnd. (or cov. candy)	67.50	Stem, 4½ oz., claret, pressed	20.00
Candelabrum w/two #1503 bobeche		Stem, 4½ oz., oyster cocktail, blown	19.00
and ten "A" prisms	132.50	Stem, 6½ oz., sherbet/saucer	
Candle block, hurricane type	90.00	champagne, blown	19.00
Candle block, 1-lite	75.00	Stem, 10 oz., pressed	18.00
Candle holder, 5″, ftd. epergne	45.00	Stem, 10 oz., blown	18.00
Candlestick, 1-lite	65.00	Sugar, ftd.	15.50
Candlestick, 2-lite	35.00	Syrup bottle w/drip, cut top	60.00
Candlestick, 3-lite	75.00	Tray, 8½″, condiment/sugar &	
Candy box w/cover, 7″	100.00	creamer	20.00
Candy w/cover, 5″, tall, ftd.	145.00	Tumbler, 5 oz., ftd. juice, pressed	22.50
Cheese w/cover, 5″, ftd.	75.00	Tumbler, 5 oz., ftd. juice, blown	25.00
Coaster, 4″	12.00	Tumbler, 10 oz., pressed	27.50
Comport, 5″	20.00	Tumbler, 12 oz., ftd. iced tea, pressed	26.00
Comport, 5″, w/cover, deep	50.00	Tumbler, 12 oz., ftd. iced tea, blown	28.00
Creamer, ftd.	16.00	Vase, 5″, ftd., flared	35.00
Cup	12.00	Vase, 9″, ftd., flared	40.00
Cup, punch	20.00		

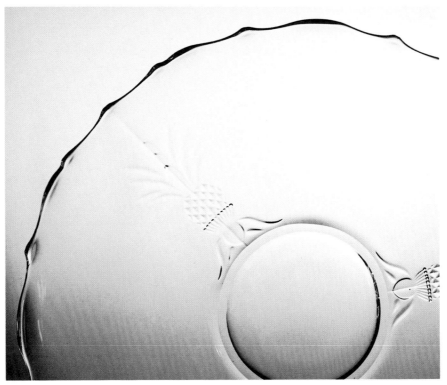

PORTIA, Cambridge Glass Company, 1932 - Early 1950's

Colors: crystal, yellow, Heatherbloom, green

	Crystal		Crystal
Basket, 2 hdld. (upturned sides)	16.00	Set: 3 pc. Frappe (bowl, 2 plain inserts)	25.00
Basket, 7″, 1 hdld.	125.00	Stem, #3121, 1 oz., cordial	50.00
Bowl, 3½″, cranberry	15.00	Stem, #3121, 1 oz., low ftd. brandy	32.00
Bowl, 3½″, sq. cranberry	12.50	Stem, #3121, 2½ oz., wine	22.50
Bowl, 5¼″, 2 hdld. bonbon	15.00	Stem, #3121, 3 oz., cocktail	20.00
Bowl, 6″, 2 pt. relish	16.00	Stem, #3121, 4½ oz. claret	25.00
Bowl, 6″, ftd., 2 hdld. bonbon	16.00	Stem, #3121, 4½ oz., oyster cocktail	15.00
Bowl, 6″, grapefruit or oyster	12.50	Stem, #3121, 5 oz., parfait	22.00
Bowl, 6½″, 3 pt. relish	15.00	Stem, #3121, 6 oz., low sherbet	13.50
Bowl, 7″, 2 pt. relish	16.00	Stem, #3121, 6 oz., tall sherbet	15.00
Bowl, 7″, ftd. bonbon, tab hdld.	20.00	Stem, #3121, 10 oz. goblet	20.00
Bowl, 7″, pickle or relish	18.00	Stem, #3124, 3 oz., cocktail	15.00
Bowl, 9″, 3 pt. celery & relish, tab hdld.	22.50	Stem, #3124, 3 oz., wine	20.00
Bowl, 9½″, ftd. pickle (like corn bowl)	20.00	Stem, #3124, 4½ oz., claret	19.00
Bowl, 10″, flared, 4 ftd.	30.00	Stem, #3124, 7 oz., low sherbet	14.00
Bowl, 11″, 2 pt., 2 hdld. "figure 8" relish	27.50	Stem, #3124, 7 oz., tall sherbet	15.00
Bowl, 11″, 2 hdld.	25.00	Stem, #3124, 10 oz., goblet	18.00
Bowl, 12″, 3 pt. celery & relish, tab hdld.	30.00	Stem, #3126, 1 oz., cordial	45.00
Bowl, 12″, 5 pt. celery & relish	32.50	Stem, #3126, 1 oz., low ft. brandy	30.00
Bowl, 12″, flared, 4 ftd.	30.00	Stem, #3126, 2½ oz., wine	23.00
Bowl, 12″, oval, 4 ftd., "ears" handles	37.50	Stem, #3126, 3 oz., cocktail	17.50
Bowl, finger w/liner #3124	20.00	Stem, #3126, 4½ oz., claret	22.50
Bowl, seafood (fruit cocktail w/liner)	15.00	Stem, #3126, 4½ oz., low ft. oyster cocktail	12.50
Candlestick, 5″	17.50	Stem, #3126, 7 oz., low sherbet	14.00
Candlestick, 6″, 2-lite, "fleur de lis"	25.00	Stem, #3126, 7 oz., tall sherbet	15.00
Candlestick, 6″, 3-lite	35.00	Stem, #3126, 9 oz., goblet	18.00
Candy box w/cover, rnd.	60.00	Stem, #3130, 1 oz., cordial	50.00
Cigarette holder, urn shape	37.50	Stem, #3130, 2½ oz., wine	23.00
Cocktail icer, 2 pt.	35.00	Stem, #3130, 3 oz., cocktail	17.50
Cocktail shaker w/stopper	75.00	Stem, #3130, 4½ oz., claret	22.50
Cocktail shaker, 80 oz., hdld. ball w/chrome		Stem, fruit/oyster cocktail, #3130, 4½ oz.	15.00
top	85.00	Stem, #3130, 7 oz., low sherbet	14.00
Cologne, 2 oz., hdld. ball w/stopper	37.50	Stem, #3130, 7 oz., tall sherbet	15.00
Comport, 5½″	27.50	Stem, #3130, 9 oz., goblet	21.00
Comport, 5⅜″, blown	35.00	Sugar, ftd. hdld. ball	14.00
Creamer, hdld. ball	15.00	Sugar, indiv.	11.50
Creamer, indiv.	11.50	Tray, 11″, celery	22.50
Cup, ftd. sq.	18.00	Tumbler, #3121, 2½ oz. bar	20.00
Decanter, 29 oz. ftd. sherry w/stopper	125.00	Tumbler, #3121, 5 oz., ftd. juice	16.00
Hurricane lamp, candlestick base	135.00	Tumbler, #3121, 10 oz., ftd. water	16.50
Hurricane lamp, keyhole base w/prisms	100.00	Tumbler, #3121, 12 oz., ftd. tea	20.00
Ice bucket w/chrome handle	55.00	Tumbler, #3124, 3 oz.	13.00
Ivy ball, 5¼″	25.00	Tumbler, #3124, 5 oz., juice	12.50
Mayonnaise, div. bowl w/liner and 2 ladles	35.00	Tumbler, #3124, 10 oz., water	15.00
Mayonnaise w/liner and ladle	30.00	Tumbler, #3124, 12 oz., tea	15.00
Oil, 6 oz., loop hdld. w/stopper	45.00	Tumbler, #3126, 2½ oz.	18.00
Oil, 6 oz., hdld. ball w/stopper	50.00	Tumbler, #3126, 5 oz., juice	14.00
Pitcher, ball	100.00	Tumbler, #3126, 10 oz., water	15.00
Pitcher, Doulton	195.00	Tumbler, #3126, 12 oz., tea	15.00
Plate, 6″, 2 hdld.	15.00	Tumbler, #3130, 5 oz., juice	16.00
Plate, 6½″, bread/butter	7.50	Tumbler, #3130, 10 oz., water	15.00
Plate, 8″, salad	12.50	Tumbler, #3130, 12 oz., tea	17.50
Plate, 8″, ftd. 2 hdld.	17.50	Tumbler, 13 oz., "roly-poly"	16.00
Plate, 8″, ftd. bonbon, tab hdld.	20.00	Vase, 5″, globe	30.00
Plate, 8½″, sq.	15.00	Vase, 6″, ftd.	30.00
Plate, 10½″, dinner	40.00	Vase, 8″, ftd.	40.00
Plate, 13″, 4 ftd. torte	30.00	Vase, 9″, keyhole ft.	47.50
Plate, 13½″, 2 hdld. cake	27.50	Vase, 10″, bud	30.00
Plate, 14″, torte	35.00	Vase, 11″, flower	40.00
Puff box, 3½″, ball shape w/lid	50.00	Vase, 11″, pedestal ft.	40.00
Salt & pepper, pr.	25.00	Vase, 12″, keyhole ft.	55.00
Saucer, sq. or rnd.	3.00	Vase, 13″, flower	70.00

Note: See Pages 166-167 for stem identification.

PROVINCIAL, Blank #1506, A. H. Heisey & Co.

Colors: crystal, "Limelight" green

	Crystal	Green
Ash tray, 3″ square	12.50	
Bonbon dish, 7″, 2 hdld., upturned sides	11.00	35.00
Bowl, 5 quart punch	62.00	
Bowl, individual nut/jelly	21.00	25.00
Bowl, 4½″, nappy	11.00	27.50
Bowl, 5″, 2 hdld. nut/jelly	12.00	
Bowl, 5½″, nappy	12.00	35.00
Bowl, 5½″, round, hdld. nappy	15.00	50.00
Bowl, 5½″, tri-corner, hdld. nappy	17.50	50.00
Bowl, 10″, 4 part relish	35.00	185.00
Bowl, 12″, floral	35.00	
Bowl, 13″, gardenia	32.50	
Box, 5½″, footed candy w/cover	85.00	325.00
Butter dish w/cover	75.00	
Candle, 1-lite, block	17.00	
Candle, 3-lite	40.00	
Candle, 3-lite, #4233 5″, vase	55.00	
Cigarette lighter	25.00	
Coaster, 4″	5.00	
Creamer, footed	15.00	85.00
Creamer & sugar w/tray, individual	35.00	
Cup, punch	10.00	
Mayonnaise, 7″ (plate, ladle, bowl)	32.00	145.00
Oil bottle, 4 oz., #1 stopper	42.00	
Plate, 5″, footed cheese	10.00	
Plate, 7″, 2 hdld. snack	12.00	
Plate, 7″, bread	10.00	
Plate, 8″, luncheon	15.00	40.00
Plate, 14″, torte	27.50	
Plate, 18″, buffet	37.50	150.00
Salt & Pepper, pr	22.00	
Stem, 3½ oz., oyster cocktail	8.00	
Stem, 3½ oz., wine	17.50	
Stem, 5 oz., sherbet/champagne	8.00	
Stem, 10 oz.	17.50	
Sugar, footed	15.00	80.00
Tray, 13″, oval celery	22.00	
Tumbler, 5 oz., footed juice	10.00	40.00
Tumbler, 8 oz.,	12.00	
Tumbler, 9 oz., footed	14.00	60.00
Tumbler, 12 oz., footed, iced tea	15.00	70.00
Tumbler, 13″, flat ice tea	15.00	
Vase, 3½″, violet	15.00	75.00
Vase, 4″, pansy	15.00	
Vase, 6″, sweet pea	22.00	

RIDGELEIGH, Blank #1469, A. H. Heisey & Co.

Colors: crystal, "Sahara," "Zircon," rare

	Crystal		Crystal
Ash tray, round	4.25	Mustard w/cover	35.00
Ash tray, square	3.25	Oil bottle, 3 oz., w/#103 stopper	45.00
Ash tray, 4", round	11.00	Pitcher, ½ gallon	110.00
Ash tray, 6", square	16.00	Pitcher, ½ gallon, ice lip	125.00
Ash trays, bridge set (heart, diamond, spade, club)	30.00	Plate, oval hors d'oeuvres	20.00
		Plate, 2 hdld. ice tub liner	15.00
Basket, bonbon	10.00	Plate, 6", round	5.00
Bottle, rock & rye w/#104 stopper	85.00	Plate, 6", scalloped	5.00
Bottle, 4 oz., cologne	75.00	Plate, 6", square	5.00
Bottle, 5 oz., bitters w/tube	60.00	Plate, 7", square	6.00
Bowl, indiv. nut	7.25	Plate, 8", round	7.00
Bowl, oval indiv. jelly	12.50	Plate, 8", square	7.00
Bowl, indiv. nut, 2 part	10.50	Plate, 13½", sandwich	22.00
Bowl, 4½", nappy, bell or cupped	6.25	Plate, 13½", ftd. torte	22.00
Bowl, 4½", nappy, scalloped	6.25	Plate, 14", salver	55.00
Bowl, 5", lemon w/cover	16.00	Salt & pepper, pr.	25.00
Bowl, 5", nappy, straight	6.50	Salt dip, indiv.	13.00
Bowl, 5", nappy, square	6.50	Saucer	3.00
Bowl, 6", 2 hdld. divided jelly	12.75	Soda, 12 oz., cupped or flared	22.50
Bowl, 6", 2 hdld. jelly	12.75	Stem, cocktail, pressed	20.00
Bowl, 7", 2 part oval relish	12.75	Stem, claret, pressed	25.00
Bowl, 8", centerpiece	21.00	Stem, oyster cocktail, pressed	14.00
Bowl, 8", nappy, square	26.00	Stem, sherbet, pressed	10.00
Bowl, 9", nappy, square	26.00	Stem, saucer champagne, pressed	11.00
Bowl, 9", salad	28.00	Stem, wine, pressed	25.00
Bowl, 10", flared fruit	32.00	Stem, 1 oz., cordial, blown	110.00
Bowl, 10", floral	32.00	Stem, 2 oz., sherry, blown	55.00
Bowl, 11", centerpiece	35.00	Stem, 2½ oz., wine, blown	45.00
Bowl, 11", punch	85.00	Stem, 3½ oz., cocktail blown	26.00
Bowl, 11½", floral	30.00	Stem, 4 oz., claret, blown	27.50
Bowl, 12", oval floral	35.00	Stem, 4 oz., oyster cocktail, blown	16.00
Bowl, 12", flared fruit	35.00	Stem, 5 oz., saucer champagne, blown	17.50
Bowl, 13", cone floral	35.00	Stem, 5 oz., sherbet, blown	12.50
Bowl, 14", oblong floral	45.00	Stem, 8 oz., luncheon, low stem	12.50
Bowl, 14", oblong swan hdld. floral	95.00	Stem, 8 oz., tall stem	17.50
Box, 8", floral	22.00	Sugar	15.00
Candle block, 3"	16.00	Sugar, indiv.	10.00
Candle vase, 6"	16.00	Tray, for indiv. sugar & creamer	10.00
Candlestick, 2", 1-lite	12.00	Tray, 10½", oblong	22.00
Candlestick, 2-lite, bobeche & "A" prisms	40.00	Tray, 11", 3 part, relish	26.00
Candlestick, 7", w/bobeche & "A" prisms	85.00	Tray, 12", celery & olive, divided	22.50
Cheese, 6", 2 hdld.	7.25	Tray, 12", celery	22.50
Cigarette box w/cover, oval	25.00	Tumbler, 2½ oz., bar, pressed	16.00
Cigarette box w/cover, 6"	10.00	Tumbler, 5 oz., juice, blown	16.00
Cigarette holder, oval w/2 comp. ash trays	35.00	Tumbler, 5 oz., soda, ftd., pressed	13.00
Cigarette holder, round	6.00	Tumbler, 8 oz., (#1469¾), pressed	15.00
Cigarette holder, square	6.00	Tumbler, 8 oz., old fashioned, pressed	16.00
Cigarette holder w/cover	15.00	Tumbler, 8 oz., soda, blown	16.00
Coaster or cocktail rest	3.00	Tumbler, 10 oz., (#1469¾), pressed	13.00
Cocktail shaker, 1 qt. w/#1 strainer & #86 stopper	145.00	Tumbler, 12 oz., ftd. soda, pressed	18.00
Comport, 6", low ft., flared	16.00	Tumbler, 12 oz., soda, (#1469¾) pressed	23.00
Comport, 6", low ft. w/cover	26.00	Tumbler, 13 oz., iced tea, blown	16.00
Creamer	15.00	Vase, #1 indiv., cuspidor shape	22.50
Creamer, indiv.	10.00	Vase, #2 indiv., cupped top	21.00
Cup	10.00	Vase, #3 indiv., flared rim	22.50
Cup, beverage	12.00	Vase, #4, indiv., fan out top	25.00
Cup, punch	10.00	Vase, #5 indiv., scalloped top	22.50
Decanter, 1 pint w/#95 stopper	85.00	Vase, 3½"	20.00
Ice tub, 2 hdld.	40.00	Vase, 6", (also flared)	15.00
Marmalade w/cover	35.00	Vase, 8"	20.00
Mayonnaise	30.00	Vase, 8", triangular (#1469¾)	20.00

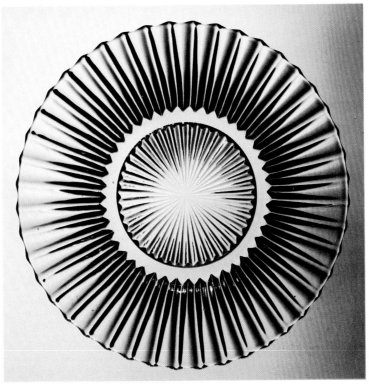

ROSALIE, or #731, Cambridge Glass Company, Late 1920's - 1930's

Colors: blue, green, Heatherbloom, pink, red, amber

It is amazing what a name for a pattern will do for its collectability! #731 was virtually unknown to collectors outside of the Cambridge collecting fraternity until my last book exposing that it really had a "name" other than #731. Now this pattern is recognized by more than Cambridge collectors and the price has increased dramatically in harder-to-find items and unusual colors.

This pattern is one of the few etched lines of Cambridge that has bi-colored pieces. Note the Moonlight blue stemmed pink tumbler.

Moonlight blue, Carmen and Heatherbloom colored pieces will bring up to double the prices listed.

	All Colors		All Colors
Bottle, French dressing	65.00	Cup	12.50
Bowl, bouillon, 2 hdld.	15.00	Gravy, double, w/platter	95.00
Bowl, cream soup	17.50	Ice bucket or pail	45.00
Bowl, finger, w/liner	25.00	Ice tub	40.00
Bowl, finger, ftd., w/liner	22.50	Mayonnaise, ftd. w/liner	37.50
Bowl, 3½", cranberry	17.50	Nut, 2½", ftd.	35.00
Bowl, 3⅝", w/cover, 3 pt.	30.00	Pitcher, 62 oz., #955	120.00
Bowl, 5½", fruit	12.50	Plate, 6¾", bread/butter	5.50
Bowl, 5½", 2 hdld., bonbon	15.00	Plate, 7", 2 hdld.	12.50
Bowl, 6¼", 2 hdld., bonbon	17.50	Plate, 7½", salad	8.50
Bowl, 7", basket, 2 hdld.	225.00	Plate, 8⅜"	13.50
Bowl, 8½", soup	25.00	Plate, 9½", dinner	35.00
Bowl, 8½", 2 hdld.	20.00	Plate, 11", 2 hdld.	22.50
Bowl, 8½", w/cover, 3 pt.	32.50	Platter, 12"	30.00
Bowl, 10"	25.00	Platter, 15"	50.00
Bowl, 10", 2 hdld.	27.50	Relish, 9", 2 pt.	17.50
Bowl, 11"	30.00	Relish, 11", 2 pt.	25.00
Bowl, 11", basket, 2 hdld.	37.50	Salt dip, 1½", ftd.	15.00
Bowl, 11½"	32.50	Saucer	2.50
Bowl, 12"	32.50	Stem, 1 oz., cordial #3077	50.00
Bowl, 13", console	32.50	Stem, 3½ oz., cocktail #3077	17.50
Bowl, 15", oval console	35.00	Stem, 6 oz., low sherbet, #3077	13.50
Bowl, 15", oval, flanged	40.00	Stem, 6 oz., high sherbet, #3077	15.00
Bowl, 15½", oval	45.00	Stem, 9 oz., water goblet, #3077	22.50
Candlestick, 4", 2 styles	20.00	Stem, 10 oz., goblet #801	22.50
Candlestick, 5", keyhole	25.00	Sugar, ftd.	12.00
Candlestick, 6", 3-lite keyhole	40.00	Sugar shaker	130.00
Candy and cover, 6"	65.00	Tray for sugar shaker/creamer	25.00
Celery, 11"	22.50	Tray, ctr. hdld., for sugar/creamer	15.00
Cheese & cracker, 11" plate	45.00	Tray, 11", ctr. hdld.	30.00
Comport, 5½", 2 hdld.	20.00	Tumbler, 2½ oz., ftd., #3077	15.00
Comport, 5¾"	22.00	Tumbler, 5 oz., ftd., #3077	16.00
Comport, 6", ftd. almond	35.00	Tumbler, 8 oz., ftd., #3077	16.00
Comport, 6½", low ft.	30.00	Tumbler, 10 oz., ftd., #3077	19.00
Comport, 6½", high ft.	35.00	Tumbler, 12 oz., ftd., #3077	22.00
Comport, 6¾"	30.00	Vase, 5½", ftd.	32.50
Creamer, ftd.	12.50	Vase, 6"	40.00
Creamer, ftd., tall	20.00	Vase, 6½", ftd.	45.00

Note: See Pages 166-167 for stem identification.

125

ROSE, Etching #1515, on WAVERLY Blank #11519, A. H. Heisey & Co., 1949 - 1957

Colors: crystal

Rose is still my favorite Heisey pattern. The multitude of pieces and the different blanks used by Heisey in making this line creates many scarcity problems for collectors. How a pattern made for nine years (and then reproduced by Imperial from the same moulds) can have so many hard-to-find pieces is astounding! Unless you consider that many people still have this pattern as their "good" crystal and are not selling it as yet, there does not seem to be justification for this!

	Crystal		Crystal
Ash tray, 3″	40.00	Cocktail icer w/liner, #3304, UNIVERSAL	75.00
Bell, dinner #5072	125.00	Cocktail shaker, #4036 & #4225, COBEL	85.00
Bottle, 8 oz., French dressing, blown, #5031	175.00	Comport, 6½″, low ft., WAVERLY	60.00
Bowl, finger, #3309	60.00	Comport, 7″, oval, ftd., WAVERLY	100.00
Bowl, 5½″, ftd. mint	32.50	Creamer, ftd., WAVERLY	32.50
Bowl, 5¾″, ftd. mint. CABOCHON	67.50	Creamer, indiv., WAVERLY	25.00
Bowl, 6″, ftd. mint, QUEEN ANN	37.50	Cup, WAVERLY	50.00
Bowl, 6″, jelly, 2 hdld., ftd. QUEEN ANN	42.50	Decanter, 1 pt., #4036½, #101 stopper	120.00
Bowl, 6″, oval lemon w/cover	165.00	Hurricane lamp w/12″ globe #5080	175.00
Bowl, 6½″, 2 pt. oval dressing, WAVERLY	57.50	Hurricane lamp, w/12″ globe, PLANTATION	175.00
Bowl, 6½″, ftd. honey/cheese, WAVERLY	55.00	Ice bucket, dolp. ft., QUEEN ANN	175.00
Bowl, 6½″, ftd. jelly, WAVERLY	45.00	Ice tub, 2 hdld., WAVERLY	175.00
Bowl, 6½″, lemon w/cover, WAVERLY	157.50	Mayonnaise, 5½″, 2 hdld., WAVERLY	50.00
Bowl, 7″, ftd. honey, WAVERLY	40.00	Mayonnaise, 5½″, div., 1 hdld., WAVERLY	50.00
Bowl, 7″, ftd. jelly, WAVERLY	40.00	Mayonnaise, 5½″, ftd., WAVERLY	55.00
Bowl, 7″, lily, QUEEN ANN	45.00	Oil, 3 oz., ftd., WAVERLY	155.00
Bowl, 7″, relish, 3 pt., round, WAVERLY	67.50	Pitcher, 73 oz., #4164	295.00
Bowl, 7″, salad, WAVERLY	52.50	Plate, 7″, salad, WAVERLY	20.00
Bowl, 7″, salad dressings, QUEEN ANN	50.00	Plate, 7″, mayonnaise, WAVERLY	20.00
Bowl, 9″, ftd. fruit or salad, WAVERLY	100.00	Plate, 8″, salad, WAVERLY	30.00
Bowl, 9″, salad, WAVERLY	75.00	Plate, 10½″, dinner	90.00
Bowl, 9″, 4 pt. rnd. relish, WAVERLY	85.00	Plate, 10½″, service, WAVERLY	75.00
Bowl, 9½″, crimped floral, WAVERLY	65.00	Plate, 11″, sandwich, WAVERLY	75.00
Bowl, 10″, gardenia, WAVERLY	65.00	Plate, 11″, demi-torte, WAVERLY	65.00
Bowl, 10″, crimped floral, WAVERLY	82.50	Plate, 12″, ftd. salver, WAVERLY	175.00
Bowl, 11″, 3 pt. relish, WAVERLY	77.50	Plate, 15″, ftd. cake, WAVERLY	250.00
Bowl, 11″, 3 ft., floral, WAVERLY	125.00	Plate, 14″, torte, WAVERLY	90.00
Bowl, 11″, floral, WAVERLY	67.50	Plate, 14″, sandwich, WAVERLY	90.00
Bowl, 11″, oval, 4 ft., WAVERLY	110.00	Plate, 14″, ctr. hdld., sandwich, WAVERLY	150.00
Bowl, 12″, crimped floral, WAVERLY	75.00	Salt & pepper, ftd., pr., WAVERLY	65.00
Bowl, 13″, crimped floral, WAVERLY	80.00	Saucer, WAVERLY	10.00
Bowl, 13″, floral, WAVERLY	80.00	Stem, #5072, 1 oz., cordial	140.00
Bowl, 13″, gardenia, WAVERLY	75.00	Stem, #5072, 3 oz., wine	110.00
Butter w/cover, 6″,. WAVERLY	155.00	Stem, #5072, 3½ oz., oyster cocktail, ftd.	27.50
Butter w/cover, ¼ lb., CABOCHON	225.00	Stem, #5072, 4 oz., claret	90.00
Candlestick, 1-lite, #112	40.00	Stem, #5072, 4 oz., cocktail	40.00
Candlestick, 2-lite, FLAME	65.00	Stem, #5072, 6 oz., sherbet	27.50
Candlestick, 3-lite, #142 CASCADE	77.50	Stem, #5072, 6 oz., saucer champagne	35.00
Candlestick, 3-lite, WAVERLY	80.00	Stem, #5072, 9 oz., water	42.50
Candlestick, 5″, 2-lite, #134, TRIDENT	65.00	Sugar, indiv., WAVERLY	25.00
Candlestick, 6″, epergnette, deep, WAVERLY	300.00	Sugar, ftd., WAVERLY	30.00
Candy w/cover, 5″, ftd. WAVERLY	160.00	Tumbler, #5072, 5 oz., ftd. juice	42.50
Candy w/cover, 6″, low, bowknot cover	165.00	Tumbler, #5072, 12 oz., ftd. tea	45.00
Candy w/cover, 6¼″, #1951, CABOCHON	110.00	Tray, indiv. creamer/sugar, QUEEN ANN	30.00
Celery tray, 12″, WAVERLY	45.00	Vase, 3½″, ftd. violet, WAVERLY	65.00
Celery tray, 13″, WAVERLY	50.00	Vase, 4″, ftd. violet, WAVERLY	67.50
Cheese compote, 4½″, & cracker (11″ plate) WAVERLY	85.00	Vase, 7″, ftd. fan, WAVERLY	67.50
Cheese compote, 5½″, & cracker (12″ plate) QUEEN ANNE	85.00	Vase, 8″, #4198	85.00
		Vase, 8″, sq. ftd. urn	75.00
Chocolate w/cover, 5″, WAVERLY	110.00	Vase, 10″, #4198	125.00
Cigarette holder, #4035	85.00	Vase, 10″, sq. ftd. urn	85.00
		Vase, 12″, sq. fd. urn	135.00

ROSE POINT, Cambridge Glass Company, 1936 - 1953

Colors: crystal, some crystal with gold

Cambridge and Rose Point go together as do Heisey and Orchid. Many times I have been told that Mom's dishes were made by the Rose Point Company.

I had better point out that the cordial with the plain green top is pressed Rose Point. The pattern was pressed on the crystal stem with a colored bowl on top. You will find additional colors of red, amethyst, cobalt blue, amber and even some with crystal tops.

I keep adding pieces to my listing of Rose Point pattern, but it is a never ending job! It seems that Rose Point is found on almost any blank that Cambridge made. You will probably find pieces on blanks not listed; so you will have to use this list as a guide. In other words, all dinner plates sell in the same price range no matter on which blank they are found.

If you have any catalogue information available to you for patterns in this book, please contact me. I have a large selection of catalogues, but I find that there is always new information in each one! A major problem is finding the time to search each one for its deep dark secrets.

	Crystal
Ash tray, 2½", sq., #721	35.00
Ash tray, 3¼" (#3500/124)	30.00
Ash tray, 3½" (#3500/125)	31.50
Ash tray, 4" (#3500/126)	32.50
Ash tray, 4¼" (#3500/127)	33.50
Ashtray, 4½" (#3500/128)	35.00
Basket, 5", 1 hdld. (#3500/51)	150.00
Basket, 6", 1 hdld. (#3500/52)	165.00
Basket, 7", 1 hdld., #119	325.00
Bowl, 3", 4 ftd. nut (#3400/71)	55.00
Bowl, 5", hdld. (#3500/49)	42.50
Bowl, 5¼", 2 hdld. bonbon (#3400/1180)	30.00
Bowl, 5½"nappy (#3400/56)	32.50
Bowl, 6", cereal (#3500/11)	40.00
Bowl, 6", hdld. (#3500/50)	40.00
Bowl, 6", 2 hdld. ftd. basket (#3500/55)	37.50
Bowl, 6", 2 hdld. ftd. bonbon (#3500/54)	32.50
Bowl, 6", 2 pt. relish (#3400/90)	32.50
Bowl, 6½", 3 pt. relish (#3500/69)	32.50
Bowl, 7", 2 pt relish (#3900/124)	35.00
Bowl, 7", relish (#3900/123)	35.00
Bowl, 7", tab hdld. ftd. bonbon (#3900/130)	35.00
Bowl, 8", 3 pt. relish (#3400/91)	40.00
Bowl, 8", 3 pt., 3 hdld. relish (#3400/91)	42.50
Bowl, 8½", soup, #381	60.00
Bowl, 9", 3 pt. celery & relish (#3900/125)	45.00
Bowl, 9½", pickle (like corn), #477	35.00
Bowl, 10", 2 hdld. (#3500/28)	65.00
Bowl, 10", 4 tab ftd., flared (#3900/54)	55.00
Bowl, 10½", flared (#3400/168)	60.00
Bowl, 10½", 3 pt. (#1401/122)	90.00
Bowl, 11", 4 ftd. shallow, fancy edge (#3400/48)	60.00
Bowl, 11", tab hdld. (#3900/34)	55.00
Bowl, 11½", ftd. w/tab hdl. (#3900/28)	57.50
Bowl, 12", 4 ftd., oval w/"ears" hdl. (#3900/65)	75.00
Bowl, 12", 3 pt. celery & relish (#3900/126)	57.50
Bowl, 12", 4 ftd. fancy rim oblong (#3400/160)	70.00
Bowl, 12", 4 ftd. flared (#3400/4)	65.00
Bowl, 12", 4 tab ftd., flared (#3900/62)	65.00
Bowl, 12", 5 pt. celery & relish (#3900/120)	67.50
Butter w/cover, ¼ lb., #506	250.00
Butter w/cover, 5" (#3400/52)	165.00
Candlestick, 5" (#3900/68)	32.50
Candlestick, 5", 1-lite keyhole (#3400/646)	30.00
Candlestick, 5", inverts to comport (#3900/67)	50.00
Candlestick, 6", 2-lite keyhole (#3400/647)	35.00
Candlestick, 6", 2-lite (#3900/72)	40.00
Candlestick, 6", 3-lite keyhole (#3400/648)	42.50
Candlestick, 6", 3-tiered lite, #1338	65.00
Candy box w/cover, 5⅜", #1066 stem	120.00

	Crystal
Candy box w/cover, 6″ ram's head (#3500/78)	150.00
Candy box w/cover, 7″, round #103	125.00
Candy box w/cover, 8″, 3 pt. (#3500/57)	72.50
Candy box w/cover, rnd. (#3900/165)	95.00
Cheese (comport) & cracker (13″ plate) (#3900/135)	100.00
Cheese dish w/cover, 5″, #980	375.00
Cigarette box w/cover, #615	90.00
Cigarette box w/cover, #747	92.50
Coaster	33.00
Cocktail icer, 2 pc. (#3600)	75.00
Cocktail shaker, metal top (#3400/175)	145.00
Cocktail shaker, 32 oz., w/stopper, #101	130.00
Comport, 5″, 4 fd. (#3400/74)	35.00
Comport, 5½″, scalloped edge (#3900/136)	47.50
Comport, 5⅜″, blown (#3500/101)	55.00
Comport, 5⅜″, blown #3121 stem	55.00
Comport, 5⅜″, blown #1066 stem	55.00
Creamer, flat	125.00
Creamer, ftd. (#3900/41)	22.50
Creamer, indiv. (#3500/15) pie crust edge	25.00
Creamer, indiv. (#3900/40) scalloped edge	25.00
Cup, 3 styles (#3400, #3500, #3900)	31.50
Decanter, 12 oz., ball, w/stopper (#3400/119)	165.00
Decanter, 28 oz. w/stopper, #1321	215.00
Decanter, 32 oz., ball, w/stopper (#3400/92)	165.00
Epergne (candle w/vases) (#3900/75)	150.00
Grapefruit w/liner, #187	80.00
Honey dish w/cover (#3500/139)	210.00
Hurricane lamp w/prisms	195.00
Hurricane lamp, candlestick base	175.00
Hurricane lamp, keyhole base w/prisms, #1603	225.00
Ice bucket w/chrome hand. (#3900/671)	125.00
Marmalade, 8 oz., #147	175.00
Mayonnaise, (sherbet type w/ladle)	50.00
Mayonnaise, div. w/liner & 2 ladles (#3900/111)	80.00
Mayonnaise w/liner & ladle (#3500/59)	65.00
Mustard, 3 oz., #151	150.00
Oil, 2 oz., ball, w/stopper (#3400/96)	47.50
Oil, 6 oz., ball, w/stopper (#3400/99)	75.00
Oil, 6 oz., loop hdld. w/stopper (#3900/100)	110.00
Oil, 6 oz., w/stopper, ftd., hdld. (#3400/161)	165.00
Pitcher, 20 oz. (#3900/117)	210.00
Pitcher, 32 oz. (#3900/118)	180.00
Pitcher, 32 oz. martini (slender) w/metal insert, (#3900/114)	450.00
Pitcher, 60 oz. martini, #1408	1250.00
Pitcher, 76 oz. (#3900/115)	155.00
Pitcher, 76 oz., ice lip (#3400/152)	165.00
Pitcher, 80 oz., Doulton (#3400/141)	255.00
Pitcher, 80 oz., ball (#3400/38)	165.00
Pitcher, nite set, 2 pc. w/tumbler insert top, #103	325.00
Plate, 6″, 2 hdld. (#3400/1181)	17.50
Plate, 6⅛″ canape	75.00
Plate, 6½″, bread/butter (#3900/20)	13.00
Plate, 7½″, salad (#3400/176)	16.00
Plate, 8″, 2 hdld. ftd. (#3500/161)	30.00
Plate, 8″, tab hdld. ftd. bonbon (#3900/131)	30.00
Plate, 8½″, breakfast (#3400/62)	20.00
Plate 9½″ crescent salad	150.00
Plate, 9½″, luncheon (#3400/63)	32.50
Plate, 10½″, dinner (#3400/64)	105.00
Plate, 10½″ dinner (#3900/24)	105.00
Plate, 11″, 2 hdld. (#3400/35)	60.00
Plate, 12″, 4 ftd. service (#3900/26)	65.00
Plate, 12½″, 2 hdld. (#3400/1186)	65.00
Plate, 13″, rolled edge, ftd. (#3900/33)	70.00

	Crystal
Plate, 13″, 4 ftd. torte (#3500/110)	72.50
Plate, 13½″, rolled edge, #1397	75.00
Plate, 13½″, tab hdld. cake (#3900/35)	72.50
Plate, 14″, service (#3900/167)	77.50
Plate, 14″ torte (#3400/65)	77.50
Punch bowl, 15″, Martha #478	1,500.00
Relish, 3 pt., 7½″ center hdld. (#3500/71)	120.00
Relish, 10″, 4 pt. (#3500/65)	60.00
Relish, 15″, 4 pt., hdld. (#3500/113)	175.00
Salt & pepper, egg shape, pr., #1468	70.00
Salt & pepper w/chrome tops, pr., ftd. (#3400/77)	50.00
Salt & pepper w/chrome tops, pr., flat (#3900/1177)	35.00
Sandwich tray, center handled (#3400/10)	135.00
Saucer, 3 styles (#3400, #3500, #3900)	7.50
Stem, #3121, 1 oz., cordial	67.50
Stem #3121, 3 oz., cocktail	35.00
Stem, #3121, 3½ oz., wine	52.50
Stem, #3121, 4½ oz., claret	55.00
Stem, #3121, 4½ oz., low oyster cocktail	32.50
Stem, #3121, 5 oz., low ft. juice	30.00
Stem, #3121, 5 oz., low ft. parfait	65.00
Stem, #3121, 6 oz., low sherbet	18.00
Stem, #3121, 6 oz., tall sherbet	20.00
Stem, #3121, 10 oz., water	26.50
Stem, #3500, 1 oz., cordial	65.00
Stem, #3500, 2½ oz., wine	47.50
Stem, #3500, 3 oz., cocktail	32.50
Stem, #3500, 4½ oz., claret	45.00
Stem, #3500, 4½ oz., low oyster cocktail	30.00
Stem, #3500, 5 oz., low ft. juice	27.50
Stem, #3500, 5 oz., low ft. parfait	55.00
Stem, #3500, 7 oz., low ft. sherbet	15.00
Stem, #3500, 7 oz., tall sherbet	20.00
Stem, #3500, 10 oz water	25.00
Stem, #7801, 4 oz. cocktail, plain stem	40.00
Stem, #7966, 2 oz., sherry, plain ft.	55.00
Sugar, flat	125.00
Sugar, ftd. (#3900/41)	21.00
Sugar, indiv. (#3500/15) pie crust edge	22.50
Sugar, indiv. (#3900/40) scalloped edge	22.50
Tray, sugar/creamer, (#3900/37)	22.50
Tumbler, #3121, 10 oz., low ft. water	22.50
Tumbler, #3121, 12 oz., low ft. ice tea	27.50
Tumbler, #3500, 10 oz., low ft. water	20.00
Tumbler, #3500, 12 oz., low ft. ice tea	23.50
Tumbler, #3900, 5 oz.	40.00
Tumbler, #3900, 13 oz.	42.50
Urn, 10″ (#3500/41)	200.00
Urn, 12″ (#3500/42)	225.00
Vase, 5″, globe (#3400/102)	55.00
Vase, 5″, ftd., #6004	50.00
Vase, 6″, high ftd. flower, #6004	55.00
Vase, 8″, flat, flared, #797	75.00
Vase, 8″, high ftd. flower, #6004	65.00
Vase, 9″, ftd., keyhole, #1237	65.00
Vase, 10″, bud, #1528	75.00
Vase, 10″, cornucopia (#3900/575)	110.00
Vase, 10″, flat, #1242	95.00
Vase, 10″, ftd., #1301	75.00
Vase, 11″, ftd. flower, #278	85.00
Vase, 11″, ped. ftd. flower, #1299	100.00
Vase, 12″, ftd., keyhole, #1238	125.00
Vase, 13″, ftd. flower, #279	145.00

ROYAL, Plate Etching #273, Fostoria Glass Company

Colors: amber, black, blue, green

Royal is a Fostoria pattern that is often confused with Vesper since both designs are similar and both are found in the same colors on the #2350 blank. There are more collectors for Vesper at the present time because that pattern has been more publicized than Royal. That may be changing as new collectors are finding that the less expensive Royal is very comparable to Vesper in many other ways. Cost is a great determining factor; so we shall see what the future holds.

Notice the black, covered, three-part candy. I found that in Eugene, Oregon. The shop's owner had no idea what it was. Since that was a pattern to be included in this book, I talked myself into bringing it back.

Several pieces to watch for include the covered cheese, cologne bottles and the pitchers. Both the amber and green can be collected in sets; but only a few pieces can be found in blue and black. Fostoria's blue color found with Royal etching was called "Blue" as opposed to the "Azure" blue which is the lighter color found with June etching.

	*Amber green		*Amber green
Ash tray, #2350, 3½"	22.50	Grapefruit w/insert	55.00
Bowl, #2350, bouillon, flat	10.00	Ice bucket, #2378	40.00
Bowl, #2350 ½, bouillon, ftd	12.50	Mayonnaise, #2315	25.00
Bowl, #2350, cream soup, flat	12.50	Pitcher, #1236	295.00
Bowl, #2350½, cream soup, ftd	14.00	Pitcher, #5000, 48 oz	215.00
Bowl, #869, 4½", finger	15.00	Plate, #2350, 6", bread/butter	3.00
Bowl, #2350, 5½", fruit	10.00	Plate, #2350, 7½", salad	4.00
Bowl, #2350, 6½", cereal	12.50	Plate, #2350, 8½", luncheon	7.00
Bowl, #2267, 7", ftd	28.00	Plate, #2350, 9½", small dinner	12.00
Bowl, #2350, 7¾", soup	17.00	Plate, #2350, 10½", dinner	22.00
Bowl, #2350, 8", nappy	28.00	Plate, #2350, 13", chop	27.50
Bowl, #2350, 9", nappy	30.00	Plate, #2350, 15", chop	38.00
Bowl, #2350, 9", oval baker	28.00	Platter, #2350, 10½"	25.00
Bowl, #2324, 10", ftd	35.00	Platter, #2350, 12"	35.00
Bowl, #2350, 10", salad	30.00	Platter, #2350, 15½"	55.00
Bowl, #2350, 10½", oval baker	38.00	Salt and pepper, #5100, pr.	55.00
Bowl, #2315, 10½", ftd	40.00	Sauce boat w/liner	70.00
Bowl, #2329, 11", console	22.00	Saucer, #2350/#2350½	3.00
Bowl, #2297, 12", deep	22.00	Saucer, #2350, demi	5.00
Bowl, #2329, 13", console	30.00	Server, #2287, 11", center hdld	25.00
Bowl, #2324, 13", ftd	38.00	Stem, #869, ¾ oz. cordial	50.00
Bowl, #2371, 13", oval w/flower frog	55.00	Stem, #869, 2¾ oz. wine	25.00
Butter w/cover #2350	150.00	Stem, #869, 3 oz. cocktail	22.50
Candlestick, #2324, 4"	14.00	Stem, #869, 5½ oz. oyster cocktail	14.00
Candlestick, #2324, 9"	40.00	Stem, #869, 5½ oz., parfait	25.00
Candy w/cover, #2331, 3 part	55.00	Stem, #869, 6 oz., low sherbet	12.50
Celery, #2350, 11"	25.00	Stem, #869, 6 oz., high sherbet	16.00
Cheese w/cover/plate #2276	65.00	Stem, #869, 9 oz., water	19.00
Cologne, #2322, tall	30.00	Sugar, #2315, ftd., fat	17.00
Cologne, #2323, short	25.00	Sugar, #2350½, ftd	12.00
Comport, #1861½, 6", jelly	25.00	Sugar lid, #2350½	95.00
Comport, #2327, 7"	28.00	Tumbler, #869, 5 oz., flat	22.50
Comport, #2358, 8" wide	30.00	Tumbler, #859, 9 oz., flat	25.00
Creamer, #2315½, ftd., fat	18.00	Tumbler, #869, 12 oz., flat	27.50
Creamer, #2350½, ftd	13.00	Tumbler, #869, 2½ oz., ftd	25.00
Cup, #2350, flat	12.00	Tumbler, #869, 5 oz., ftd	14.00
Cup, #2350½, ftd	13.00	Tumbler, #869, 9 oz., ftd	16.00
Cup, #2350, demi	20.00	Vase, #2324, urn, ftd	65.00
Egg cup, #2350	18.00	Vase, #2292, flared	85.00

* Add 50% more for blue or black!

SANDWICH, #41, Duncan & Miller Glass Company, 1924 - 1955

Colors: crystal, amber, pink, green, red, cobalt blue

Collecting Duncan & Miller Sandwich glass is on the increase. There is demand for serving pieces and the unusual items. Since this pattern was made for so long, stemware and basic pieces are commonly found. Thus, price decreases have been found in some stems as can be noted in the price listing!

	Crystal		Crystal
Ash tray, 2½″ x 3¾″ rect.	10.00	Candelabra, 10″, 3-lite, w/bobeche & prisms	100.00
Ashtray, 2¾″, sq.	8.00	Candelabra, 16″, 3-lite w/bobeche & prisms	150.00
Basket, 6½″ w/loop hdld.	110.00	Candlestick, 4″, 1-lite	12.50
Basket, 10″, crimped w/loop hdl.	125.00	Candlestick, 4″, 1-lite w/bobeche & stub.	
Basket, 10″, oval w/loop hdl.	125.00	prisms	25.00
Basket, 11½″, w/loop hdl.	145.00	Candlestick, 5″, 3-lite	30.00
Bonbon, 5″, heart shape w/ring hdl.	15.00	Candlestick, 5″, 3-lite w/bobeche & stub.	
Bonbon, 5½″, heart shape, hdld.	15.00	prisms	50.00
Bonbon, 6″, heart shape w/ring hdl.	18.00	Candlestick, 5″, 2-lite w/bobeche & stub.	
Bonbon, 7½″, ftd., w/cover	32.50	prisms	37.50
Bowl, 2½″, salted almond	7.50	Candlestick, 5″, 2-lite	20.00
Bowl, 3½″, nut	8.00	Candy box w/cover, 5″, flat	30.00
Bowl, 4″, finger	12.50	Candy jar w/cover, 8½″, ftd.	47.50
Bowl, 5½″, hdld.	15.00	Cheese w/cover (cover 4¾″, plate 8″)	85.00
Bowl, 5½″, ftd. grapefruit w/rim liner	14.00	Cheese/cracker (3″ compote, 13″ plate)	40.00
Bowl, 5½″, ftd. grapefruit w/fruit cup liner	14.00	Cigarette box w/cover, 3½″	22.00
Bowl, 5″, 2 pt. nappy	12.00	Cigarette holder, 3″, ftd.	27.50
Bowl, 5″, ftd., crimped ivy	22.00	Coaster, 5″	12.00
Bowl, 5″, fruit	10.00	Comport, 2¼″	15.00
Bowl, 5″, nappy w/ring hdl.	12.00	Comport, 3¼″, low ft., crimped candy	17.50
Bowl, 6″, 2 pt. nappy	14.00	Comport, 3¼″, low ft., flared candy	17.50
Bowl, 6″, fruit salad	12.00	Comport, 4¼″, ftd.	20.00
Bowl, 6″, grapefruit, rimmed edge	15.00	Comport, 5″, low ft.	20.00
Bowl, 6″, nappy w/ring hdl.	16.00	Comport, 5½″, ftd., low crimped	22.50
Bowl, 10″, salad, deep	55.00	Comport, 6″, low ft., flared	22.50
Bowl, 10″, 3 pt., fruit	65.00	Condiment set (2 cruets; 3¾″ salt & pepper;	
Bowl, 10″, lily, vertical edge	45.00	4 pt. tray)	85.00
Bowl, 11″, cupped nut	40.00	Creamer, 4″, 7 oz, ftd.	8.00
Bowl, 11½″, crimped flower	45.00	Cup, 6 oz., tea	10.00
Bowl, 11½″, gardenia	45.00	Epergne, 9″, garden	75.00
Bowl, 11½″, ftd., crimped fruit	45.00	Epergne, 12″, 3 pt., fruit or flower	150.00
Bowl, 12″, fruit, flared edge	35.00	Jelly, 3″, indiv.	7.00
Bowl, 12″, shallow salad	35.00	Mayonnaise set, 3 pc.: Ladle, 5″ bowl, 7″	
Bowl, 12″, oblong console	35.00	plate	30.00
Bowl, 12″, epergne w/ctr. hole	45.00	Oil bottle, 5¾″	32.00
Butter w/cover, ¼ lb.	35.00	Pan, 6¾″ x 10½″, oblong camelia	50.00
Cake stand, 11½″, ftd., rolled edge	85.00	Pitcher, 13 oz., metal top	45.00
Cake stand, 12″, ftd., rolled edge, plain		Pitcher w/ice lip, 8″, 64 oz.	110.00
pedestal	75.00	Plate, 3″, indiv. jelly	6.00
Cake stand, 13″, ftd., plain pedestal	75.00	Plate, 6″, bread/butter	6.00
Candelabra, 10″, 1-lite w/bobeche & prisms	50.00	Plate, 6½″, finger bowl liner	8.00

	Crystal		Crystal
Plate, 7", dessert	7.50	Stem, 3½", 5 oz., sundae (flared rim)	12.00
Plate, 8", mayonnaise liner w/ring	5.00	Stem, 4¼", 3 oz., cocktail	15.00
Plate, 8", salad	10.00	Stem, 4¼", 5 oz., ice cream	12.50
Plate, 9½", dinner	27.50	Stem, 4¼", 3 oz., wine	18.00
Plate, 11½", hdld. service	35.00	Stem, 5¼", 4 oz., ftd. parfait	22.00
Plate, 12", torte	45.00	Stem, 5¼", 5 oz., champagne	20.00
Plate, 12", ice cream, rolled edge	45.00	Stem, 6", 9 oz., goblet	16.50
Plate, 12", deviled egg	60.00	Sugar, 3¼", ftd., 9 oz.	8.00
Plate, 13", salad dressing w/ring	32.00	Sugar, 5 oz.	7.50
Plate, 13", service	50.00	Sugar (cheese) shaker, 13 oz., metal top	55.00
Plate, 13", service, rolled edge	50.00	Tray, oval (for sugar/creamer)	10.00
Plate, 13", cracker w/ring	25.00	Tray, 6" mint, rolled edge w/ring hdl.	15.00
Plate, 16", lazy susan w/turntable	75.00	Tray, 7", oval pickle	15.00
Plate, 16", hostess	75.00	Tray, 7", mint, rolled edge w/ring hdl.	18.00
Relish, 5½", 2 pt., rnd., ring hdl.	12.00	Tray, 8", oval	18.00
Relish, 6", 2 pt., rnd., ring hdl.	15.00	Tray, 8", for oil/vinegar	20.00
Relish, 7", 2 pt. oval	20.00	Tray, 10", oval celery	18.00
Relish, 10", 4 pt. hdld.	22.00	Tray, 12", fruit epergne	35.00
Relish, 10", 3 pt., oblong	25.00	Tray, 12", ice cream, rolled edge	35.00
Relish, 10½", 3 pt. oblong	25.00	Tumbler, 3¾", 5 oz., ftd. juice	12.00
Relish, 12", 3 pt.	35.00	Tumbler, 4¾", 9 oz., ftd. water	14.00
Salad dressing set:		Tumbler, 5¼", 13 oz., flat iced tea	18.00
(2 ladles; 5" ftd. mayonnaise; 13" plate		Tumbler, 5¼", 12 oz., ftd. iced tea	16.00
w/ring)	75.00	Urn w/cover, 12", ftd.	95.00
Salad dressing set:		Vase, 3", ftd., crimped	15.00
(2 ladles; 6" ftd. div. bowl; 8" plate		Vase, 3", ftd., flared rim	14.00
w/ring)	60.00	Vase, 4", hat shape	18.00
Salt & pepper, 2½" w/glass tops, pr.	18.00	Vase, 4½", flat base, crimped	18.00
Salt & pepper, 2½" w/metal tops, pr.	18.00	Vase, 5", ftd., flared rim	20.00
Salt & pepper, 3¾" w/metal top (on 6" tray), 3 pc.	30.00	Vase, 5", ftd., crimped	20.00
Saucer, 6", w/ring	4.00	Vase, 5", ftd., fan	30.00
Stem, 2½", 6 oz., ftd. fruit cup/jello	11.00	Vase, 7½", epergne, threaded base	37.50
Stem, 2¾", 5 oz., ftd. oyster cocktail	14.00	Vase, 10", ftd.	40.00

SATURN, Blank #1485, A. H. Heisey & Co.

Colors: crystal, "Zircon" or "Limelight" green, "Dawn"

Shakers in "Zircon" are quite rare as you can see by the price. "Limelight" and "Zircon" are the same color. Originally made in 1937, this color was called "Zircon". In 1955, it was made again by Heisey, but called "Limelight".

	Crystal	Zircon/ Limelight
Ash tray	15.00	----
Bitters bottle w/short tube, blown	32.50	
Bowl, baked apple	5.00	48.00
Bowl, finger	4.00	
Bowl, rose, lg.	32.50	
Bowl, 4½″, nappy	4.00	
Bowl, 5″, nappy	6.00	
Bowl, 5″, whipped cream	10.00	50.00
Bowl, 7″, pickle	10.00	
Bowl, 9″, 3 part relish	15.00	
Bowl, 10″, celery	13.00	
Bowl, 11″, salad	27.50	
Bowl, 12″, fruit, flared rim	30.00	
Bowl, 13″, floral, rolled edge	32.50	
Bowl, 13″, floral	32.50	
Candelabrum w/"e" ball drops, 2-lite	110.00	435.00
Candle block, 2-lite	90.00	275.00
Candlestick, 3″, ftd., 1-lite	12.50	125.00
Comport, 7″	30.00	140.00
Creamer	15.00	85.00
Cup	9.00	85.00
Hostess Set, 8 pc. (low bowl w/ftd. ctr. bowl, 3 toothpick holders and clips)	55.00	185.00
Marmalade w/cover	30.00	
Mayonnaise	17.50	75.00
Mustard w/cover and paddle	35.00	285.00
Oil bottle, 2 oz., w/#1 stoppper	45.00	305.00
Parfait, 5 oz.	9.00	65.00
Pitcher, 70 oz., w/ice lip, blown	55.00	200.00
Pitcher, juice	30.00	225.00
Plate, 6″	3.00	22.50
Plate, 7″, bread	5.00	30.00
Plate, 8″, luncheon	7.00	45.00
Plate, 13″, torte	15.00	
Plate, 15″, torte	20.00	
Salt & pepper, pr.	45.00	500.00
Saucer	3.00	20.00
Stem, 3 oz., cocktail	6.00	50.00
Stem, 4 oz., fruit cocktail	5.00	45.00
Stem, 4½ oz., sherbet	5.00	45.00
Stem, 5 oz., sherbet	5.00	45.00
Stem, 6 oz., saucer champagne	7.00	50.00
Stem, 10 oz.	10.00	70.00
Sugar	15.00	85.00
Sugar shaker	35.00	
Sugar w/cover, no handles	20.00	
Tray, tid bit, 2 sides turned as fan	20.00	70.00
Tumbler, 5 oz., juice	4.00	60.00
Tumbler, 7 oz., old fashioned	6.00	
Tumbler, 8 oz., old fashioned	7.00	
Tumbler, 9 oz., luncheon	8.00	
Tumbler, 10 oz.	10.00	
Tumbler, 12 oz., soda	12.00	50.00
Vase, violet	20.00	65.00
Vase, 8½″, flared	25.00	165.00
Vase, 8½″, straight	25.00	165.00

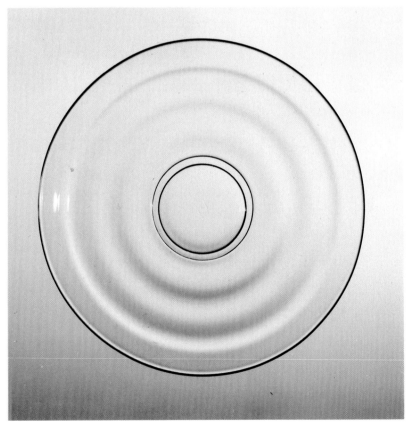

"SPIRAL FLUTES", Duncan & Miller Glass Company, Introduced 1924

Colors: amber, green, pink

Demand for this pattern has increased slightly. A few of the harder-to-find items have surfaced recently. I found a few of the 5½″, 11 oz., ginger ales in Rochester, New York, that were being sold as "Spiral" Depression Glass. They sold very quickly at Indianapolis for $40.00 and the customer wanted more. One is pictured in crystal with a flashed amber top.

Remember that there are several pieces in this pattern which are rather common: 6¾″ flanged bowls, 7½″ plates and the 7 oz. footed tumblers.

	Amber, Green, Pink		Amber, Green, Pink
Bowl, 2″, almond	9.00	Ice tub, handled	35.00
Bowl, 3¾″, bouillion	13.00	Lamp, 10½″, countess	200.00
Bowl, 4⅜″, finger	6.00	Mug, 6½″, 9 oz., handled	25.00
Bowl, 4¾″, ftd. cream soup	15.00	Mug, 7″, 9 oz., handled	30.00
Bowl, 4″ w., mayonnaise	15.00	Oil w/stopper, 6 oz.	110.00
Bowl, 5″, nappy	5.00	Pickle, 8⅝″	12.00
Bowl, 6½″, cereal, sm. flange	12.50	Pitcher, ½ gal.	110.00
Bowl, 6¾″, grapefruit	7.50	Plate, 6″, pie	3.00
Bowl, 6″, handled nappy	22.00	Plate, 7½″, salad	4.00
Bowl, 6″, handled nappy w/cover	60.00	Plate, 8⅜″, luncheon	4.00
Bowl, 7″, nappy	15.00	Plate, 10⅜″, dinner	20.00
Bowl, 7½″, flanged (baked apple)	20.00	Plate, 13⅝″, torte	25.00
Bowl, 8″, nappy	15.00	Plate w/star, 6″, (fingerbowl liner)	6.00
Bowl, 8½″, flanged (oyster plate)	20.00	Platter, 11″	30.00
Bowl, 9″, nappy	25.00	Platter, 13″	40.00
Bowl, 10″, oval veg.	35.00	Relish, 10″ x 7⅜″, oval, 3 pc. (2 inserts)	55.00
Bowl, 10½″, lily pond	37.00	Saucer	3.00
Bowl, 11¾″ w. x 3¾″ t., console, flared	25.00	Saucer, demi	5.00
Bowl, 11″, nappy	25.00	Seafood sauce cup, 3″ w. x 2½″ h.	20.00
Bowl, 12″, cupped console	26.00	Stem, 3¾″, 3½ oz. wine	15.00
Candle, 3½″	13.00	Stem, 3¾″, 5 oz., low sherbet	8.00
Candle, 7½″	45.00	Stem, 4¾″, 6 oz., tall sherbet	12.00
Candle, 9½″	50.00	Stem, 5⅝″, 4½ oz., parfait	15.00
Candle, 11½″	85.00	Stem, 6¼″, 7 oz., water	15.00
Celery, 10¾″ x 4¾″	15.00	Sugar, oval	8.00
Chocolate jar w/cover (crystal)	135.00	Sweetmeat w/cover, 7½″	75.00
Cigarette holder, 4″	30.00	Tumbler, 3⅜″, ftd., 2½ oz., cocktail (no stem)	7.00
Comport, 4⅜″	15.00	Tumbler, 4¼″, 8 oz., flat	25.00
Comport, 6⅝″	17.50	Tumbler, 4⅜″, ftd., 5½ oz., juice (no stem)	14.00
Comport, 9″, low ft., flared	45.00	Tumbler, 4¾″, 7 oz., flat soda	25.00
Console stand, 1½″ h. x 4⅝″ w.	12.00	Tumbler, 5⅛″, ftd., 7 oz. water (1 knob)	8.00
Creamer, oval	8.00	Tumbler, 5⅛″, ftd., 9 oz. water (no stem)	17.50
Cup	9.00	Tumbler, 5½″, 11 oz., gingerale	40.00
Cup, demi	20.00	Vase, 6½″	10.00
Fernery, 10″ x 5½″, 4 ft. flower box	185.00	Vase, 8½″	15.00
Grapefruit, ftd.	20.00	Vase, 10½″	20.00

TEAR DROP, #301, Duncan & Miller Glass Company, 1936 - 1955

Colors: crystal

The abundance of stemware and luncheon plates in Tear Drop has only emphasized the dearth of dinner plates and certain serving pieces in this Duncan and Miller pattern. Beginning collectors should note that this pattern is one of the more reasonably priced patterns in this book. There are some expensive and hard-to-find items also. You will not put a large set together without some difficulties.

	Crystal
Ash tray, 3″ indiv.	6.00
Ashtray, 5″	8.00
Bonbon, 6″ 4 hdld.	10.00
Bottle w/stopper, 12″, bar	85.00
Bowl, 4¼″, finger	7.00
Bowl, 5″, fruit nappy	6.00
Bowl, 5″, 2 hdld. nappy	8.00
Bowl, 6″, dessert nappy	6.00
Bowl, 6″, fruit nappy	6.00
Bowl, 7″, fruit nappy	7.00
Bowl, 7″, 2 hdld. nappy	10.00
Bowl, 8″ x 12″, oval flower	32.00
Bowl, 9″, salad	25.00
Bowl, 9″, 2 hdld. nappy	20.00
Bowl, 10″, crimped console, 2 hdld.	25.00
Bowl, 10″, flared fruit	25.00
Bowl, 11½″, crimped flower	30.00
Bowl, 11½″, flared flower	30.00
Bowl, 12″, salad	35.00
Bowl, 12″, crimped, low foot	37.00
Bowl, 12″, ftd. flower	40.00
Bowl, 12″, sq., 4 hdld.	40.00
Bowl, 13″, gardenia	35.00
Bowl, 15½″, 2½ gal. punch	75.00
Butter w/cover, ¼ lb., 2 hdld.	22.00
Cake salver, 13″, ftd.	40.00
Canape set: (6″ plate w/ring, 4 oz., ftd. cocktail)	25.00
Candlestick, 4″	9.00
Candlestick, 7″, 2-lite, ball loop ctr.	18.00
Candlestick, 7″, lg. ball ctr. w/bobeches, prisms	30.00
Candy basket, 5½″ x 7½″, 2 hdld. oval	50.00
Candy box w/cover, 7″, 2 pt., 2 hdld.	35.00
Candy box w/cover, 8″, 3 pt., 3 hdld.	40.00
Candy dish, 7½″, heart shape	21.00
Celery, 11″, 2 hdld.	15.00
Celery, 11″, 2 pt., 2 hdld.	18.00
Celery, 12″, 3 pt.	20.00
Cheese & cracker (3½″ comport, 11″ 2 hdld. plate)	40.00

	Crystal
Coaster/ashtray, 3″, rolled edge	7.00
Comport, 4¾″, ftd.	12.00
Comport, 6″, low foot. hdld.	15.00
Condiment set: 5 pc. (salt/pepper, 2 3oz. cruets, 9″, 2 hdld. tray)	85.00
Creamer, 3 oz.	5.00
Creamer, 6 oz.	6.00
Creamer, 8 oz.	8.00
Cup, 2½ oz., demi	10.00
Cup, 6 oz. tea	6.00
Flower basket, 12″, loop hand.	85.00
Ice bucket, 5½″	50.00
Marmalade w/cover, 4″	35.00
Mayonnaise, 4½″ (2 hdld. bowl, ladle, 6″ plate)	27.50
Mayonnaise set, 3 pc. (4½″ bowl, ladle, 8″ hdld. plate)	32.50
Mustard jar w/cover, 4¼″	35.00
Nut dish, 6″, 2 pt.	10.00
Oil bottle, 3 oz.	20.00
Olive dish, 4¼″, 2 hdld. oval	15.00
Olive dish, 6″, 2 pt.	15.00
Pickle dish, 6″	15.00
Pitcher, 5″, 16 oz., milk	45.00
Pitcher, 8½″, 64 oz., w/ice lip	85.00
Plate, 6″, bread/butter	4.00
Plate, 6″, canape	10.00
Plate, 7″, 4 hdld., lemon	12.50
Plate, 7½″, salad	5.00
Plate, 8½″, luncheon	7.00
Plate, 10½″, dinner	22.00
Plate, 11″, 2 hdld.	27.50
Plate, 13″, 4 hdld.	25.00
Plate, 13″, rolled edge salad liner	27.50
Plate, 13″, torte, rolled edge	30.00
Plate, 14″, torte	35.00
Plate, 14″, torte, rolled edge	35.00
Plate, 16″, torte, rolled edge	37.50
Plate, 18″, lazy susan	45.00
Plate, 18″, punch liner, rolled edge	45.00

	Crystal		Crystal
Relish, 7″, 2 pt., 2 hdld.	15.00	Sugar, 8 oz.	8.00
Relish, 7½″, 2 pt. heart shape	18.00	Sweetmeat, 5½″, star shape, 2 hdld.	25.00
Relish, 9″, 3 pt., 3 hdld.	25.00	Sweetmeat, 6½″, ctr. hdld.	25.00
Relish, 11″, 3 pt. 2 hdld.	25.00	Sweetmeat, 7″, star shape, 2 hdld.	27.00
Relish, 12″, 3 pt.	25.00	Tray, 5½″, ctr. hdld. (for mustard jar)	11.00
Relish, 12″, 5 pt. rnd.	25.00	Tray, 6″, 2 hdld. (for salt/pepper)	10.00
Relish, 12″, 6 pt., rnd.	25.00	Tray, 7¾″, ctr. hdld. (for cruets)	12.50
Relish, 12″, sq., 4 pt., 4 hdld.	25.00	Tray, 8″, 2 hdld. (for oil/vinegar)	12.50
Salad set, 6″ (compote, 11″ hdld. plate)	37.50	Tray, 8″, 2 hdld. (for sugar/creamer)	7.50
Salad set, 9″, (2 pt. bowl, 13″ rolled edge plate)	65.00	Tray, 10″, 2 hdld (for sugar/creamer)	8.00
Salt & pepper, 5″	25.00	Tumbler, 2¼″, 2 oz., flat whiskey	15.00
Saucer, 4½″, demi	3.00	Tumbler, 2¼″, 2 oz., ftd. whiskey	15.00
Saucer, 6″	1.50	Tumbler, 3″, 3 oz., ftd. whiskey	15.00
Stem, 2½″, 5 oz., ftd. sherbet	5.00	Tumbler, 3¼″, 3½ oz., flat juice	8.00
Stem, 2¾″, 3½ oz., ftd. oyster cocktail	7.50	Tumbler, 3¼″, 7 oz., flat old fashioned	10.00
Stem, 3½″, 5 oz. sherbet	6.00	Tumbler, 3½″, 5 oz., flat juice	8.00
Stem, 4″, 1 oz., cordial	27.50	Tumbler, 4″, 4½ oz., ftd. juice	9.00
Stem, 4½″, 1¾ oz., sherry	25.00	Tumbler, 4¼″, 9 oz., flat	9.00
Stem, 4½″, 3½ oz., cocktail	20.00	Tumbler, 4½″, 8 oz., flat split	9.00
Stem, 4¾″, 3 oz., wine	22.00	Tumbler, 4½″, 9 oz., ftd.	9.00
Stem, 5″, 5 oz., champagne	10.00	Tumbler, 4¾″, 10 oz., flat hi-ball	10.00
Stem, 5½″, 4 oz., claret	15.00	Tumbler, 5″, 8 oz., ftd. party	10.00
Stem, 5¾″, 9 oz.	11.00	Tumbler, 5¼″, 12 oz., flat iced tea	12.50
Stem, 6¼″, 8 oz., ale	15.00	Tumbler, 5¾″, 14 oz., flat hi-ball	15.00
Stem, 7″, 9 oz.	15.00	Tumbler, 6″, 14 oz., iced tea	16.00
Sugar, 3 oz.	5.00	Urn w/cover, 9″, ftd.	90.00
Sugar, 6 oz.	6.00	Vase, 9″, ftd. fan	22.00
		Vase, 9″, ftd. round	30.00

TROJAN, Fostoria Glass Company, 1929 - 1944

Colors: "Rose" pink, "Topaz" yellow; some green seen

I have seen more pink Trojan at shows this year than I ever have. Yellow is still the more collected color and more readily available. Years ago, I bought a pink grill plate at a show in Georgia, but it did not seem to still be around for this photo session.

The yellow, three-part relish shown behind the ice bucket is not commonly found.

	Rose, Topaz		Rose, Topaz
Ash tray, lg.	27.50	Oyster, cocktail, ftd.	22.50
Ash tray, sm.	22.50	Parfait	37.00
Bowl, 9", baker	45.00	Pitcher	265.00
Bowl, bonbon	13.00	Plate, canape	15.00
Bowl, bouillon, ftd.	16.00	Plate, 6", bread/butter	5.00
Bowl, cream soup, ftd.	18.00	Plate, 6¼", finger bowl liner	6.50
Bowl, finger w/6¼" liner	22.00	Plate, 7½", salad	7.50
Bowl, lemon	16.00	Plate, 7½", cream soup liner	7.50
Bowl, mint, 3 ftd	17.00	Plate, 8¾", , luncheon	10.00
Bowl, 5", fruit	15.00	Plate, 9½", sm. dinner	16.00
Bowl, 6", cereal	22.00	Plate, 10", cake, handled	25.00
Bowl, 7", soup	23.00	Plate, 10¼", grill, rare	35.00
Bowl, lg. dessert, handled	35.00	Plate, 10¼", dinner	32.50
Bowl, 10"	30.00	Plate, 13", chop	37.50
Bowl, combination w/candleholder handles	100.00	Platter, 12"	42.00
Bowl, 12" centerpiece, sev. types	33.50	Platter, 15"	65.00
Candlestick, 2"	15.00	Relish, 8½"	15.00
Candlestick, 3"	15.00	Relish, 3 pt.	37.50
Candlestick, 5"	19.50	Sauce boat	60.00
Candy w/cover, ½ lb.	100.00	Sauce plate	20.00
Celery, 11½"	22.50	Saucer, after dinner	7.50
Cheese & cracker, set	45.00	Saucer	4.50
Comport, 6"	25.00	Shaker, ftd., pr.	70.00
Comport, 7"	30.00	Sherbet, 6", high	20.00
Creamer, ftd.	17.50	Sherbet, 4¼", low	16.00
Creamer, tea	35.00	Sugar, ftd.	17.50
Cup, after dinner	27.50	Sugar cover	75.00
Cup, ftd.	16.00	Sugar pail	95.00
Goblet, claret, 6", 4 oz.	40.00	Sugar, tea	35.00
Goblet, cocktail, 5¼", 3 oz.	25.00	Sweetmeat	13.50
Goblet, cordial, 4", ¾ oz.	65.00	Tray, 11", ctr. hdld.	32.50
Goblet, water, 8¼", 10 oz.	27.50	Tray, service	27.50
Goblet, wine, 5½", 3 oz.	40.00	Tray, service & lemon	40.00
Grapefruit	40.00	Tumbler, 2½ oz., ftd.	30.00
Grapefruit liner	35.00	Tumbler, 5 oz., ftd., 4½"	22.50
Ice bucket	65.00	Tumbler, 9 oz., ftd., 5¼"	15.50
Ice dish	30.00	Tumbler, 12 oz., ftd., 6"	20.00
Ice dish liner (tomato, crab, fruit)	7.00	Vase, 8", 2 styles	120.00
Mayonnaise w/liner	30.00	Whipped cream bowl	11.00
Oil, ftd.	235.00	Whipped cream pail	100.00

Note: See page 79 for stem identification.

TWIST, Blank #1252, A. H. Heisey & Co.

Colors: crystal, "Flamingo" pink, "Moongleam" green; "Marigold" amber/yellow; some "Sahara", a florescent yellow and some "Alexandrite", (rare)

Alexandrite ice tubs and the 12", four-footed, floral bowls are the only pieces that are turning up in Twist with any regularity. You may find others, but those are all I've seen!

	Crystal	Pink	Green	Marigold Sahara
Baker, 9", oval	10.00	16.00	22.00	47.50
Bonbon	5.00	10.00	16.00	20.00
Bonbon, 6", 2 hdld.	5.00	10.00	16.00	20.00
Bottle, French dressing	25.00	65.00	85.00	110.00
Bowl, cream soup/bouillon	15.00	25.00	32.00	50.00
Bowl, ftd. almond/indiv. sugar	15.00	30.00	37.50	60.00
Bowl, indiv. nut	5.00	20.00	27.50	45.00
Bowl, 4", nappy	5.00	12.00	16.00	17.00
Bowl, 6", 2 hdld.	7.00	15.00	18.00	20.00
Bowl, 6", 2 hdld. jelly	7.00	15.00	18.00	20.00
Bowl, 6", 2 hdld. mint	7.00	15.00	18.00	20.00
Bowl, 8", low ftd.	20.00	30.00	37.00	65.00
Bowl, 8", nappy, grnd. bottom	12.00	20.00	27.00	40.00
Bowl, 8", nasturtium, rnd.	20.00	28.00	37.00	60.00
Bowl, 8", nasturtium, oval	20.00	28.00	37.00	60.00
Bowl, 9", floral	22.00	30.00	39.00	65.00
Bowl, 9", floral, rolled edge	22.00	30.00	39.00	65.00
Bowl, 12", floral, oval, 4 ft.	25.00	35.00	45.00	65.00
Bowl, 12", floral, rnd., 4 ft.	25.00	35.00	45.00	65.00
Candlestick, 2", 1-lite	7.50	10.00	15.00	20.00
Cheese dish, 6", 2 hdld.	5.00	10.00	17.50	20.00
Cocktail shaker, metal top			300.00	
Comport, 7", tall	25.00	55.00	75.00	135.00
Creamer, hotel oval	15.00	35.00	45.00	50.00
Creamer, individual (unusual)	10.00	25.00	32.00	55.00
Creamer, zig-zag handles, ftd.	20.00	30.00	37.50	60.00
Cup, zig-zag handles	10.00	25.00	32.00	35.00
Grapefruit, ftd.	10.00	15.00	22.50	30.00
Ice tub	25.00	60.00	75.00	100.00
Pitcher, 3 pint	35.00	90.00	140.00	------
Mayonnaise	15.00	20.00	30.00	40.00
Mayonnaise #1252½	15.00	22.50	32.00	50.00
Mustard w/cover, spoon	25.00	50.00	70.00	90.00
Oil bottle, 2½ oz., w/#78 stopper	30.00	62.00	80.00	110.00
Oil bottle, 4 oz., w/#78 stopper	35.00	67.00	85.00	120.00
Plate, cream soup liner	5.00	7.00	10.00	15.00
Plate, 8", Kraft cheese	15.00	25.00	35.00	55.00
Plate, 8", grnd. bottom	7.00	12.00	15.00	20.00
Plate, 10", utility, 3 ft.	20.00	30.00	42.00	-----
Plate, 12", 2 hdld. sandwich	20.00	37.00	50.00	55.00
Plate, 12", muffin, 2 hdld., turned sides	20.00	40.00	55.00	65.00
Plate, 13", 3 part relish	10.00	17.00	22.00	35.00
Platter, 12"	15.00	35.00	55.00	70.00
Salt & pepper, 2 styles	30.00	55.00	120.00	100.00
Saucer	3.00	5.00	7.00	10.00
Stem, 2½ oz., wine	15.00	27.00	32.00	35.00
Stem, 3 oz., oyster cocktail	5.00	15.00	22.00	25.00
Stem, 3 oz., cocktail	5.00	15.00	22.00	25.00
Stem, 5 oz., saucer champagne	7.00	16.00	22.00	25.00
Stem, 5 oz., sherbet	7.50	12.00	18.00	22.50
Stem, 9 oz., luncheon (1 block in stem)	15.00	20.00	32.00	40.00
Sugar, ftd.	20.00	30.00	37.50	60.00
Sugar, hotel oval	15.00	35.00	40.00	50.00
Sugar, individual (unusual)	15.00	32.00	36.00	65.00
Sugar w/cover, zig-zag handles	15.00	27.00	40.00	70.00
Tray, 7", pickle, grnd. bottom	7.00	15.00	22.00	25.00
Tray, 10", celery	10.00	20.00	27.00	30.00
Tray, 13", celery	12.00	25.00	37.00	50.00
Tumbler, 5 oz., fruit	4.00	12.00	19.00	24.00
Tumbler, 6 oz., ftd. soda	5.00	13.00	20.00	25.00
Tumbler, 8 oz., flat, grnd. bottom	7.00	15.00	21.00	30.00
Tumbler, 8 oz., soda, straight & flared	7.00	15.00	21.00	30.00
Tumbler, 9 oz., ftd. soda	8.00	16.00	24.00	31.00
Tumbler, 12 oz., iced tea	11.00	22.00	30.00	42.50
Tumbler, 12 oz., ftd. iced tea	12.00	25.00	35.00	45.00

VALENCIA, Cambridge Glass Company

Colors: crystal

This little-known Cambridge pattern has many unusual and interesting pieces in its repetoire. Note the covered honey dish, six-piece relish on #3500 12″ plate, and the 15″ long, three-part, two-handled relish. All of these pieces are highly coveted in Rose Point, but are just beginning to be noticed in Valencia. Pieces in a highly-promoted pattern such as Rose Point were made in larger quantities than those of Valencia. Since there are thousands of collectors searching for Rose Point, and only a small number looking for Valencia, there is a large discrepancy in price on the same pieces in the two patterns. Of course, the Rose Point is the higher priced.

The little metal-handled piece on the left is called a sugar basket by Cambridge. This is similar to Fostoria's sugar pail. Terminology used by the different companies causes collectors problems in figuring out which piece is called what.

	Crystal		Crystal
Ash tray, #3500/124, 3¼″, round	8.00	Relish, #3500/64, 10″, 3 comp	27.50
Ash tray, #3500/126, 4″, round	12.00	Relish, #3500/65, 10″, 4 comp	30.00
Ash tray, #3500/128, 4½″, round	15.00	Relish, #3500/67, 12″, 6 pc.	85.00
Basket, #3500/55, 6″, 2 hdld., ftd	22.00	Relish, #3500/112, 15″, 3 pt/2 hdld	75.00
Bowl, #3500/49, 5″, hdld	18.00	Relsih, #3500/13, 15″, 4 pt/2 hdld	85.00
Bowl, #3500/37, 6″, cereal		Salt and pepper, #3400/18	45.00
Bowl, #1402/89, 6″, 2 hdld	18.00	Saucer, #3500/1	3.00
Bowl, #1402/88, 6″, 2 hdld., div	20.00	Stem, #1402, cordial	55.00
Bowl, #3500/115, 9½″, 2 hdld., ftd	35.00	Stem, #1402, wine	30.00
Bowl, #1402/82, 10″	32.50	Stem, #1402, cocktail	20.00
Bowl, #1402/88, 11″	35.00	Stem, #1402, claret	25.00
Bowl, #1402/95, salad dressing, div	40.00	Stem, #1402, oyster cocktail	16.00
Bowl, #1402/100, finger w/liner	25.00	Stem, #1402, low sherbet	12.50
Bowl, #3500, ftd, finger	27.50	Stem, #1402, tall sherbet	15.00
Candy dish w/cover #3500/103	75.00	Stem, #1402, goblet	20.00
Celery, #1402/94, 12″	30.00	Stem, #3500, cordial	45.00
Cigarette holder, #1066, ftd	35.00	Stem, #3500, wine, 2½ oz.	27.50
Comport, #3500/36, 6″	27.50	Stem, #3500, cocktail, 3 oz	18.00
Comport, #3500/37, 7″	35.00	Stem, #3500, claret, 4½ oz	22.50
Creamer, #3500/14	15.00	Stem, #3500, oyster cocktail, 4½ oz	15.00
Creamer, #3500/15, individual	15.00	Stem, #3500, low sherbet, 7 oz	12.50
Cup, #3500/1	17.50	Stem, #3500, tall sherbet, 7 oz	15.00
Decanter, #3400/92, 32 oz., ball	85.00	Stem, #3500, goblet, lon bowl	20.00
Decanter, –4300/119, 12 oz., ball	55.00	Stem, #3500, goblet, short bowl	18.00
Honey dish w/cover #3500/139	75.00	Sugar, #3500/14	15.00
Ice pail, #1402/52	45.00	Sugar, #3500/15, individual	15.00
Mayonnaise, #3500/59, 3 pc	40.00	Sugar basket, #3500/13	45.00
Nut, #3400/71, 3″, 4 ftd	30.00	Tumbler, #3400/92, 2½ oz	15.00
Perfume, #3400/97, 2 oz., perfume	40.00	Tumbler, #3400/100, 13 oz	18.00
Plate, #3500/167, 7½″, salad	10.00	Tumbler, #3400/115, 14 oz	20.00
Plate, #3500/5, 8½″, breakfast″	12.00	Tumbler, #3500, 2½ oz., ftd	14.00
Plate, #1402, 11½″, sandwich, hdld	22.50	Tumbler, #3500, 3 oz., ftd	14.00
Plate, #3500/39, 12″, ftd	27.50	Tumbler, #3500, 5 oz., ftd	12.50
Plate, #3500/67, 12″	22.50	Tumbler, #3500, 10 oz., ftd.	14.00
Plate, #3500/38, 13″, torte	25.00	Tumbler, #3500, 12 oz., ftd	15.00
Relish, #3500/68, 5½″, 2 comp	17.50	Tumbler, #3500, 13 oz., ftd	16.00
Relish, #3500/69, 6½″, 3 comp	20.00	Tumbler, #3500, 16 oz., ftd	17.50
Relish, #1402/91, 8″, 3 comp	25.00		

VERSAILLES, Fostoria Glass Company, 1928 - 1944

Colors: blue, yellow, pink, green

Azure blue is the color most avidly sought by collectors; but the two pieces of pink (in the blue picture) are among the rarest items shown. The flat, old fashioned in the foreground and the flat tea in the right rear have never been photographed before. Pink is the only color in which these two tumblers have been seen.

Another newly discovered piece in Versailles is a canape plate. It is 6″ with an indent on which the 2½ oz. footed tumbler sits. It never ceases to amaze me how new discoveries still occur in major patterns that have been collected for years. There is no way of knowing what will be found next or who will be the lucky one to find it!

	Pink, Green	Blue	Yellow		Pink, Green	Blue	Yellow
Ash tray	24.00	30.00	25.00	Mayonnaise w/liner	35.00	50.00	40.00
Bottle, salad dressing with				Oil, ftd.	250.00	350.00	250.00
sterling top	275.00	------	325.00	Oyster cocktail	20.00	27.50	22.00
Bowl, 9″, baker	35.00	55.00	45.00	Parfait	27.50	35.00	30.00
Bowl, bonbon	13.00	20.00	15.00	Pitcher	250.00	350.00	275.00
Bowl, bouillon, ftd.	16.00	30.00	17.50	Plate, 6″, bread/butter	4.00	5.00	4.00
Bowl, cream soup, ftd.	16.00	25.00	20.00	Plate 6″ canape	40.00	65.00	55.00
Bowl, finger w/liner	20.00	32.00	25.00	Plate, 7½″, salad	6.00	8.00	7.00
Bowl, lemon	13.00	20.00	15.00	Plate, 7½″, cream soup			
Bowl, mint, 3 ftd	16.00	25.00	18.00	liner	6.00	8.00	7.00
Bowl, 5″, fruit	15.00	20.00	16.00	Plate, 8¾″, , luncheon	8.00	10.00	9.00
Bowl, 6″, cereal	20.00	30.00	22.00	Plate, 9½″, sm. dinner	14.00	20.00	15.00
Bowl, 7″, soup	25.00	37.00	30.00	Plate, 10″, grill	20.00	30.00	25.00
Bowl, lg. dessert, 2 hdld. . . .	30.00	50.00	33.00	Plate, 10″, cake, 2 hdld.	26.00	35.00	30.00
Bowl, 10″	30.00	42.00	32.00	Plate, 10¼″, dinner	35.00	45.00	37.50
Bowl, 11″, centerpiece	30.00	45.00	35.00	Plate, 13″, chop	30.00	40.00	35.00
Bowl, 12″, centerpiece, sev.				Platter, 12″	30.00	40.00	35.00
type	25.00	47.00	35.00	Platter, 15″	60.00	85.00	60.00
Bowl, 13″, oval centerpiece	35.00	55.00	40.00	Relish, 8½″	30.00	40.00	35.00
Candlestick, 2″	15.00	20.00	16.00	Sauce boat	60.00	80.00	60.00
Candlestick, 3″	16.00	25.00	17.50	Sauce plate	20.00	25.00	20.00
Candlestick, 5″	20.00	30.00	22.00	Saucer, after dinner	4.00	6.00	5.00
Candy w/cover, 3 pt.	75.00	120.00	85.00	Saucer	4.00	6.00	5.00
Candy w/cover, ½ lb.	65.00	110.00	75.00	Shaker, ftd., pr.	80.00	110.00	85.00
Celery, 11½″	30.00	40.00	50.00	Sherbet, high, 6″	20.00	25.00	22.50
Cheese & cracker, set	50.00	65.00	52.00	Sherbet, low, 4¼″	20.00	24.00	22.00
Comport, 6″	25.00	35.00	27.50	Sugar, ftd.	15.00	20.00	15.00
Comport, 7″	27.00	45.00	30.00	Sugar cover	85.00	125.00	95.00
Comport, 8″		75.00		Sugar pail	95.00	155.00	95.00
Creamer, ftd.	15.00	20.00	15.00	Sugar, tea	27.50	30.00	27.50
Creamer, tea	27.50	30.00	27.50	Sweetmeat	12.00	17.50	14.00
Cup, after dinner	25.00	40.00	30.00	Tray, 11″, ctr. hdld.	25.00	35.00	30.00
Cup, ftd.	17.50	21.00	19.00	Tray, service	30.00	40.00	35.00
Decanter	250.00	350.00	250.00	Tray, service & lemon	32.50	42.50	37.50
Goblet, cordial, 4″, ¾ oz. . .	75.00	80.00	65.00	Tumbler, flat, old fashioned	75.00		
Goblet, claret, 6″, 4 oz.	40.00	65.00	45.00	Tumbler, flat tea	80.00		
Goblet, cocktail, 5¼″, 3 oz. . .	25.00	35.00	28.00	Tumbler, 2½ oz., ftd. . . .	30.00	40.00	37.50
Goblet, water, 8¼″, 10 oz. . .	27.50	32.50	30.00	Tumbler, 5 oz., ftd., 4½″ . . .	20.00	25.00	22.00
Goblet, wine, 5½″, 3 oz.	35.00	55.00	42.00	Tumbler, 9 oz., ftd., 5¼″ . . .	20.00	25.00	21.50
Grapefruit	40.00	60.00	40.00	Tumbler, 12 oz., ftd., 6″ . . .	22.50	27.50	25.00
Grapefruit liner	30.00	40.00	30.00	Vase, 8″	100.00	150.00	110.00
Ice bucket	62.50	80.00	75.00	Vase, 8½″, fan, ftd.	85.00	140.00	85.00
Ice dish	30.00	40.00	30.00	Whipped cream bowl	12.00	15.00	13.00
Ice dish liner (tomato,				Whipped cream pail	85.00	115.00	85.00
crab, fruit)	5.00	10.00	7.50				

Note: For stem identification see page 79.

VESPER, Fostoria Glass Company, 1926 - 1934

Colors: amber, green, some blue

	Green	Amber	Blue
Ash tray	25.00	30.00	
Bowl, finger	15.00	17.50	
Bowl, ftd., bouillon	12.00	13.00	
Bowl, cream soup	12.50	14.00	
Bowl, 5½″, fruit	8.00	10.00	16.00
Bowl, 6½″, cereal	15.00	18.00	22.00
Bowl, 7¾″, soup, shallow	16.00	20.00	30.00
Bowl, 8″, soup, deep	17.00	21.00	
Bowl, 8″	22.00	25.00	
Bowl, 9″	30.00	32.00	
Bowl, 11″, console	25.00	27.50	
Bowl, 13″, console	27.50	30.00	
Candlestick, 3″	15.00	15.00	30.00
Candlestick, 9″	30.00	35.00	50.00
Candy jar w/cover	65.00	80.00	150.00
Candy jar, ftd. w/cover	100.00	125.00	
Cheese, ftd.	18.00	20.00	
Comport, 6″	22.50	25.00	35.00
Comport, 7″	25.00	28.00	40.00
Comport, 8″	35.00	40.00	50.00
Creamer, ftd.	14.00	16.00	
Creamer, fat, ftd.	18.00	20.00	25.00
Cup	12.00	14.00	
Cup, after dinner	18.00	20.00	35.00
Dish, celery	15.00	17.50	
Finger bowl liner, 6″	4.50	5.50	
Grapefruit	35.00	35.00	
Grapefruit liner	25.00	30.00	
Ice bucket	55.00	60.00	
Oyster cocktail	16.00	18.00	
Pitcher, ftd.	275.00	295.00	
Plate, 6″, bread/butter	4.50	5.00	
Plate, 7½″, salad	6.00	6.50	
Plate, 8½″, luncheon	7.50	8.50	
Plate, 9½″, sm. dinner	11.00	12.00	
Plate, 10½″, dinner	23.00	29.00	
Plate, 11″, ctr. hand.	22.50	25.00	
Plate, 13″, chop	32.00	37.50	
Plate, 15″, server	40.00	45.00	
Plate w/indent for cheese	18.00	20.00	
Platter, 10½″	22.50	25.00	
Platter, 12″	35.00	40.00	
Platter, 15″	50.00	60.00	
Salt & pepper, pr., 2 styles	65.00	75.00	
Sauce boat w/liner	75.00	85.00	
Saucer, after dinner	7.50	9.00	15.00
Saucer	4.00	4.50	
Stem, sherbet	15.00	16.00	
Stem, water	22.50	25.00	
Stem, low sherbet	14.00	15.00	
Stem, parfait	25.00	27.50	
Stem, ¾ oz., cordial	65.00	70.00	
Stem, 2½ oz., ftd.	20.00	22.50	
Stem, 2¾ oz., wine	27.50	30.00	
Stem, 3 oz., cocktail	22.50	25.00	
Sugar, fat ftd.	18.00	20.00	25.00
Sugar, ftd.	14.00	16.00	
Sugar, lid	125.00	125.00	
Tumbler, 5 oz., ftd.	14.00	15.00	
Tumbler, 9 oz., ftd.	15.00	16.00	
Tumbler, 12 oz., ftd.	18.00	20.00	
Urn, sm.	60.00	65.00	
Urn, lg.	70.00	75.00	120.00
Vase, 8″	70.00	75.00	110.00

NOTE: Page 79 for stem identification.

WAVERLY, Blank #1519, A. H. Heisey & Co.

Colors: crystal; rare in amber

	Crystal
Bowl, 6″, oval lemon w/cover	26.00
Bowl, 6½″, 2 hdld. ice	47.50
Bowl, 7″, 3 part relish, oblong	25.00
Bowl, 7″, salad	20.00
Bowl, 9″, 4 part relish, round	23.00
Bowl, 9″, fruit	32.00
Bowl, 9″, vegetable	32.00
Bowl, 10″, crimped edge	15.00
Bowl, 10″, gardenia	15.00
Bowl, 11″, seahorse foot, floral	57.50
Bowl, 12″, crimped edge	37.50
Bowl, 13″, gardenia	20.00
Box, 5″, chocolate w/cover	37.50
Box, 5″ tall, ft. w/cover, seahorse hand.	62.50
Box, 6″, candy w/bow tie knob	45.00
Box, trinket, lion cover (rare)	650.00
Butter dish w/cover, 6″, square	65.00
Candleholder, 1-lite, block (rare)	135.00
Candleholder, 2-lite	20.00
Candleholder, 2-lite, "flame" center	50.00
Candleholder, 3-lite	50.00
Candle epergnette, 5″	7.50
Candle epergnette, 6″, deep	12.50
Candle epergnette, 6½″	10.00
Cheese dish, 5½″, ft.	9.00
Cigarette holder	30.00
Comport, 6″, low ft.	7.00
Comport, 6½″, jelly	9.00
Comport, 7″, low ft., oval	30.00
Creamer, ft.	15.00
Creamer & sugar, individual w/tray	30.00
Cruet, 3 oz., ft. w/#122 stopper	40.00
Cup	10.00
Honey dish, 6½″, ft.	9.00
Mayonnaise w/liner & ladle, 5½″	25.00
Plate, 7″, salad	4.00
Plate, 8″, luncheon	6.00
Plate, 10½″, server	20.00
Plate, 11″, sandwich	12.00
Plate, 13½″, ft. cake salver	50.00
Plate, 14″, center handle sandwich	50.00
Plate, 14″, sandwich	20.00
Salt & pepper, pr.	25.00
Saucer	3.00
Stem, 1 oz., cordial	95.00
Stem, 3 oz., wine, blown	55.00
Stem, 3½ oz., cocktail	32.50
Stem, 5½ oz., sherbet/champagne	15.00
Stem, 10 oz., blown	20.00
Sugar, ft.	15.00
Tray, 12″, celery	13.00
Tumbler, 5 oz., ft. juice, blown	15.00
Tumbler, 13 oz., ft. tea, blown	20.00
Vase, 3½″, violet	27.00
Vase, 7″, ft.	25.00
Vase, 7″, ft., fan shape	27.50

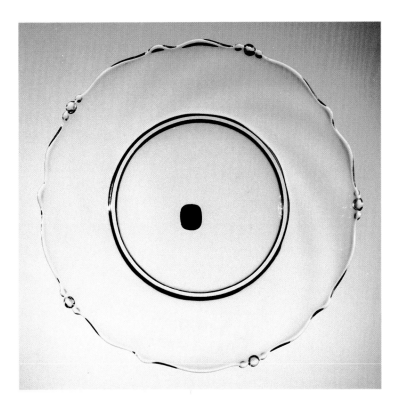

WILDFLOWER, Cambridge Glass Company, 1940's - 1950's

Colors: crystal, mainly; some few pieces in color

You will find a few Wildflower pieces in yellow and green and they fetch 50% more than the crystal prices listed below. Gold-encrusted Wildflower is visually stunning, but sells for only a little more than the plainer crystal.

The ball shaped, stemmed piece behind the gold-encrusted, three-part relish is a mayonnaise, listed as sherbet type. I received several letters asking about that particular item.

	Crystal		Crystal
Basket, 6″, 2 hdld. ftd.	22.00	Plate, 8″, salad	11.00
Bowl, 5¼″, 2 hdld., bonbon	16.00	Plate, 10½″, dinner	42.00
Bowl, 6″, 2 hdld. ftd. bonbon	17.50	Plate, 12″, 4 ftd. service	30.00
Bowl, 6″, 2 pt. relish	17.50	Plate, 13″, 4 ftd. torte	32.50
Bowl, 6½″, 3 pt. relish	17.50	Plate, 13½″, 2 hdld. cake	32.50
Bowl, 7″, relish	18.00	Plate, 14″, torte	35.00
Bowl, 7″, 2 hdld. bonbon	20.00	Salt & pepper, pr.	30.00
Bowl, 7″, 2 pt. relish	20.00	Saucer	3.50
Bowl, 8″, 3 hdld. 3 pt. relish	25.00	Set: 2 pc. Mayonnaise (ft. sherbet w/ladle)	25.00
Bowl, 9″, 3 pt. celery & relish	25.00	Set: 3 pc. Mayonnaise (bowl, liner, ladle)	28.00
Bowl, 9½″, ftd. pickle (corn)	22.00	Set: 4 pc. Mayonnaise (div. bowl, liner, 2 ladles)	32.00
Bowl, 10″, 4 ft. flared	30.00	Stem, #3121, 1 oz., cordial	47.50
Bowl, 11″, 2 hdld	30.00	Stem, #3121, 3 oz., cocktail	22.50
Bowl, 11½″, ftd. w/tab hand.	35.00	Stem, #3121, 3½ oz. wine	25.00
Bowl, 12″, 3 pt. celery & relish	30.00	Stem, #3121, 4½ oz. claret	25.00
Bowl, 12″, 4 ft. flared	29.50	Stem, #3121, 4½ oz., low oyster cocktail	16.00
Bowl, 12″ 4 ft. oval, "ears" hand.	42.00	Stem, #3121, 5 oz., low parfait	24.00
Bowl, 12″, 5 pt celery & relish	35.00	Stem, #3121, 6 oz. low sherbet	15.00
Candlestick, 3-lite, ea.	32.00	Stem, #3121, 6 oz. tall sherbet	17.50
Candlestick, 5″	25.00	Stem, #3121, 10 oz. water	20.00
Candlestick, 6″, 2-lite "fleur de lis"	30.00	Sugar	12.50
Candy box w/cover, 8″, 3 hdld. 3 pt.	55.00	Sugar, indiv.	12.50
Candy box w/cover, rnd.	50.00	Tumbler, #3121, 5 oz., juice	13.50
Cocktail icer, 2 pc.	35.00	Tumbler, #3121, 10 oz., water	15.00
Comport, 5½″	30.00	Tumbler, #3121, 12 oz., tea	17.50
Comport, 5⅜″, blown	40.00	Tumbler, 13 oz.	20.00
Creamer	12.50	Vase, 5″, globe	30.00
Creamer, indiv.	12.50	Vase, 6″, ftd. flower	30.00
Cup	16.50	Vase, 8″, ftd. flower	35.00
Hurricane lamp, candlestick base	100.00	Vase, 9″, keyhole ft.	40.00
Hurricane lamp, keyhole base & prisms	120.00	Vase, 10″, bud	30.00
Ice bucket w/chrome hand.	55.00	Vase, 11″, ftd. flower	42.00
Oil, 6 oz. w/stopper	42.00	Vase, 11″, ped. ft.	45.00
Pitcher, ball	95.00	Vase, 12″, keyhole ft.	55.00
Pitcher, Doulton	155.00	Vase, 13″, ftd. flower	75.00
Plate, 6″, 2 hdld.	12.50		
Plate, 6½″, bread/butter	7.50		
Plate, 8″, 2 hdld. bonbon	17.50		
Plate, 8″, 2 hdld. ftd.	20.50		

Note: See Pages 166-167 for stem identification.

YEOMAN, Blank #1184, A. H. Heisey & Co.

Colors: crystal, "Flamingo" pink, "Sahara" yellow, "Moongleam" green; "Hawthorne" orchid/pink; "Marigold" deep, amber/yellow; some cobalt

Etched patterns on Yeoman blanks will bring 15% to 25% more than the prices listed below. Empress etch is the most commonly found pattern on Yeoman blanks.

	Crystal	Pink	Sahara	Green	Hawth.	Marigold
Ash tray, 4", hdld. (bow tie)	9.50	18.00	20.00	22.50	27.50	30.00
Bowl, 2 hdld. cream soup	10.00	16.00	21.00	24.00	28.00	32.00
Bowl, finger	5.00	11.00	15.00	19.00	27.50	27.50
Bowl, ftd., banana split	7.00	22.00	27.00	32.00	37.00	42.00
Bowl, ftd., 2 hdld. bouillon	10.00	20.00	25.00	30.00	35.00	40.00
Bowl, 4½", nappy	4.00	7.50	10.00	12.50	15.00	17.00
Bowl, 5", low ftd. jelly	12.00	20.00	25.00	27.00	30.00	40.00
Bowl, 5", oval lemon	7.00	10.00	15.00	18.00	19.00	25.00
Bowl, 5", rnd. lemon	6.00	10.00	15.00	18.00	19.00	25.00
Bowl, 5", rnd. lemon w/cover	12.00	17.50	22.50	27.50	37.50	37.50
Bowl, 6", oval preserve	7.00	12.00	17.00	22.00	27.00	30.00
Bowl, 6", vegetable	5.00	10.00	14.00	16.00	20.00	24.00
Bowl, 6½", hdld. bonbon	5.00	10.00	14.00	16.00	20.00	24.00
Bowl, 8", rect. pickle/olive	12.00	15.00	20.00	25.00	30.00	35.00
Bowl, 8½", berry, 2 hdld	14.00	19.00	24.00	29.00	34.00	40.00
Bowl, 9", 2 hdld. veg. w/cover	30.00	40.00	50.00	60.00	80.00	125.00
Bowl, 9", oval fruit	20.00	25.00	35.00	45.00	55.00	55.00
Bowl, 9", baker	20.00	25.00	35.00	45.00	55.00	55.00
Bowl, 12", low floral	15.00	25.00	35.00	45.00	55.00	55.00
Cigarette box, (ash tray cover)	25.00	40.00	50.00	60.00	70.00	80.00
Cologne bottle w/stopper	40.00	85.00	90.00	95.00	100.00	125.00
Comport, 5", high ftd., shallow	15.00	25.00	37.00	45.00	55.00	70.00
Comport, 6", low ftd., deep	20.00	30.00	34.00	40.00	42.00	48.00
Creamer	10.00	15.00	17.00	19.00	22.00	28.00
Cruet, 2 oz. oil	20.00	35.00	40.00	45.00	50.00	55.00
Cruet, 4 oz. oil	25.00	37.50	42.50	47.50	55.00	60.00
Cup..............................	5.00	15.00	20.00	25.00	30.00	40.00
Cup, after dinner	7.00	21.00	26.00	32.00	38.00	45.00
Egg cup	15.00	24.00	32.00	39.00	42.00	52.00
Grapefruit, ftd.	10.00	17.00	24.00	31.00	38.00	45.00
Gravy (or dressing) boat w/underliner .	13.00	18.00	23.00	28.00	35.00	40.00
Marmalade jar w/cover	25.00	35.00	40.00	45.00	55.00	65.00
Parfait, 5 oz.	10.00	15.00	20.00	25.00	30.00	35.00
Pitcher, quart	35.00	48.00	58.00	68.00	110.00	140.00
Plate, 2 hdld. cheese	5.00	10.00	13.00	15.00	17.00	25.00
Plate, cream soup underliner	5.00	7.00	9.00	12.00	14.00	16.00
Plate, finger bowl underliner	3.00	5.00	7.00	9.00	11.00	13.00
Plate, 4½", coaster	3.00	5.00	10.00	12.00		
Plate, 6"	3.00	6.00	8.00	10.00	13.00	15.00
Plate, 6", bouillon underliner	3.00	6.00	8.00	10.00	13.00	15.00

	Crystal	Pink	Sahara	Green	Hawth.	Marigold
Plate, 6½″, grapefruit bowl	7.00	12.00	15.00	19.00	27.00	32.00
Plate, 7″	5.00	8.00	10.00	14.00	17.00	22.00
Plate, 8″, oyster cocktail	9.00					
Plate, 8″, soup	9.00					
Plate, 9″, oyster cocktail	10.00					
Plate, 10½″	12.00					
Plate, 10½″, ctr. hand. oval, div.	15.00	26.00		32.00		
Plate, 11″, 4 pt. relish	20.00	27.00		32.00		
Plate, 14″	20.00					
Platter, 12″, oval	10.00	17.00	19.00	26.00	33.00	
Salt, ind. tub (cobalt: $20.00)	5.00	7.00		12.00		
Salver, 10″, low ftd.	15.00	26.00		42.00		
Salver, 12″, low ftd.	10.00	20.00		32.00		
Saucer	3.00	5.00	7.00	7.00	10.00	10.00
Saucer, after dinner	3.00	5.00	7.00	8.00	10.00	10.00
Stem, 2¾ oz., ftd. oyster cocktail	3.00	5.00	7.00	8.00	12.00	
Stem 3 oz., cocktail	7.00	12.00	17.00	20.00		
Stem, 3½ oz., sherbet	5.00	8.00	11.00	12.00		
Stem, 4 oz., fruit cocktail	3.00	5.00	7.00	9.00		
Stem, 4½ oz., sherbet	3.00	5.00	7.00	9.00		
Stem, 5 oz., soda	4.00	6.00	8.00	10.00		
Stem, 5 oz., sherbet	3.00	5.00	7.00	9.00		
Stem, 6 oz., champagne	6.00	11.00	16.00	18.00		
Stem, 8 oz.	5.00	10.00	16.00	17.00		
Stem, 10 oz., goblet	7.00	12.00	17.00	20.00		
Stem, 12 oz., tea	8.00	14.00	19.00	22.00		
Sugar w/cover	13.00	25.00	27.00	30.00	35.00	40.00
Sugar shaker, ftd.	30.00	90.00		95.00		
Syrup, 7 oz., saucer ftd.	25.00	60.00				
Tray, 7″ x 10″, rect.	26.00	30.00	40.00	35.00		
Tray, 9″, celery	10.00	14.00	16.00	15.00		
Tray, 11″, ctr. hand., 3 pt.	15.00	20.00	24.00			
Tray, 12″, oblong	16.00	19.00	24.00			
Tray, 13″, 3 pt. relish	20.00	27.00	32.00			
Tray, 13″, celery	20.00	27.00	32.00			
Tray, 13″, hors d'oeuvre w/cov. ctr.	32.00	42.00	52.00	75.00		
Tray insert, 3½″ x 4½″	4.00	6.00	7.00	8.00		
Tumbler, 2½ oz., whiskey	3.00	6.00	8.00	10.00		
Tumbler, 4½ oz., soda	4.00	6.00	10.00	15.00		
Tumbler, 8 oz.	4.00	12.00	17.00	20.00		
Tumbler, 10 oz., cupped rim	4.00	15.00	20.00	22.50		
Tumbler, 10 oz., straight side	5.00	15.00	20.00	22.50		
Tumbler, 12 oz., tea	5.00	16.00	22.00	25.00		
Tumbler cover (unusual)	30.00					

165

CAMBRIDGE STEMS

1066
11 oz. Goblet

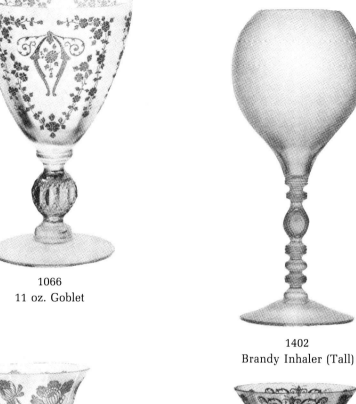

1402
Brandy Inhaler (Tall)

3025
10 oz. Goblet

3035
3 oz. Cocktail

3077
6 oz. Tall Sherbet

3104
1 oz. Cordial

3106
9 oz. Goblet Tall Bowl

3115
3½ oz. Cocktail

3120
6 oz. Tall Sherbet

3121
10 oz. Goblet

CAMBRIDGE STEMS

3122
9 oz. Goblet

3124
3 oz. Wine

3126
7 oz. Tall Sherbet

3130
6 oz. Tall Sherbet

3135
6 oz. Tall Sherbet

3400
9 oz. Lunch Goblet

3500
10 oz. Goblet

3600
2½ oz. Wine

3775
4½ oz. Claret

3625
4½ oz. Claret

3779
1 oz. Cordial

HEISEY'S "ALEXANDRITE" COLOR (rare)

Bowl, 12″, floral, Twist (1252) 275.00
Candlesticks, pr. (134) 500.00
Cream & sugar, pr., Empress (1401) 400.00
Compote, Albermarle (3368) 125.00
Cup & saucer, Queen Ann (1509) 120.00
Jelly, 6″, w/dolphin feet Queen Ann (1509) 90:00
Mayonnaise w/dolp. ft. & ladle Queen Ann (1509) 185.00
Plate, 8″, Empress (1401) 55.00
Salt & pepper, pr. Queen Ann (1509) 235.00
Stem, 2½ oz. wine, Creole (3381) 140.00
Stem, 2½ oz. wine, Old Dominion (3380) 115.00
Stem, 6 oz. champagne, Old Dominion (3380) 75.00
Stem, 11 oz. water goblet Carcassone (3390) 80.00
Stem 11 oz. water goblet Creole (3381) 135.00
Vase, 4″, ball Wide Optic (4045) 190.00

HEISEY'S "ALEXANDRITE" COLOR (rare)

Ash tray, Empress (1401)	130.00
Candlestick, 7″, pr. (135)	350.00
Celery tray, 10″, Empress (1401)	150.00
Nut, individual, Empress (1401)	80.00
Plate, 6″, square, Empress (1401)	35.00
Plate, 7″, square, Empress (1401)	45.00
Plate, 8″, square, Empress (1401)	60.00
Plate, 10″, square, Empress (1401)	125.00
Tumbler, 1 oz., cordial, Carcassonne (3390)	100.00
Tumbler, 2½ oz., bar, Glenford (3481)	100.00
Tumbler, 5 oz. ftd. soda, Creole (3381)	60.00
Tumbler, 8½ oz., ftd. soda, Creole (3381)	50.00
Tumbler, 12 oz., ftd. soda, Creole (3381)	60.00
Vase, 9″, ftd., Empress (1401)	525.00

HEISEY'S "COBALT", COLOR (rare)

Ash tray, Empress (1401)	125.00
Bowl, 12″, Thumbprint & Panel (1433)	100.00
Candlestick, pair, 6″, Old Sandwich (1404)	200.00
Creamer, 12 oz., Old Sandwich (1404)	260.00
Mug, 12 oz., Old Sandwich	275.00
Salt & pepper shaker pr. (24)	95.00
Salt tub, individual, Revere (1183)	90.00
Tumbler, 12 oz. footed soda, Old Williamsburg, (341)	350.00
Vase, 2″ ball, Wide Optic (4045)	400.00
Vase, 4″ ball, Wide Optic (4045)	115.00
Vase, 9″, pr., Warwick (1428)	350.00
Vase, 9″ ftd. tulip (1420)	325.00
Vase, favor, Diamond Optic (4228)	75.00
Vase, favor, Diamond Optic (4230)	75.00
Vase, ivy, Wide Optic (4224)	140.00

HEISEY'S "COBALT", COLOR (rare)

Ash tray or butter pat, Old Sandwich (1404)	30.00
Bowl, 11″, dolphin ftd., floral, Empress (1401)	310.00
Candlestick, pair, 6″, Empress (135)	300.00
Cigarette holder, Carcassonne (3390)	85.00
Plate, 8″, round, Queen Ann (1509)	50.00
Plate, 8″, square, Empress, (1401)	60.00
Stem, 2½ oz., wine, Carcassonne (3390)	110.00
Stem, 3½ oz., cocktail, Spanish stem (3404)	60.00
Stem, 6 oz., sherbet, Carcassonne (3390)	80.00
Stem, 8 oz., ftd. soda, Spanish stem (3404)	95.00
Stem, 12 oz., ftd. soda, Carcassonne (3390)	60.00
Tumbler, 9 oz., Arch (1417)	65.00
Vase, flared, Cathedral (1413)	300.00

HEISEY'S "DAWN" COLOR (rare)

Ash tray, 5¼″ Lodestar (1632)	75.00
Ash tray, Prism Square (1593)	110.00
Bowl, 6¾″ jelly (1565)	45.00
Bowl, crimped, Lodestar (1626)	95.00
Candy, 5″ w/cover Lodestar (1632)	125.00
Cruet, 3 oz., crys. stopper Saturn (1483)	275.00
Jar & cover, Lodestar (1626)	185.00
Pitcher, 1 qt., Lodestar (1626)	140.00
Relish, 12″, 4 pt., Octagon (500)	300.00
Salt shaker, Saturn (1485), pr	295.00
Sherbet, 20th Century (1415)	30.00
Tumbler, Coleport (1487)	35.00
Tumbler, 6 oz., Lodestar (1632)	30.00
Vase, 7½″, Lodestar (1626)	175.00

HEISEY'S TANGERINE COLOR (rare)

Plate, 8″, Empress blank (1401) 130.00
Stem, champagne Duquesne blank (3389) 175.00
Stem, cocktail Gascony (3397) looks red 225.00
Stem, sherbet Duquesne blank (3389) 165.00
Stem, water Duquesne blank (3389) 190.00
Tumbler, ice tea Spanish stem (3404) 375.00
Tumbler, juice Duquesne blank (3389) 125.00
Tumbler, soda Gascony (3397) looks red 300.00
Vase, favor (4232). 300.00
Vase, ivy 175.00

HEISEY'S ZIRCON (LIMELIGHT) COLOR (rare)

Ash tray, Kohinoor (1488)	75.00
Ash tray, Ridgeleigh (1469)	35.00
Bowl, 6″, hdld. jelly, Fern (1495)	45.00
Bowl, 13″, floral, Kohinoor (1488)	375.00
Cigarette box, Ridgeleigh (1469)	140.00
Cigarette holder, Kohinoor (1488)	175.00
Candelabra pr., Kohinoor (1488)	925.00
Candle vase, Ridgeleigh (1469)	85.00
Vase, 8″, Ridgeleigh (1469½)	140.00

Books by Gene Florence

Pocket Guide To Depression Glass, Fifth Edition

by Gene Florence

After attending a recent Depression Glass Show in Houston, Texas, Gene Florence found that the attendance was up 30% over last year, proving that Depression Glass is still gaining in popularity and increasing in value each day. With this in mind, Mr. Florence has compltely updated and reivsed his popular *Pocket Guide to Depression Glass*. Gene has rephotogaphed most of the pictures and added many new finds making this an all new book, not just a revised edition. This full-color presentation is in the same easy-to-use format with bold photographs that make pattern identification simple. Over 4,000 values have been updated to meet the ever-changing market. Also included is a special section on re-issues and how to detect valuable, old, authentic glass from worthless re-issues and fakes. This pocket guide is a MUST for both the beginner and advanced collector.
5½ x 8½, 160 Pages, paperback $9.95

Kitchen Glassware of the Depression Years 3rd Ed

by Gene Florence

Kitchen Glassware has been one of our bestsellers since it was originally published in June 1981. Depression Glass has long been a popular collectible in this country. Many glass enthusiasts have turned to Kitchen Glassware of the same period as a natural "go with"! These kitchen containers, gadgets and utensils can be found in many of the same shades as the tableware that has become so highly collectible. Now these collectors will be delighted to know that Gene Florence has compliled a new revised 3rd edition which features all the new finds that have turned up since the 2nd edition. It also adds many new group shots as well as updates the values. This full color volume features over 3,000 pieces of glass listing size, color, pattern description and current market value. Now with over 100,000 copies in print it is one of the best selling glass price guides on the market today. Gene Florence is the country's most respected authority on Depression Glass.
8½ x 11, 224 Pages, Hardbound $19.95

The Collector's Encyclopedia of Occupied Japan Collectibles

by Gene Florence

During the occupation after World War II, most items manufactured in Japan were marked "Made in Occupied Japan". These include Ceramics, Toys, Games, Wooden Items, Leather and many others. This popular set is produced in full color with over 3,000 items included. Gene Florence has been collecting and researching Occupied Japan collectibles for about 20 years and is regarded as the foremost authority on this collectible. With this 3 volume set, one will become more knowledgeable and more aware of what was produced during this period. This set should be the last word on Occupied Japan collectibles.
#1037, 8½x11, 108 Pgs., HB, 1984, Vol. I $12.95
#1038, 8½x11, 112 Pgs., HB, 1987 Values, Vol. II $14.95
#1719, 8½x11, 144 Pgs., Hb, 1987 Values, Vol. III $19.95

Collector's Encyclopedia of Depression Glass 8th Edition

by Gene Florence

Depression glass is still the most popular glassware collected today. This new 8th edition of that ever popular glassware is bigger and better than ever. This 8th edition features all the new finds that have turned up since the 7th edition plus adds many new group shots as well as updating the values on all the pieces in each pattern. This full color volume features over 5,000 pieces of glass listing: size, color, pattern description and current market value. Now with over 400,000 copies in print it is one of the best selling price guides on the market today. A section is devoted to exposing re-issues and fakes, alerting the unknowing buyer as to what has been released and how to determine the old valuable glass from the worthless new issues.
8½ x 11, 224 Pgs., HB, 1988 $19.95

Copies of these books may be ordered from:
Gene Florence
P.O. Box 22186
Lexington, KY 40522

COLLECTOR BOOKS
P.O. Box 3009
Paducah, KY 42001

Glass Clubs

Heisey Collectors of America
Box 27GF
Newark, Ohio 43055
Dues: $15.00 yearly

National Cambridge Collectors, Inc.
Box 416GF
Cambridge, Ohio 43725
Dues: $13.00 yearly

Add $1.00 postage for the first book, $.40 for each aditional book.

Schroeder's Antiques Price Guide

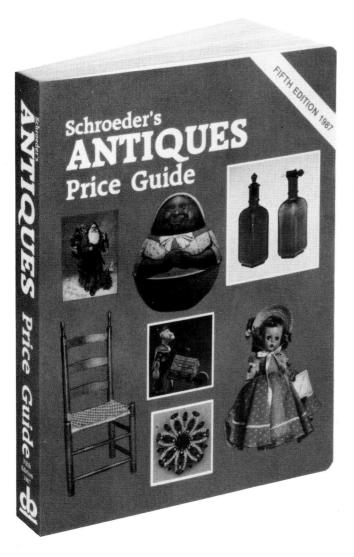

Schroeder's Antiques Price Guide has climbed its way to the top in a field already supplied with several well-established publications! The word is out, *Schroeder's Price Guide* is the best buy at any price. Over 500 categories are covered, with more than 50,000 listings. But it's not volume alone that makes Schroeder's the unique guide it is recognized to be. From ABC Plates to Zsolnay, if it merits the interest of today's collector, you'll find it in Schroeder's. Each subject is represented with histories and background information. In addition, hundreds of sharp original photos are used each year to illustrate not only the rare and the unusual, but the everyday "fun-type" collectibles as well -- not postage stamp pictures, but large close-up shots that show important details clearly.

Each edition is completely re-typeset from all new sources. We have not and will not simply change prices in each new edition. All new copy and all new illustrations make Schroeder's THE price guide on antiques and collectibles.

The writing and researching team behind this giant is proportionately large. It is backed by a staff of more than seventy of Collector Books' finest authors, as well as a board of advisors made up of well-known antique authorities and the country's top dealers, all specialists in their fields. Accurancy is their primary aim. Prices are gathered over the entire year previous to publication, from ads and personal contacts. Then each category is thoroughly checked to spot inconsistencies, listings that may not be entirely reflective of actual market dealings, and lines too vague to be of merit.

Only the best of the lot remains for publication. You'll find *Schroeder's Antiques Price Guide* the one to buy for factual information and quality.

No dealer, collector or investor can afford not to own this book. It is available from your favorite bookseller or antiques dealer at the low price of $11.95. If you are unable to find this price guide in your area, it's available from Collector Books, P. O. Box 3009, Paducah, KY 42001 at $11.95 plus $1.00 for postage and handling.

8½ x 11, 608 Pages $11.95

COLLECTOR BOOKS

A Division of Schroeder Publishing Co., Inc.